Walter Camp

Walter Camp's Book of College Sports

Walter Camp

Walter Camp's Book of College Sports

ISBN/EAN: 9783337426187

Printed in Europe, USA, Canada, Australia, Japan

Cover: Foto ©Andreas Hilbeck / pixelio.de

More available books at **www.hansebooks.com**

WALTER CAMP'S BOOK OF COLLEGE SPORTS

Copyright, 1889, 1890, 1893, by
THE CENTURY CO.

THE DE VINNE PRESS.

PREFACE

IN selecting the four branches of sport treated of in this book I have taken those in which coaching has been most generally demanded, and which, with the exception of tennis,—a game already thoroughly written up by others,—make up the main body of our college sports. It is not my intention to bore the reader with very much regarding the great value of athletic sports to the development of a sound manhood. Our generation has already arrived at very satisfactory conclusions upon that point. I want to write to the boy or man who not only loves his sports, but who when he goes into them goes in heart and soul and who means to win every time if he can, who wants a fair field but no favors, who is ready to do his level best, and when he sees a better man, can give up the ball or the bat or the oar to him and stand aside with a good grace and cheer himself hoarse for his school or college, winning or losing, with an enthusiasm that knows only fair play and the best man to win.

CONTENTS

	PAGE
INTRODUCTION	1
TRACK ATHLETICS.................	13
ROWING	50
A REMARKABLE BOAT RACE	76
A BOAT RACE AT NEW LONDON........	81
FOOT-BALL IN AMERICA	88
BASE-BALL — FOR THE SPECTATOR	164
BASE-BALL — FOR THE PLAYER	184
APPENDIX:	
FOOT-BALL.— Rules of the American Inter-Collegiate Association	283
BASE-BALL.— Playing-rules of Base-ball for principal College Matches of 1893	289
ROWING.— Form of Boating Agreement	305
TRACK ATHLETICS.— Conditions governing the Harvard-Yale Contests for the University Track Athletic Cup..	310
CONSTITUTION.— Form of Constitution as adopted in Old League of Harvard, Princeton, and Yale...........	324
CONTRACT.— Form of Contract between Clubs and Ground Owners....................................	328

ILLUSTRATIONS

	PAGE
A Run Around the End	Frontispiece
The One-hundred-yard Dash — the Start	21
Taking the Hurdles	23
The High Leap, Front View	26
The High Leap, Rear View	27
Vaulting the Bar at Eleven Feet Five Inches	28
Vaulting the Bar at Ten Feet Six Inches	29
Shot-putter Balancing	30
Putting the Shot	30
Putting the Shot	31
Shot-putter, Left View	31
Swinging the Hammer	32
The Hammer-thrower — the Start	32
The Bicycle-rider	33
Quarter-back Taking the Ball	91
A Touch-down	93
A Fair Tackle	95
Diagram of Foot-Ball Field, with Measurements	103
Diagrams Showing Different Plays	105–110
Tackle of a Runner	129
A Try-at-Goal by a Place-kick	131
The Open Scrimmage	135
Making an Opening for a Runner, under the Old Rules, by Using the Arms	137

	PAGE
LAMAR DODGING THE YALE TACKLERS	143
LAMAR AFTER PASSING YALE'S TWENTY-FIVE-YARD LINE	145
BULL, OF YALE	148
THE POLO GROUNDS DURING A MATCH	153
THE FOOT-BALL TEAM STARTING FOR THE POLO GROUNDS	155
THE OLD WOOLEN COSTUME	158
FOOT-BALL PLAYER'S SHOES	159
A TACKLE	162
THE CATCHER	167
AN "OUT-CURVE"—THE BEGINNING	169
AN "OUT-CURVE"—THE END	169
PITCHING A "DROP" BALL	171
STOPPING A GROUNDER	171
RUNNING TO FIRST BASE	174
SLIDING TO BASE	175
FIELDER CATCHING A FLY	178
FIRST BASEMAN CATCHING A HIGH BALL	181
DIAGRAM OF THE [BASE-BALL] FIELD	187
LAYING OUT AN AMATEUR FIELD	189
ARTICLES OF A BASE-BALL OUTFIT	192
THE BODY PROTECTOR AND CATCHER'S MASK	195
PITCHER AT PRACTICE IN THE "CAGE"	197
PRACTISING THROWING WITH THE SPOOL	200
BATTING FOR THE FIELDERS' PRACTICE	203
SHORT-ARM THROW—THE BEGINNING	208
SHORT-ARM THROW—THE END	209
FIRST BASEMAN THROWING TO SECOND FOR A DOUBLE-PLAY	210
MAKING SURE OF A CATCH.—LEFT-FIELDER CATCHING, CENTER-FIELDER BACKING HIM UP	213
ON THE ALERT. "GET OFF! GET A LEAD!"	215
A WILD THROW AND A SAFE SLIDE TO SECOND	217

ILLUSTRATIONS

	PAGE
"Out!"	219
"Jump in Front of the Ball"	221
Third Baseman Intercepting the Slide of a Runner from Second	225
Playing a Trick on the Base-runner	227
First Baseman Taking a Low Throw by Reaching Forward	228
First Baseman Taking a Low Throw on the Long Bound	229
A Runner Caught between Third Base and the Home Plate	231
Diagram of Pitcher's Curves	241
Catcher Signaling to Pitcher by Relative Position of the Mask and His Eyes	249
A Pitcher's Victim. Out on Strikes	251
Catcher Running for a "Foul Fly"	253
Catcher Throwing down to Second	257
Diagram of Batting	261
Base-runner Keeping on to Third	263
Shutting off a Runner at the Home Plate	266
"We Crossed the Home Plate within Three Feet of Each Other"	269
"The Umpire Did not See Gardner at all, and was therefore Wholly Unable to Say whether the Run Counted or not"	271

WALTER CAMP'S BOOK OF COLLEGE SPORTS

INTRODUCTION

"Who misses or who wins the prize,
Go lose or conquer as you can;
But if you fail or if you rise
Be each, pray God, a gentleman!"

BEFORE taking up the direct plan of this book I want to seize upon the opportunity when, my dear sirs, I find you all together and in such good spirits that you will bear with an old preacher for sermonizing a little. I will not bore you long, but to each of you I have a word to say—to you, my boy, just home from school for the short holidays; to you, young man, whose college years are hastening by; to you, *paterfamilias*, who, relieved for a day of business or professional cares, can spare a moment to look back upon your own school and college days, over which the lapse of years has thrown a glamour that, hiding some of the hard realities, still lends a halo of romance to the incidents.

There is the Rev. Dr. Sixthly, who on every seventh day spreads out before you, in choicest rhetoric, the tenets and doctrines of the church; there is the learned Professor Syntax, who looks after your construing; there is the new Professor Dumbell, who drags you willy-nilly through a complex system of chest-measurement and pulley-prescriptions; and there is Dr. Birch himself, who switches you well for whittling the desk. I shall not trespass upon the field of any of these worthy developers of the young idea. The field I enter with you, my boy, is the playground, where you go out to meet your school rivals; I want you, collegian, when you are after championships; I want you, sir, when you are talking with your boy about his sports.

"Be each, pray God, a gentleman!" It is an easy word, and a pleasant one. I don't doubt but that you all pronounce it trippingly enough, and have each one his own high ideal of what a gentleman should be. Do you live up to it? Or are you letting it come down a little here and there; so little, perhaps, that you hardly notice it until you make comparison? A gentleman against a gentleman always plays to win. There is a tacit agreement between them that each shall do his best, and the best man shall win. A gentleman does not make his living, however, from his athletic prowess. He does not earn anything by his victories except glory and satisfaction. Perhaps the first falling off in this respect began when the laurel wreath became a mug. So long as the mug was but the emblem, and valueless otherwise, there was no harm. There is still no harm where the mug or trophy hangs in the room of the winner as indicative of his skill; but if the silver mug becomes a silver dollar, either at the hands of the winner or the donor, let us have the laurel back again.

A gentleman never competes for money, directly or indirectly. Make no mistake about this. No matter how winding the road may be that eventually brings the sovereign into the pocket, it is the price of what should be dearer to you than anything else,—your honor. It is quite the fashion to say "sentimental bosh" to any one who preaches such an old-fashioned thing as honor; but among true gentlemen, my boy, it is just as real an article as ever, and it is one of the few things that never ring false. The man who tells you that insufferable rot about being practical and discarding sentiment, is not the man you would choose as a friend. He would n't stand by you in a pinch, and when we come to the reality, it is only the man who believes in such a thing as honor that is worth anything. So stick to it, my boy, and keep it bright. Carry it down into the small affairs of school and college.

If you are enough of a man to be a good athlete, and some one asks you to use that athletic ability upon their behalf, don't take money for it, or anything that amounts to pay. If you are on the school team or nine and go into training, don't break faith with your captain, yourself, and your fellows by surreptitious indulgences. This does n't mean that if you see some other fellow smoke on the sly you are obliged to tell of it, nor does it mean that you must call him to account, unless you are the captain. If his standard is not so high as yours, that is his misfortune. If he asks your opinion, give it to him, if you like, but not in such a way as to leave the impression that you are put out by your own longing for a similar indulgence. If you are the captain and you find a man breaking training in spite of your orders, and you consider it advisable to put him off, don't be afraid to do it. Gentlemen are not cowards, mentally or physically.

If a man comes to you and endeavors to affect your choice of a college by offers of a pecuniary nature, he does not take you for a gentleman or a gentleman's son, you may be sure. Gentlemen neither offer nor take bribes.

Now, my young college friend, it is your turn. Remember it is upon you that the eyes of the preparatory school-boy are fixed, it is toward you that the younger brother looks for example, and whatever you do in your four years' course, you will see magnified by the boys who come after you. Support your class and your college in every way compatible with your position. Gentlemen are not stingy, nor are they selfish. Play if you can and your class or college needs you. Pay if you can afford it, but do not allow a false pride to lead you into subscriptions beyond your means. Don't be ashamed of enthusiasm. A man without it is a man without a purpose.

I remember a little incident of my own college course. I was a freshman, and knew almost no one in college except a certain junior. I had entered in two events in the fall athletic games, one a quarter mile, the other a hurdle race. I had run the quarter and been beaten, although I finished second. My opponents had all been upper classmen, and received no little encouragement from their friends. I felt very lonely and disgusted with myself and life in general when I got on the mark for the hurdle. I had but two competitors, and both had been cheered when they came to the scratch. Suddenly as we were getting on our marks I heard a voice half-way down the course call out, "You can do 'em," and I saw my junior friend waving his hat to me. It was not a classical remark, but it made me feel better. I was clumsy in getting off, and when we came to the sixth hurdle was nearly five yards behind the other two, but from that time on I could hear my friend roaring out, "Go in!" "You 've got 'em yet!" "Now you 're over," as I went up each flight. I *did* finish first, and I had hardly touched the tape before he was patting me on the back. I don't suppose it cost him much to yell for a poor freshman, but I know that I always thought of him as one of the best fellows I ever knew, and in after years I have remembered enough of the feeling that was in my heart toward him, to go out and try to make some others feel that even a freshman has friends.

Apropos of this, a word to non-contestants. In a boat-race or a foot-ball match the chances are that your own men will not hear your cheer, but the men who may try for the team or crew the next season do, and they are encouraged to better efforts by it. Now about the treatment of your rivals. A gentleman is courteous. It is not courtesy upon a ball-field to cheer an error of the opponents. If it is upon your own grounds, it is the worst kind of boorishness. Moreover, if there are remarkable plays made by your rivals you yourselves should cheer; conceal any chagrin you may feel at the loss it may be to your side, but be courteous to appreciate and applaud an exceptional play by the opponents.

After winning a race or a match, there is no reason why a good, healthy lot of young men should not do plenty of cheering, but there is every reason why they should not make their enjoyment depend upon insulting those who have lost. You cannot take your hilarity off into a corner and choke it to death, and no one wants you to; but gratuitous jibes and jeers at the crestfallen mark you as a man who does not know how to bear a victory, a man whose pate is addled by the excitement or whose bringing up has been at fault.

Finally, to non-contestants, I want to say a word regarding "celebrating." Primarily, do not, I beg of you, do anything because it looks smart. Enjoy yourselves, but do not try to "show off." Don't be "tough." A little unusual hilarity, a tendency to believe that everything is expressly for the collegian, can be upon these occasions overlooked and forgiven, but be ready to appreciate the point beyond which it is carried too far; be ready to apologize quickly and instantly where offense is taken. Show that behind the jolly fun there is the instinct and cultivation of a gentleman's son, and that the ebullition of enthusiasm, although it may be a bore to those who fail to kindle at it, has nothing of the vicious element, and is thoroughly innocent of intentional offense to any one. If you find you are losing your head, go home; you will not be sorry for it.

Now for the contestants. I wish I could impress indelibly upon your minds the fact that with you rests the most enduring standard for amateur sports. With no disrespect to any class or condition — with the best regard for all strong legislation in outside athletic bodies — I say that the collegian's standard of purity in his sports should be the highest. The very fact of having the leisure to devote four years to a higher education, should be taken to involve the duty of acquiring a keener perception of right and wrong in matters where right and wrong depend upon a delicacy of honor. Gentlemen do not cheat, nor do they deceive themselves as to what cheating is. If you are elected the captain of a nine, team, or crew, read over your rules, and note exactly who are allowed as contestants by those rules, not by the custom of some predecessor, not by what you think some rival will do, but by the rules themselves. Having done that, never let a thought enter your head of making use of any man not clearly and cleanly eligible. You will save yourself many a future worry if you start fairly by looking into the record of every candidate at the outset. It is your duty to know that every one of your men is straight and square. I know what I am talking about when I say that a college captain can, in ninety-nine cases out of a hundred, become possessed of the exact truth regarding any man he thinks of trying. Don't investigate to see how much your opponent could prove, but investigate for your own satisfaction. In legislating, remember that what a gentleman wants is fair play and the best man to win. When it is possible, without losing sight of this, to legislate for improvements in method, so much the better; but primarily make every rule such that the probability of unfinished, drawn, or disputed contests is reduced to a minimum.

What if, at the time, your side may be the weaker? Don't be a coward on that account. Face it like a man, and say with your whole heart that you are on the side of the men who want no chance of retreat or escape, only a fair contest and certain victory or defeat at the end of it. To what do all the technicalities amount when compared with the sincerity of men who come together to effect that result? When the delegates earnestly desire rules that shall insure such a contest and such an issue, their work is more than half done. Don't take the coward's part and try to legislate means of avoiding the issue.

Perhaps if you, sir, the father of these boys, have had patience to listen thus far to me, you will allow me to put in a word for the love they bear these sports and the pride they take in their school and college. Talk with them about these interests. You will lose no dignity by it, and you will gain a confidence from them worth having. When you see anything in their speech or conduct that betokens a lowering of the high ideal of gentlemanliness, don't hesitate to say so. You don't want your boy "hired" by any one. If he plays, he plays as a gentleman, and not as a professional; he plays for victory, not for money; and whatever bruises he may have in the flesh, his heart is right, and he can look you in the eye as a gentleman should.

"Be each, pray God, a gentleman!"

So intimate are the relations now existing between the athletic development of the preparatory school and that of the college or university that neither can be independent of the other. The 'varsity captain looks for his future material among the athletes of the preparatory school, and the school captain studies the manner and method of the 'varsities for suggestions that will enable his team, crew, or nine to wrest a victory from his rival school. In this book I have endeavored to give as far as possible the detailed work in each sport, because from the many inquiries that come, both from school and college, it is easy to see that something like practical coaching may be acceptable, even though it be only in print. Of course the member of the 'varsity will, if he look through the book, find many things that are to him an old story, but I know that many of us who now have been through the mill, would have read most eagerly a description of how the 'varsity was trained, and when we were school-boys would have saved ourselves many an error by knowing more of the detail observed in such training. Many a man comes to college or enters the upper class in a preparatory school fresh from home, with no experience of school or college life. Not infrequently such a man has in him a taste for athletics, which has had but a small chance of development. He wants to go in for the sports, but hesitates to ask the detail from his fellows lest they think him stupid. It is with this in mind that I have tried to take up the matter at the very beginning, so that any man or boy can organize a nine, crew, or team, and properly equipping that set of players, finally place them in the contest well drilled and disciplined to do themselves and him credit. I have seen, both in school and college, men well fitted in disposition and character for the position of captain, men of excellent executive ability, who were impossible as candidates for that honor simply because they did not know the detail of the work required. I have seen many a man whose chances of "getting on" were small, who could have been sure of a place had he known in the beginning how to go to work to fit himself. Neither captain nor player who is to become thoroughly successful ever neglects the trivial detail, and although those who watch and applaud the victory see only the final results, the captain and player can tell of long hours spent in mastering what seemed a very insignificant part of the early work. The plan of this book is fashioned after a device which served to give many a victory to one of our largest colleges, and which if adopted at any school or college is sure to bring about good results. The method was to keep a book, in which either the captain or coach entered a record of the practice, transcribing as accurately as possible the daily work of the men; the improvement under certain conditions; any falling back, and the apparent reasons for it — in fact, telling through the pages of the diary, as it were, everything he knew regarding the progress each day. This book was kept up, and each year the former year's record was studied and additions made; and, as I have heard captains and coaches frequently remark, there were in its pages a constant reminder of little points which without it would have been lost sight of, but which with it were kept fresh in the mind of each succeeding leader. In a similar fashion, there will be many apparently insignificant details mentioned and dwelt on in this book of college sports, which perhaps every captain knows and recognizes when he sees them in print as an old story, but which are on that very account so easily forgotten as to make it worth while to read them at least once a season.

TRACK ATHLETICS

ENGLAND has been in advance of us in track athletics, as in many other branches of sports, having long ago learned the advantages of all outdoor exercises. But Americans are already realizing that the unfailing laws of nature demand more attention to the physical welfare of the body, and base-ball, foot-ball, and boating have done much for us; but track athletics offer a wider field, as they give more opportunity for individual endeavor, and demand nothing of that team work or united exercise which must always place something of a limit upon the universal enjoyment of and participation in the other sports.

The professional side offers but little of interest to us beyond the records. The reason for this is that, in America at least, professional running is, like professional sculling, under a heavy cloud of questionable practices in the way of buying and selling races. Certain of the more recent additions to the professional ranks are men of better character, and men whose conduct will eventually tell favorably toward an increase of interest in professional running.

The amateur ranks, however, offer a very different phase of the subject. Two classes may be at once selected; not because they are actually distinct, but because their growth has been different, and because the conditions under which they exist must always differ considerably. These two classes are college athletes and other amateurs. College athletes are competing more and more in the general amateur meetings, and from these competitions deriving excellent practice.

Of English universities Oxford was the first to possess an organized athletic club. This was forty years ago, and in a few years Cambridge followed, for a time even taking the lead in the number of organizations. Fourteen years later the first inter-university contests were held between these two at the cricket grounds of Christ Church. Ten years later American colleges held their first intercollegiate contest at Saratoga. This American meeting was, however, only a sort of side-show to the intercollegiate boat-racing of that date. The incentive of these contests, nevertheless, brought about the formation of athletic associations at both Harvard and Yale, Harvard's organization antedating Yale's by a few months. The Intercollegiate Association was not formed until college sports had been in progress for some three years. Then in 1876 the Intercollegiate Association of American Athletes of America was organized. The same year the New York Athletic Club gave an annual meeting for the decision of the amateur athletic championship of America. The year 1876, then, may be taken as the date when organization was first firmly established in both college and amateur clubs. The necessity for such organization was the rapid increase in interest and the number of the contesting clubs. This was most marked in the college meetings, for in 1873 only three colleges competed, in 1874 eight, and in 1875 thirteen. The year after organization only six colleges competed, but since then the number has never been below nine, and ten years from the date of the formation of the Intercollegiate Association there were fifteen colleges represented by contestants. The number of events, which in 1873 was one, increased in the following year to five, and was twelve when the organization was formed. These events have been altered somewhat since that time, and the number is at present fourteen.

The various games which are generally classed under the term "track athletics" are walking, running, jumping, bicycling, pole-vaulting, throwing of weights. Of these, running occupies the first place in point of public interest. The very idea of a race between two men stimulates interest at once, and to watch a close contest between trained runners is pleasant, even to those uninitiated in the mysteries of the track.

The fastest running thus far done by any amateur for one hundred yards from a standstill is nine and three quarter seconds. Amateur runners have been coming up to the ten-second limit occasionally ever since 1868, but not one had passed it until within the nineties. In that twenty-odd years some eight American amateurs and an equal number of Englishmen have dashed down the track in the even time of ten seconds, while hundreds have run the course in the next fraction of a second. This record was made first in London in 1868.

A story was once written of a man who traveled many a mile to attend performances of a lion-tamer. He was possessed of the insane desire to see the man eaten by the wild beasts, and eventually his passion was gratified. There is a similar feeling of expectation in the minds of most of the enthusiasts who attend the amateur meetings of track athletes. Some time a record will be beaten, and it is always a story worth the telling if one has seen it done. Naturally, the fifth of a second by which this new champion dashes into prominence will not be appreciable to the eye of the best of judges. Just the slightest movement less of the fine split second-hand on the watches of the timers, and some man's name is added to the list of record-breakers. When one thinks that these sprinters, as they are called, go at the rate of thirty feet a second, he realizes something of the meaning of the term "dash" as applied to the short-distance races. Nor are the longer distances without especial interest, each in its own way. From a quarter of a mile down the races are run at the top of a man's speed, but the half-mile, mile, and above require the husbanding of strength and proper putting forth of just enough to run out the entire distance at the best uniform speed. The walking requires a rather more accurate idea of the rules to make it of the most interest to the average spectator, who fails to feel that the walkers are putting forth their best endeavors *because they do not run*. This feeling is but human, and it often seems to take possession of the contestants themselves, as one may see from the occasional warnings given by the judge.

The other features of track athletics are not brought so prominently before the public as are running and walking, but no one can fail to find a keen enjoyment in each when once or twice he has been a spectator of the contests. There is no better way to acquaint the reader with these various events than to answer in detail the questions which one might ask who for the first time attends one of these field meetings. The very heading in the newspaper, speaking of the men as the "Athletes of the Cinder Path," provokes a question. They come by this designation legitimately, and on account of the peculiar construction of the track upon which they run. This track is a scientific affair, and not a mere stretch of black dirt. It is made of six inches of the most approved constituents, carefully laid, and occupies months in its construction.

First the ground is accurately surveyed and measured, and the track so marked out that the required distance is given. The best tracks have straight sides, while the ends are upon moderate curves, either circular, elliptical, or parabolic, there being considerable difference of opinion regarding the respective merits of these curves. This distance is measured just eighteen inches from the inner edge, in order that the runner may have room to run freely, and yet not be obliged to traverse more than the correct distance. When the track is thus mapped out the proposed space is excavated to the depth of six inches, and curbings of seasoned lumber, an inch thick and eight inches wide, are set up around both inner and outer edge. Then the first layer, consisting of four inches of ordinary rough ashes freed from the coarser lumps, is deposited for a foundation. This layer is carefully raked and leveled, and then covered with two inches of loam. This loam in turn is carefully picked over and all small stones taken out. It is then rolled and watered frequently, usually for some weeks, but occasionally for two or three months, in order to have it thoroughly firm and hard. Finally the top layer, of cinders, is put on. This should be just sufficient thoroughly to cover the loam in every spot. The track is then complete, but it requires the constant care and attention of an experienced man to see that it is kept in condition. The object of all this is to give the runners a firm, dry, and elastic surface upon which to make their best efforts successfully.

One of the first things on the programme of events received on entry to the grounds is a summary of records. This plainly means the best time or distance, as the case may be, by which the contest has been won at any preceding meeting. But records have become things of nicety, and it requires certain conditions to make them of value.

A professional runner named Seward was at one time accredited with running one hundred yards in nine and a quarter seconds. From the time when belief in that record was exploded down to the present day there have been many discussions relative to timing. The English are partial to a single watch in the hands of an experienced timer; but to make a record in this country requires the presence of three timers or measurers, and two of these must agree or the intermediate one of the three be taken as the correct one. These timers and measurers, together with the other officials of the meeting, may be distinguished by the various ribbons which they wear. In this respect track athletics differ considerably from either base-ball or foot-ball. Two officials on the field suffice in these sports, but on the track there are nearly a score. First there is the referee, who decides all questions in dispute which are not otherwise covered by the rules, and who has power to disqualify a competitor. Then there are two or more assistants to the referee, who are called clerks, and who act as witnesses before him in case of fouls. There are three judges at the finish, who determine the order in which the contestants finish. Three other judges are called field judges; these measure and tally the trials of competitors in jumps, pole-vaults, and weight competition. There are three time-keepers, who take the time in the events requiring it. There is a clerk of the course, who notifies the contestants to appear at the starting-time, and assigns them their positions. There is one starter, who assumes control of the competitors after the clerk has placed them in their positions, and who, either by word or by pistol-report, starts each race, and whose duty it also is to set back any contestant making a false start. There is a judge of walking, who determines the fairness or unfairness of the walking, and warns or disqualifies any contestant guilty of adopting an unfair gait. There is one scorer, who records the order in which contestants finish, as well as their time. Finally, there is one marshal, who has police charge of the inclosure. There is occasionally an official reporter, who announces the record of each event. Any number of assistants may be given to such officers as the judge of walking, clerk of the course, scorer, and marshal. All these officials are necessary to the careful conduct of the events and to the accurate recording of them.

As the first array of contestants in the 100-yard run come up to the starting-point, and the clerk of the course assigns them their positions, one is struck by the difference of build among them. Tall and short, light and heavy, there are few men who are prevented by physical make-up from competition in one of these dashes. Brooks at 170 pounds, and Myers at 110 pounds, made one of the prettiest 220-yard contests ever seen in America, and both could run a fast 100. In this 100-yard race one of the chief points to be mastered is the start. How to get off quickly is the problem, for a fifth of a second means five feet of ground. They are on the mark, and the starter stands behind them where they cannot see his movements nor the flash of his pistol. "Are you ready?" "Set!" An instant, and at the crack of the pistol down they come, and almost before an inexperienced man can select his favorite from the rush, they breast the tape which is held across the finish-line, and the race is over. Nothing is prettier in any race than the running up out of the crowd of a fast sprinter who is too good for his companions, but who has perhaps lost a fraction at the start. There is none of the gradual cutting down of competitors such as one sees in the longer distances —just a mad dash for the front, as it seems; and yet when one comes to analyze it, to know the training gone through to get that stride, he begins to realize that it is by no means what it appears at the first

THE ONE-HUNDRED-YARD DASH — THE START.

glance, almost a matter of luck. The start, too, requires weeks of practice, and one might almost say years of experience. If an ordinary spectator were to watch the start of an experienced sprinter against a novice, he would almost invariably suspect collusion of some kind between the starter and the sprinter. More than this, he would think that the experienced man got off considerably more ahead of the novice than he really did; for the sprinter gains not only in leaving the mark, but in getting instantly up into his stride, whereas the novice is not fairly under way for several feet after he has actually left the mark. The rules regarding unfair starting are necessarily strict, on account of this great advantage to be gained. In all short races, those up to 300 yards, the penalty for a false start is to be put back one yard. It is greater in the longer races. Two yards is the penalty in races up to 600 yards, three yards in races up to 1000 yards, five yards in races up to a mile, and ten yards in those over a mile. In all races a third false start disqualifies the competitor; and any attempt to advance ahead of his mark after the words "Are you ready?" is met with immediate disqualification.

The 220-yard race is similar to the 100 in all respects. The contestants belong to the sprinter class, and go at high speed the entire distance.

With the 440-yard, or quarter-mile, one sees the first signs of grief in those whose condition is not of the best, or who cannot hold out for the entire distance. It is at this distance that the runner shows that he is not a machine. The best illustration of this is found in the records of the events. The speed of a runner at his best, as shown in the 100-yard race, is ten yards a second. This speed he holds with machine-like precision in the 220-yard race, the record being a bare fraction under 22 seconds. When the 440-yard race is reached, however, he cannot gather the power necessary to finish in 44 seconds, but at this distance we find the best man nearly 4 seconds behind time. The quarter-mile has more in common with the sprint runner than the distance man, however, for the sensation is that of running at full speed the entire distance, rather than by a perceptible effort so husbanding power as to make the pace a steady one, which is the feeling of, for example, the mile runner. The distance runners appear to run easily all the way, and to the spectator it seems that they might go faster if they would make the effort; but where the sprinter would have run himself out, and would begin to go unsteadily and manifestly with an effort, the distance man is still springing easily over the ground, apparently with no thought of fatigue, but rather with a consciousness of strength.

Hurdle-racing is a sport which stands between running and jumping, being a combination of the two. It does not require a man of marked jumping ability, however, as the flights are only 3 feet 6 inches, and any average athlete, although he may have paid no attention to jumping, finds no difficulty in clearing them. The point, in

TAKING THE HURDLES.

fact, at which the hurdler aims is to clear them just as little as possible, skimming over the tops so closely that he almost grazes each. In the early days of hurdling the runner ran as fast as he could between each flight, and with no definite number of steps took the hurdles as he might obstructions thrown in his pathway at haphazard. The scientific hurdler now takes a certain number of steps between the flights, and, fetching each at the most favorable point for his rise, actually clears them without a break in his stride, one leg being put out while the other is bent just as though it were but an exaggerated step. The distance covered is 120 yards, and there are ten hurdles set 10 yards apart with a 15-yard clear start and finish. Other distances are sometimes run, as 220 yards most commonly. In this case the hurdles are a foot lower, and are set 20 yards apart. The amateur record for the 120-yard hurdle race is 16 seconds. This shows that the runner loses almost half a second at each one of the obstacles in his course.

The walkers next attract our attention. To the ordinary pedestrian who tramps out for twenty or thirty miles into the country the gait of these racers is entirely unfamiliar. There seems the most intense exaggeration of every muscular movement. Watch this man who walks a mile in seven minutes! It certainly seems as if he would twist his spinal column apart just above his hips. But if one attempts to walk alongside of him, one soon realizes with what rapidity he covers the ground. Even a modest trot will not keep one even with him. Roughly speaking, it takes only a little over two minutes longer to walk than to run a mile. The distinction between running and walking is, that in the latter the heel strikes the ground first, and some part of one foot is always touching the ground, whereas in running the toe strikes first, and there is a period in the stride when both the runner's feet are off the ground. It requires the most expert of judges to see that the walking is fair, for there are a dozen tricks of gait, not in the least apparent to the uninitiated, which are unfair. Perhaps none is more common than what to us would seem the faintest suspicion of a limp, by which means the failure to straighten the leg at each step, thus not striking the heel first, from which an unfair walker can gain a very marked increase in speed. Long-distance pedestrianism, such as six-day walking-matches, has nothing in common with the walking of the short-distance cinder-track men. Most of these long-distance matches are now of the go-as-you-please class; that is, there is no restriction as to the gait, the majority taking to a kind of jog-trot, which yields the greatest results with the least fatigue.

To watch the jumping is rather a relief after the strain of sympathetic effort one feels inclined involuntarily to make when the walkers are exerting every particle of power to pass each other. Here the effort is a concentrated one, a sudden putting forth of muscular energy. The contestants jump in turns, and in the case of a long or a broad jump the greatest distance covered in three attempts wins the event. The run is unlimited, each man suiting his own taste in the matter. The scratch or line from which the jump is taken is a joist, some five inches wide, sunk flush with the ground. Just in front of this the earth is removed to the depth of three inches from a space of six inches, and the rule regarding the jump is that it counts a trial with no result if a competitor step

THE HIGH LEAP,
FRONT VIEW.

over the scratch line, or if he make any mark on the ground in front of the scratch. The measuring is done at right angles to the scratch line and to the nearest mark made by any part of the person of the competitor.

The high jump is made over a flat bar, which is supported on two uprights in such a position as to be easily dislodged. Competition begins at some height, selected by the measurers, which all the contestants can easily clear. The bar is then steadily lifted at the regulation of the measurers. A competitor may decline to use his jump at any height in his turn, but by so doing forfeits his right to jump again at that height. Three trials are allowed, and if on the third the jumper fails to clear the bar he drops out. The removal of the bar constitutes a failure. To run under the bar is a balk, and three of these successive balks constitute a trial jump. A fair jump is one made without the assistance of

THE HIGH LEAP.
REAR VIEW.

weights, diving, somersaults, or handsprings of any kind.

Pole-vaulting is another species of jumping, in which the jumper aids himself by the use of a long pole which he plants in the ground a little distance from the bar, and with which he lifts himself as he springs into the air. As the pole is reaching the perpendicular he swings himself over the bar, letting go the pole at the same moment. The same rule governs the pole-vault as the running high jump, and there is no limit to the size or weight of the poles.

Putting the shot is a contest requiring not only the same amount of skill as the other events, but also unusual muscular strength. The shot is an iron sphere, weighing either sixteen pounds or twenty-four pounds, the more usual weight being sixteen pounds. It must be put with one hand only, and in front of the shoulder. The competitor stands in a seven-foot square, and must not step out of this

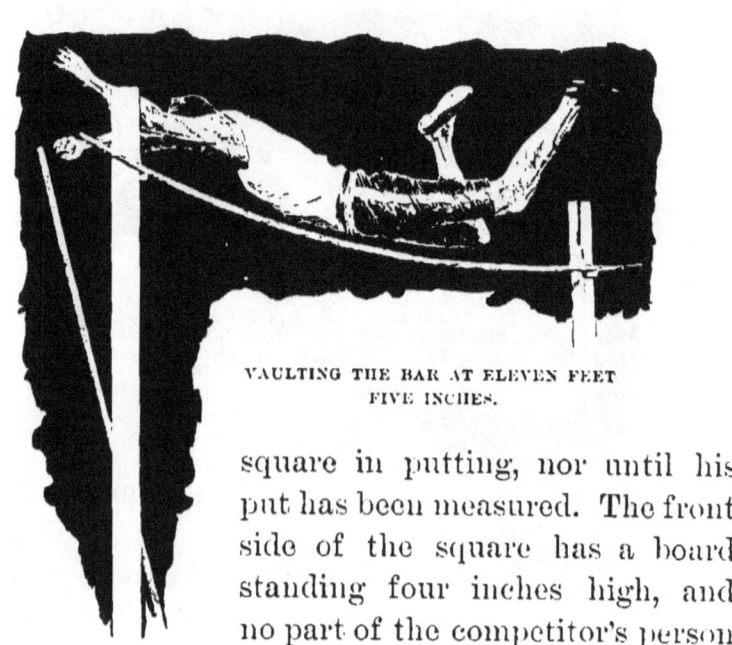

VAULTING THE BAR AT ELEVEN FEET FIVE INCHES.

square in putting, nor until his put has been measured. The front side of the square has a board standing four inches high, and no part of the competitor's person must be on this board in making the attempt. Puts are measured in a line at right angles from the front line of the square, or that line prolonged, to the nearest mark made by the shot. Three trials are allowed, and the contestants take turns as in the broad jump.

Throwing the hammer, like putting the shot, requires a combination of skill and muscular strength. The hammer is a metal sphere into which is set a handle, the projecting length of which, together with the diameter of the head, is four feet, the combined weight of head and handle being sixteen pounds. The throwing is done from a circle seven feet in diameter, and the competitor may not overstep the front of this circle until his throw is measured. The throw is measured from the nearest mark made by the hammer-head to the circumference of a circle on a line with that mark and the center of the circle. In throwing the hammer under the Amateur Athletic Union rules there are no further restrictions as to the man's method, but it is usual to swing the hammer two or three times over the head at the extended length of the arms, and then to let it go over the shoulder. Other contests in weight-putting and hammer-throwing are indulged in, but these are the most common in the programmes in this country.

VAULTING THE BAR AT TEN FEET SIX INCHES.

Bicycling has grown to be so common and wide-spread that it has a life, rules, and records quite apart from ordinary track athletics. There is one feature of these sports not yet mentioned, but which forms an important element in the interest and progress of the games. This is what is known as handicapping. Were it not for this many a meeting would lose much of its interest, and undoubtedly it stimulates to the improvement in general ability much more than would only level racing.

SHOT-PUTTER BALANCING.

As the term implies, handicapping is the taking away certain of the advantages of the superior men, and so arranging the acknowledged superior contestants that they must not only do better than the rest in order to win, but do enough better to make it a fair struggle on both sides. Sometimes a time allowance is made to the weaker men; more often, as in running-matches, the best man is started from the scratch and is obliged, therefore, to run the full distance, whereas his competitors are placed at certain intervals ahead of him, these distances being proportioned to their relative ability as displayed by the records they have already made. In order that this system of handicapping may be properly carried out, it is, of course, necessary that the handicapper be not only thoroughly familiar with the usual speed developed in all the various races, but also that he keep accurate tables of the records of each one of the runners whom he must place. Even

PUTTING THE SHOT.

PUTTING THE SHOT.

then, unless he be possessed of excellent judgment, he makes occasional mistakes that result in unsatisfactory races. The Amateur Athletic Union, which at present embraces the majority of prominent clubs, employs an official handicapper, whose duty it is, upon receipt of the names of contestants, to map out from his table of records the proper handicaps for the entries in each race. The rules of the A. A. U. provide for this official handicapper. He is expected to keep records and to handicap all entries as directed by the secretary of the Union, also to do other work such as the board of managers may direct.

There are a few pertinent questions that arise, to which a review of the annual amateur championship meetings affords more or less satisfactory answers. The question of the age at which a man is fitted for his best athletic work has always been a mooted one in all sports. In the games belonging particularly to track athletics the record

SHOT-PUTTER, LEFT VIEW.

SWINGING THE HAMMER.

of events shows that maturity is most needed in the events requiring unusual muscular development, such as weight-putting contests and hammer-throwing, while the extreme of youth seems no detriment to the running contests, jumping, and pole-vaulting. Hammer-throwing and weight-putting championships have been won by men over forty years of age, while boys of eighteen years have taken 100-yard, mile, jumping, and pole-vaulting championships. W. B. Curtis has shown the most mature development by winning championships at the age of 40, 41, 42, 43, and 44 years.

The longest continuous connection with track athletic sports has been that of C. A. J. Queckberner, who has competed in twelve successive years, ever since 1878, winning one or more championships at nine meetings. L. E. Myers, whose career is noted later in this article, and L. F. Lambrecht, both held a championship against all competition for six successive annual contests. The entries for these annual championship meetings have ranged from 100

THE HAMMER-THROWER — THE START.

to 150, once even as high as 169. As a rule, four fifths of those entering start in the events. The tendency to go from the ranks of the amateur into professionalism was much more marked in the earlier days of these meetings. The first annual champion-

THE BICYCLE-RIDER.

ship meeting, in 1876, had on its programme the following events: 100-yard, quarter-mile, half-mile, one-mile runs; 120-yard hurdle race; one-, three-, and seven-mile walks; running high jump; running long jump; throwing hammer; and putting the shot. The rules of the A. A. U. in 1890 gave events as follows: 100-yard, 220-yard, 440-yard, 880-yard, one-mile, and five-mile runs, one-mile and three-mile walks, two-mile bicycle race, pole-vault, running high jump, running broad jump, throwing 16-pound hammer, throwing 36-pound weight, putting 16-pound shot, 120-yard hurdle race, 220-yard hurdle race, individual tug of war, and team tug of war — a total of nineteen. The seven-mile walk is the only event that has been absolutely lost, while eight have been added.

Some of the contests of American athletes have stirred the enthusiastic spirit of more than the mere spectators. No one can read the story of one of his own countrymen contending against a foreigner, and showing pluck and skill enough to win, without a secret satisfaction. The performances of one amateur of our day are so remarkable as to be worthy of chronicling. That man is L. E. Myers, who has now joined the ranks of professional runners; but who, while strictly an amateur, lowered more records, and ran away from more really good runners, than any other man ever upon the cinder track. His first appearance was at the games of the New-York Athletic Club, election day, November, 1878. He was given a start of 18 yards in the quarter-mile race, and won in 55 seconds. The next spring we find him in the games of the Staten Island Athletic Club, where he won the quarter-mile in 54 seconds. From this time on he attacked records and men, and mowed them down steadily. In 1880 he won four American and four Canadian championships. It was then decided to send him to England, where they had little faith in the genuineness of his records, and predicted that their second-rate men would run the American off his feet. Previous to his first appearance, Englishmen interested in track athletics laughed at the possibility of his winning. With many runners the time when much is expected of them is very apt to be the occasion when they appear at their worst. Myers, however, never displayed this unfortunate trait, and his first English race was a grand triumph. Not only did he win by a clean eleven yards, but he broke the English record. From that time on he ran on every kind of track, through fields of all sorts of men, was placed at scratch with what appeared at least a line of men stationed all the way down the course, and yet the summary of nearly every race was the legend, "Myers romped in an easy winner."

It is needless to say that the Englishmen became thoroughly satisfied with the genuineness of his records. In 1884 he again visited England, and lowered three records. The following year he crossed once more to meet the best of England's men on various tracks. Two of these meetings were notable. At the Civil Service sports he was entered in a handicap quarter when Cowie, the English champion, was given eight yards' start. Myers ran him down and won in $48\frac{4}{5}$ seconds. A month and a half later, having in the mean time won many races, he was entered at Blackburn in two handicaps, and after winning the half-mile he ran the final heat of the quarter, giving Barton, of Scotland, 20 yards. Snook and others were given good starts in this, and it was generally believed that for once the American was to be defeated. Myers picked them all up, and won over a grass course in $49\frac{2}{5}$ seconds.

A half-mile race of Myers at Widnes shows the caliber of the man. As we have it on the authority of an

English journal of that date, Myers entered this particular half-mile handicap to beat a local man who had been freely boasting that the American could not give him 35 yards at that distance. Myers had just beaten Cowie again in the quarter, also Snook and others in the level half. But one great feature of Myers's running has always been his wonderful ability to keep on running race after race as long as there was any one before him, and he stepped up to the scratch in the handicap half as ready as ever. One by one he ran through his field, and 30 yards from home had them all behind him, coming in with an easy 8-yard lead in 1 minute $57\frac{2}{5}$ seconds. As the English journal took occasion to remark of the local runner's impression about the 35-yard start, "At five o'clock on Saturday evening Mr. —— had quite altered his opinion on the subject, which only shows what changeable mortals we all are."

The only man who actually ran Myers off his feet in a burst of speed was Brooks, a college sprinter. This man had beaten Myers in 1882, but in that race he had made his lead and kept in front to the end. In 1883, however, Myers had the pole, and when the two entered the straight with 90 yards to go Brooks was some 3 yards in the rear. The watches of some reliable experts say that the collegian ran the 90 yards in $8\frac{1}{2}$ seconds. At any rate he gained inch by inch, and 25 yards from the finish was within a yard of Myers. Then it was that both felt the final struggle, and as Brooks came up by Myers's side, both men tried for that impossible speed which is beyond the limit. Myers's limit came a shade nearer than that of Brooks, for he fell headlong in the attempt, and Brooks breasted the tape a winner.

Concerning the financial status of track athletics, while they do not, like base-ball, have an existence for the purpose of money-making, there is nevertheless a large amount of capital involved indirectly. Almost all of the clubs now prominent in this branch of sports have a winter existence, games, and habitat as well as an outdoor one. In most of the large cities there are athletic clubs which own desirable property. The club-houses in many instances are as much marvels of comfort and luxury as clubs with a different *raison d'être*.

One feature of these sports has not yet been mentioned, and that is the prizes. These have varied much from time to time. The first prizes given in English university sports were money prizes, but this practice was almost immediately altered, and there is now even a rule forbidding an athlete from pawning his medals or in any way converting them into money. While the correct theory for the amateur is that the prize should be valued and valuable only as a token of the victory it represents, as a matter of fact it has become the custom to have the prizes for record-breaking of more than a merely nominal value. So long as the present very stringent rules are in force regarding professionalism of any kind, there is but little danger of prizes becoming so great in value as to induce men to wish to obtain them with an eye to their marketable nature.

The progress of track athletics in this country has been rapid. The extension of the games of the cinder track throughout all large cities marks a different standing for them than any that they have obtained in the colleges and universities. There they had to wage direct warfare with boating and ball, and for a time the battle was an unequal one. The other sports were older and had the support of those who had gone before, while sports of the track were looked upon as interlopers which would interfere with the more regular games by directing men to other athletic enjoyment. The day has now come, however, when they have an assured position at all the large universities and colleges, while in amateur athletic organizations track athletics have the first rank, and the other sports are of but minor interest. Nor is the day far distant when the audiences that assemble to witness these contests will be equal to those assembled at any amateur ball-game or boat-race. Moreover, the number of contestants is increasing, and that means that more men are enjoying the benefits of open-air exercise, and by the help of the pleasant stimulus of contest are being drawn toward a better physical development.

The matter of training the track athlete at school and college has become one of careful study and of even more varied scope than the training of crews, ball nines, or foot-ball teams. The types of men in the various events are so markedly dissimilar, and the kinds of work for which they are to be prepared so different, that there must be several divisions of track athletes, and each division enjoy detailed study and direction toward fitting them for their special performance. The sprinter, or short-distance runner, although exceptionally a large man, is, as a rule, of a light, nervous, exceedingly active, and high-strung type. The weight-putter and hammer-thrower, on the other hand, is generally found among the large, heavily built, and rather slow-moving type of extraordinary muscular strength.

The college athletes in training for the games may be classed as follows: Long-distance runners, middle-distance runners, sprinters, jumpers and pole-vaulters, weight-throwers, walkers, and bicycle men. Of these the long-distance men are trained chiefly to increase their staying powers. But they are not put through exactly the same work day after day. They run three or four miles across country, for instance, two or three days in the week, and on the alternate days take sharp three-quarter or half-mile runs. In this way their early training is directed especially toward "improving their wind," as the expression has it. Later, as the season opens, they are put on the track and sent at varying distances, usually half or two thirds of the race for which they are to be entered. They are taught by running under the watch to become accurate judges of the rate at which they are running, in order not to be tempted to take too fast or too slow a pace by the efforts of some rival's partner or by the honest but ill-judged attempt of some inexperienced man. About once a week or once in ten days the runner is put over his distance on time. The rest of the time he either takes these half distances or practises short dashes to increase his ability to spurt.

The sprinters in the early and preliminary weeks do plenty of walking, broken up by short sprints, and should have a short section of track — regulation cinder track—conveniently near at hand upon which to practise starting, for it is upon the ability to get off the mark quickly that the race may often depend in these short distances. In practising these starts it is well for the man to have his regular running-shoes on, else his practice will amount to but little on account of the altered conditions. After the season opens at the track the sprinters practise daily starting under the pistol, and vary this with short bursts and then moderate stretches, being very careful not to lapse into careless running, but making every step clean and sharp, even though at a slower pace.

The jumpers and pole men go through general training by long walks and little dashes in order to get into good condition, but their special practice is sprinting and that of the take-off. Both spend much time upon this latter all-important point of their work. Later, when at work at the field, they take sprinting practice, and every other day or two or three times a week jump and vault, taking the day between for easing up by a run rather than their regular work.

The weight men take runs of one or two miles in the preliminary weeks, and through the winter use the chest weights and pulleys besides the heavy dumb-bells, all of which is directed toward strengthening the muscles they will use the most. After a time they go through regular trials with each other, for this sport particularly requires something of an incentive in the shape of contest to keep a man steadily improving. Their work does not differ materially when at the field, although they are not expected to make their best effort too often, as they run the same risk of getting stale as that experienced by a pitcher who uses his arm too much. The walkers take walks of from three to four miles at a fast pace, paying particular attention to the steady increase of their stride, and, of course, walking fairly. When in the season they get on the track, special attention is paid to their free hip action and the use of the arms. They, too, practise to acquire a good and accurate knowledge of pace and practise spurts. They should walk on time once a week or so for a trial. The bicycle men do road work during the fall and winter when the weather permits, going eight or ten miles a day, and then taking body exercise in the gymnasium. Usually all the candidates for the athletic team go through a short daily course of gymnasium work during the winter. As early as possible the bicyclists get on the track, and then their practice consists of daily rides at medium speed, interspersed with spurts. To them also the acquiring a knowledge of pace is absolutely necessary, and they make their weekly trial as well. The winter work of an athletic team can in these days of excellent gymnasia be made of great help toward their preparation for the spring. Felt- or canvas-covered weights enable the weight men to practise indoors, and the use of mattresses and boards makes it possible to do the high jump and the pole-vault. Short sprints are also possible, and even hurdling. On the track distance races, both running and walking, can be indulged in, and meetings, called indoor meetings, are now regularly held every winter.

One of the best methods for the development of new material is the occasional handicap meeting, either at home or upon an outside track. At home these meetings are productive of a friendly rivalry that stimulates men to their best efforts, as well as directing their attention to the improvement of their faults; and competition in outside meetings gives them that most necessary experience which is so valuable when the day of the important contest arrives. Many a first-time track athlete is afflicted with a sensation exactly similar to stage-fright, and wholly unable to do himself or his college justice from this very lack of experience.

Whenever it is possible, an experienced coach should be employed, for he is even more desirable in track and field events than in foot-ball or base-ball, although perhaps in rowing the services of a coach are of equal value. The men should be worked in squads, and it is well to have a sub-captain or man in charge of each of these squads, while the captain himself has full charge over all. The coach should be a man of thorough experience, and should spend all his time upon the coaching of the individuals in their respective lines.

There is one point in which the development of an athletic team requires far more careful study than that of any of the other branches. In base-ball, foot-ball, and boating there is a need of good substitutes, but they are few compared with the number of the men making up the first choice. In all track meetings second and third places count a certain number of points for the team securing them, and for that reason the development of the men who are not perhaps the most promising is an all-important point for the consideration of captain and coach. A man who wins third place may by that very triumph secure for his college the cup, and be as much the victor as the member of the nine who scores the winning run or of the team who makes the touch-down. Moreover, it is in the development of these second and third men that a school or college eventually establishes a fund of material for first places.

To a school or college about to start an athletic team a few very brief hints may be valuable. Remember that the first thing to be done is not to know that you have some one single star, but to induce as large a number of men as possible to come out and try for the team. If a start can be made before the spring and a number of men persuaded to put themselves into reasonably good condition by gymnasium and general winter work, so much the better. Then the man who is chosen captain should, as soon as the weather and men are in condition for a few trials, make a thorough test of his candidates. Here let me say that one of the best captains of a university track athletic team once said to me: "No man knows what he can do in track athletics until he tries, and I think, almost without exception, that of all my record-holders not one of them had ever tried his respective event previous to entering college." It is therefore well to bear in mind this fact, and by having the men take part in little competitions, determine what each is likely to do best. Many times an unexpected star is thus discovered. In track athletics, as in the other sports, it is hard, persistent work that wins, and the men must have this fact thoroughly impressed upon them at the outset, in order that no individual may become discouraged when some veteran runner, jumper, or vaulter beats him. Be careful to avoid overtraining, however, for it is both more common and more serious in this branch than in some of the others. A man is making individual efforts, and there is no limit perhaps to his pluck and ambition, so that without a watchful eye over him he goes on overexerting himself, and when the time of trial comes he has no snap or dash, but only a half-hearted listlessness that numbs his physical and mental qualities. Pluck, or "sand," as the average American boy calls it, is a characteristic of the winners in track events, as it is of the best men in the other sports: only in the other sports there are usually comrades close at hand to help, while on the track a man must run his own race on his own bottom. He must grit his teeth, squeeze his corks, and go ahead, even though he feels that he will drop. The preparation in the gymnasium will have put the men into some measure of condition, but work should be gradual even after that, and it is a cardinal fact worth remembering that vitality or energy should never be exhausted. The best performer is usually the eager performer.

Candidates for the 100-yard dash should be classed together, and the light body-exercise they have taken in the winter, with the occasional short outdoor run, and the starting practice, will have fitted them for track work. They should be brought up to their mark and put through the regular form of "Ready," "Get set," and then the pistol, and all off at their top speed for twenty or twenty-five yards. They should always run their distance as though in a race. Every other day they should be given a 50-yard instead, and they should do some jogging of 100 or

125 yards occasionally, lengthening out as the day of contest draws near, so that they can go through their distance at a good clip. In starting there are many different styles, the crouching and the Sheffield being perhaps the most favored. In the former the runner crouches down, touching his fingers to the ground, one foot on the mark, the other just behind it. In the latter he stands, bending slightly forward, his body partly turned, one arm projecting in front and the other lifted behind, his forward foot on the mark and the other some inches back.

The 220-yard men practise like the 100-yard men, with this exception — that the 220 men must acquire a knowledge of pace which the 100 men do not so certainly need. A 100-yard man, except in trials, when he is sure of getting his place, is usually best instructed to run it out at speed. Turning and looking behind and slackening up have lost many a winner his race; and there are men who, in a 100, when possessed of the notion that they know just what clip they are going at, will do tricks of this kind. But in a 220 the runner should know something of pace as do the longer distance men. The best thing to say to the sprinters just before the race is what I heard a captain at the Intercollegiates say one year: "Now remember that you are running for your college. Don't leave that mark until the pistol goes, and then you go too, and as if Death were after you. Don't turn your head until your chest strikes the tape!"

For the 440 the practice should be, after the winter breaking in, easy quarters, — sometimes an easy half — sometimes a 300; on occasional afternoons, the 220-yard dashes, — of course with a rest between; and once a week, a quarter on time. With the increased distance comes that increased value of a knowledge of pace which the runner must acquire from daily running under the watch, until he knows what time he is making. But he must not (any more than the 220 man) get an idea that he can run the first part of his race easy and then finish fast. As one man puts it: "You 've got to run the first 220 as fast as you can, and then finish on your sand."

For the 880, after getting on the track, short, sharp 300-yard dashes every few days, then a 660-yard, every little while quick quarters, — all run under the watch, to acquire the knowledge of pace. At first a slow half, or possibly five eighths once in a while, starting from the mark and running hard for the first 30 or 40 yards. This the 440 men should also do. When the quarter- and half-milers are going on the track for the race, the captain should tell them to leap off the mark, sprinting for 10 or 15 yards, — to get rid, if possible, of the crowd, as these are usually full races, — then dropping into regular gait. They must not be troubled by some man rushing past them at first, so long as they are sure of their own gait. In the 440, if there is anybody ahead of you, at the 220th yard you must begin to look to overhauling him, and when at the 400th-yard mark grit your teeth, squeeze your corks, and get home as fast as you know how. Of course in trial heats of a 440, get your place as easily as you can.

To the 880 men I would say that if at the end

of the first quarter anybody who has gone up is still ahead of you, you must begin to pick him up, and by the time you reach the 660th-yard mark you ought to be close behind him, or if he is known to be a fast finisher you must pass him. Then, when you come into the stretch, you must fairly fly. These races take plenty of thinking as one runs; and keeping cool and calculating the thing out will win doubtful races many a time. If you know there is a great runner in your race, it is often good policy to pick him out and dog his tracks, unless you feel that he is setting an unusual pace purposely. If you find him going slow of your gait, you had better move up rather than let him keep you back, because he can probably make too long a burst for you later in the race.

Mile runners take half and three-quarter distances always under time, and finish fast. In a race they should stick to their own pace, particularly in the first quarter; but when they reach the last quarter, it is time to begin to pick up the leader, and in the stretch run the last bit out. Mile men should also break out of the crowd at the start, the same as the 440 and 880 men. It is well to say, also, that all these men should be kept off the hard sidewalks both in their winter and other running or walking, as far as possible. It is not necessary in winter to practise every day, particularly for preparatory school-boys, who should practise only three times a week. An occasional day off, at the discretion of the captain or coach, after track work has commenced, is not a bad thing either.

Hurdlers should practise their take-off and sprinting, and should negotiate about three hurdles at a time in practice. The usual three-step method is preferred for the high hurdles, and the jump and stride should be a jump clearing close to fourteen feet, next step five feet, next six, next five again, then flight. Of course these steps will vary slightly, but that illustrates the principle. When learning this three-step the novice should place the hurdles sufficiently near together to enable him to get his stride, then he can increase the distance as his strength increases until he reaches the regulation ten yards. In mid-season the hurdler should occasionally go over six or seven hurdles, and three weeks before the race, the full course. Then again, he should go over that number once ten days and once the week before. When a hurdler goes to the mark, it is well to tell him as a parting injunction not to look around, and never to mind if he touches or knocks down a flight or misses his stride; but to go on and win. Mile walkers practise fast quarters, with occasional half and three-quarters, then good jogs of distance. The walkers, together with the weight-throwers, should have some expert to teach them at the start the proper motions, as these cannot be accurately and concisely described in print without the aid of practical illustration. The pole-vaulters should have good winter practice upon the parallel bars; and indoor practice at vaulting is also simple nowadays. At the field they should practise sprinting and take-off, as should also the jumpers. American pole-vaulters do not climb their poles — that is, move the hands up the pole after taking-off, as do some of the Englishmen; but the motion is a single one. All jumpers and vaulters should start easily for their run, and then, striking their mark and getting into their stride, go to the take-off with speed and confidence. They should be told just before going into the contest to keep cool and not to permit the bar to be put up any faster than they want it. Broad jumpers should, in addition to their sprinting and take-off practice, try getting up well into the air. Sometimes it is even best to put a string, about a foot and a half high and twelve or fourteen feet from the take-off, to tempt them up. Some excellent authorities, however, are against this plan.

ROWING

"No boy or man should be allowed to go in for school or college rowing until he can swim."

THE English universities had had many a hard contest at the oar before the American universities took up boating. In 1829 Oxford defeated Cambridge; then no race was rowed until 1836, when Cambridge turned the tables and won not only that race, but the next succeeding three. The first college boat-club in America was formed at Yale in 1843, and in the fall of the next year the Oneida Boat Club was organized at Harvard. This was a club of juniors, and was followed a few weeks later by the Iris Boat Club, organized by the seniors. In the spring of 1846 there were three boat-clubs at Harvard, which united in building a boat-house. In 1852 a challenge was received from Yale, and, upon its acceptance, a race was rowed at Lake Winipiseogee, August 3d. Harvard won this race, as also the next one, which was rowed in 1855 at Springfield. In 1853 there were at Yale six active boat-clubs, which formed themselves into the Yale Navy,— although this was not legally incorporated until 1863. Harvard's clubs by the time of the 1855 race had also increased in number to five, but it was not until 1869 that the Harvard University Boat Club was formed. Although the first race, that in 1852, had been rowed in eight-oared barges with coxswains, the race in 1855 had two six-oared barges with coxswains entered from Yale, while Harvard sent one eight-oared barge with coxswain, and a four-oared lapstreak boat without coxswain. In 1859 all the entries were six-oared boats, although the rigging differed as well as the style of boats. Six-oared boats were adhered to throughout the number of years of the intercollegiate regattas until, in 1876, Yale and Harvard rowed their first eight-oared race at Springfield. The distance rowed has, like the boats, gone through a variety of changes since the inauguration of college races. The first race was over an approximately two-mile straightaway course, but from that time until 1872, the races were over a course of a mile and a half and return. In that year a three-mile straightaway course was adopted and adhered to until Yale and Harvard began the eight-oared races, when the course was altered to a four-mile straightaway. English oars have consistently adhered to the straightaway course and to long distance, rowing now a course a furlong over four miles. Since 1857 they have rowed in what was practically the present style of eights, although the present oar, rigging, sliding seats, etc., have been later additions. The first six-oared shell in America was built for Harvard in 1857. It was forty feet long and twenty-six inches wide, made of white pine, at a cost of two hundred dollars. It weighed one hundred and fifty pounds. Spoon oars were used in this boat. Since that time both cedar and paper boats have been used, and there is talk about the possibility of aluminium. For smaller boats this has already been tried, but there is doubt of its availability for eight oars. College boat-racing in America was at its height, so far as the number of crews entered was concerned, in the days of the National Rowing Association of American Colleges. This was formed in 1872, and the regattas were held at Springfield, on the Connecticut River. Then Saratoga was adopted as the course, and in 1875 the following thirteen colleges sent crews: Amherst, Bowdoin, Brown, Columbia, Cornell, Dartmouth, Hamilton, Harvard, Princeton, Union, Wesleyan, Williams, and Yale. The Massachusetts Agricultural and Trinity had crews in the two preceding years. With the withdrawal of Yale and Harvard this organization fell to pieces, and to-day the race between these two universities at New London is the only one which is rowed regularly every year.

Of all the college sports this one of rowing makes the most stringent demands upon a man's unselfish devotion. In base-ball and foot-ball there is the stimulus and excitement of frequent, almost daily, games, and in track athletics there are plenty of brushes with friends, and occasional outside contests, to give a pleasant interest. In boating, although there are many days during the season when the old as well as the new oar finds an enjoyment in the sport itself, there is usually but one day of contest,—one day of supreme effort,—and the struggle for which all the labor of six months has been undergone is all over in a brief twenty minutes. To be prepared for this day, to be fit to represent the university, a man goes through months of training and many a day of hard work, when there are no enthusiastic admirers applauding the effort, and when oftentimes even the weather seems to be possessed of a vindictiveness against the oarsman. Such a sport requires preëminently men of strong character, men in whom perseverance and patience are marked traits. A boating man must make himself. Not all the coaches in the world can do for him that part of the work which persistent, plodding effort to master each detail can alone accomplish. A coach may correct a fault, but faults in rowing are apt to be like the formed habits of mature life, almost ingrained, and to eradicate them requires the steadily fixed and unflagging attention of the individual himself. At first it is a distinct effort at every stroke for him to avoid a lapse into his old or natural way. For days, and it may be for weeks, he feels that he must think every time; but then there comes a day when it is more natural and easy to do it the right way than the old way, and his lesson is learned. But this is only one fault, and lucky indeed would be the oarsman who found he had but one fault to correct. In fact it is a wonder that more men do not become discouraged in their early attempts; but the man who goes in for this sport, and sticks doggedly at it, putting his whole thought and attention upon the instructions he is receiving, reaps in the end the reward for all his labors. To some men, rowing, so far as eventually securing a seat in the 'varsity boat, is as much out of the question as becoming a 'varsity ball-player. There is a knack about rowing as about any other game of skill, but patience and perseverance have made boatingmen out of some terribly unpromising material, so that one can hardly feel justified in saying to any man, "You 'll never be an oarsman."

Some of the best men in Harvard and Yale boats have been men who during their first year—yes, even their second year—have been looked upon by the coaches as decidedly doubtful. Besides the monotony of the rower's training, there must also be considered the fact that in the great final contest the oarsman does not come into actual contact with his opponent; and so there is lacking the usual stimulus to outdo that is so marked in foot-ball, and present to less extent in the other sports. It is here that the result of the dogged determination is seen; and the same earnest patience which makes the old oarsman take kindly the coach's severest criticisms and put his whole mind into correcting a trifling fault, now drives him on when every stroke is a pain and his whole strength seems exhausted. In selecting a man for the boat, therefore, this quality of being willing to die with no one but himself to fight is a *sine qua non*, and often gives a seat to a man whose skill may be less than a rival's. Besides this, quickness of action and adaptability to changing circumstances are of great importance. Thus it is seen that many components—strength, skill, quickness, perseverance, and bull-dog pluck, with a cheerful acquiescence to hardships and sacrifices—must be nicely balanced in the oarsman; and the selecting of their men to answer these requirements is the most difficult task of captains and coaches.

The fact that a suitable bit of water must be near at hand makes taking up the sport of rowing, in any college or school, something more difficult than is the case with foot-ball or base-ball. But the English bumping-races show the possibility of using even a narrow course, and the roughness of the Sound, and the oyster stakes in Mill River at New Haven, as well as the bad water often on the Charles at Boston, go far toward showing that a still-water lake is by no means necessary to the development of the pastime. Naturally the choice location for a course upon which to bring up and train crews would be a placid lake, long enough to yield a dead-water straightaway four-mile course. The great advantage of dead water lies in the possibility not only of trying experiments in rigging and stroke, but of comparing one crew with the crew of the previous year at the same period of development. This gives the coaches and the captains a means of judging how much value there is in every change made either in work, training, or rig. But any body of water where the prevailing winds of summer and spring do not with too great frequency put a shell in imminent danger of swamping, should tempt the boating enthusiast to organize a crew. If the course can be but a mile, by rowing with a turn a two-mile race is possible; and many a class crew has turned out 'varsity material upon races of that distance. In the matter of boats, class crews have in the past produced excellent oarsmen in six-oared barges, and 'varsity men are to-day trained in pair-oars, while the 'varsity crew complete does its preliminary work when first on the water in an eight-oared barge. The eight-oared shell is the boat for the oarsman when he has rubbed off some of his faults and become accustomed to his work. Nothing can be prettier to the spectator, or more fascinating to the men themselves, than the rhythmic swing of those eight bodies, the dip of the eight oars, and that well nigh invisible bit of the boat-maker's art which holds the eight stalwart fellows out of water. But to return to the barge. The best thing that a school or college determining upon the organization of a boat-club can do, is to purchase a second-hand barge for their initial work. If their club is likely to depend for its races upon some rival school or college, the two should agree upon the number of men and purchase their first boats accordingly. If, on the other hand, there are to be no outside races, but inter-club contests, then pair-oars, fours, sixes, eights,—anything that is warranted by the number of men and the finances of the club. Racing in singles, while an excellent sport, is not so good training for future crew work as the others, and although it teaches an individual many things regarding balance and watermanship, it does not directly fit him with any great measure of assurance to become a member of a crew.

When a boat is obtained, a crew should know how to take care of it. It is just as well to practise upon an old boat and follow out the details as carefully as though it were just from the maker. When not in use it should be shelved, bottom up, upon a number of brackets (at least four for a sixty-foot boat), sufficiently close together to prevent any danger of warping from sagging. It should be kept well varnished, with bolts, screws, etc., in tight order. Outriggers, locks, and stretchers should be carefully inspected before each row. When taken from the water, it should be carefully wiped both inside and out. Before a race it should be rubbed down with pumice-stone, smoothed with soapstone, and greased with oil, paraffin, or similar substance. An eight-oared shell made of paper should weigh, all rigged, from 210 to 240 pounds; if made of cedar, it should weigh from 230 to 275 pounds. A cedar boat cannot be re-rigged with as little damage as can the paper boat, and as a rule the paper boat proves stiffer and more durable. The length should be from 59 to 61 feet, the depth approximately 9 inches from gunwale to keel, with 4-inch wash-board above the gunwale. The breadth in middle should be from 22 to 25 inches, narrowing to 16 or 18 inches at the ends of the cockpit. The cockpit should be about 35 feet. The oars should weigh approximately $7\frac{1}{2}$ pounds, and the length be, inboard—that is, from button to end of handle—$3\frac{1}{2}$ feet, and outboard—that is, from button to tip of blade—$8\frac{1}{2}$ feet.

A word as to care of the oars. They should be treated most carefully, for any slight scratch through the varnish admits the water, and makes them heavy and lessens their spring. In landing at the float, and even when laid on a floor, the concavity of the spoon should be down so as to avoid scratching. If leather buttons are used, they should be examined often, and kept up true and smooth. Metal buttons always keep their shape, and so are preferable to the leather in that point, and have another advantage, in that the small screws for attaching them weaken the oar less than the nails of the leather button. It is important to have the end of the blade and the back of the shank at the button exactly parallel. One can determine whether the oar is "true" or not by resting the shank on a straightedge and sighting over the end of blade. If "off," it can be remedied by shaving off the leather that covers the oar at the button on one side or the other as required. Each man should cut the handle of his oar to fit his own hand, so he can hold it easily and firmly with least effort.

In handling a boat, there is something to be considered beyond the mere rowing when in the water. As I have already indicated, the boat must be properly cared for at all times. If a foot-ball player uses a ball badly, plays with it when the weather is inclement, as many a time he must for practice, the expense of a new ball is not so great as to count for the labor necessary to prevent the ball becoming out of shape and ruined. The same is true of a base-ball or a bat. But a boat is not in the same class, and bad handling and lack of proper care will ruin any boat, not only in appearance, but for practical work and — that for which it is wanted — for speed. I have already noted how the boat is to be kept upon brackets or a rack, how it is to be kept well wiped, varnished, and tight as to bolts, screws, etc. Now as to moving the boat. In taking a boat from the rack, if it be a high rack, as is often the case, the crew should stand under it, take it above their heads, and, lifting it clear, then let it settle between the port and starboard men. If the rack be low, the port men on one side and the starboard men on the other lift it and carry it out. It is best to carry it keel up, — that is, upside down, — with port men on starboard side and starboard men on port side, each man opposite his own rigger. Then when the boat is turned, one side reaching over and the other under, each man gets his own rigger in his hand. If carried keel down each man should be behind his own rigger. The boat is put in the water from the keel-up position by raising above the heads and the men on one side—the side next the water—stepping under, and all grasping the cross-bars and swinging down to the water together. It is put into the water from the keel-down position by one side—the shore side men—holding the boat up by the cross-bars while the other side crawl under the boat — then as above to place it in the water. The keel-up position is the best, and with a well-disciplined crew is a very pretty sight. The boat being in the water alongside the float, it is as well to say to the uninitiated that it is not advisable to jump into an eight-oared racing shell in exactly the same careless manner in which the average excursion party boards a broad-beamed sail-boat. The shell would surely tip over, and probably some feet would go through the thin sides. As one looks down into the boat he sees eight small seats on slides, and eight inclined foot-boards (with straps for the feet), called stretchers. Along the exact center of the bottom of the boat runs a strip called the keelson. Running out from the sides are the outriggers, through which the oars obtain their purchase. To get into the boat, put one foot on the keelson, and, bracing on seat braces, transfer all the weight to the foot on the keelson and lift the other daintily over, slipping it into the stretcher strap; then, bending the knee of the leg bearing the weight of the body, and with hands on the side of the boat, let the body down into the seat. The oar—this depends upon the nature of the rowlock, however—should already be in place, and an experienced man will steady himself with the oar instead of the sides of the boat. The feet should always be tightly strapped in the stretcher. Our crew and coxswain being now in the boat, an assistant or two, taking hold of the blades of the oars that rest on the float (not lifting them up, however, so as to unbalance the boat), the end of handle being held against the opposite gunwale, while the men on the other side keep their blades flat on the water and steady the shell, gently push the boat out into the stream until the oars are clear of the float. At this point, barring an interposition of Providence, a crew of landsmen who had not begun as suggested earlier in this article with pair-oar and barge work, will tip over — in fact they probably would before reaching this point. But having gone through all the details in a less cranky affair, they are ready for shell work. The coxswain says, "Ready!" The eight oars go back to full reach and lie flat on the water — or the oars may be buried for the stroke. The knees of the men are bent and the slides all aft and the arms extended. "Give way!" and the men swing up from the "Ready" position and the boat is off. Here we will leave the crew to discover how hard it is to learn to keep a shell on its bottom, while I revert to the terms used in rowing and coaching.

"Ready all" and "Give way" have just been defined.

"Avast" means stop rowing, and should be called while the oars are in the water — never on the recover except in an emergency.

"Hold" means to keep the oar buried at right angles to the side of the boat, thus stopping her progress; the plane of blade being parallel to the surface of the water.

"Back water" means to reverse the motion of rowing, driving the oar in water from stern to bow instead.

The "Catch" is when the oars take the water on the stroke and the shoulders swing up.

The "Finish" is when the oars leave the water at the end of the stroke.

The "Recover" is the combination of movements through which an oarsman goes from the time of the "Finish" until he is again in position for another stroke,—that is, to the position for "Catch" again.

The "Bevel" of the oar is the angle it makes with the plane of the water when it goes in. If this angle be too great the oar goes too deep, or "dives," as the expression has it. If too small, it does not get a grip. When the angle is too great it is called too little bevel, and *vice versa*. In general the bevel of the oar should be 5 degrees to 10 degrees from in front of the perpendicular, and the shoulders ought to be about 15 degrees beyond the perpendicular at both ends of the stroke.

The term "Time" is used technically to indicate the unison of a crew in every movement.

The following are the most common terms used in coaching a crew, with the meaning appended:

"Bucks" or "Meets the oar" is the expression used to indicate meeting the oar with the body at finish when the arms are pulled in. The body here should be perfectly rigid.

"Slumps." Settles down with shoulders and upper body at the finish, so that back is crooked and muscles relaxed.

"Rushes slide." On recover allows slide to run the oarsman by the momentum of the boat, rather than holding it in check with the feet on the stretcher.

"Loses control of slide" has similar meaning.

"Swings out," that is, fails to keep in line over the keel so that the men are not in line. When a crew swing out, as one looks along the boat their bodies appear to be making a scissors motion as they row.

"Gets in late." The oar goes into the water after the others, or the swing up with the shoulders is too slow and breaks the time.

"Gets out late." The oar drags at finish and backs water.

"Short on catch" means not getting the oar in the water far enough toward bow. This may be due to either too short rigging or too little body reach.

"Drops on catch" means that the oarsman allows his shoulders to go toward the stern of the boat just as his oar takes the water.

"Clips" means to miss the first part of a stroke, rowing it in the air.

The management of the boat while in use is important both as a help to perfection in rowing and for the preservation of the shell in the best possible condition. When not rowing the blades should rest flat on the water, the handles being held firmly, and the boat *always* balanced on an even keel. If in the racing boat, holding water should be done as little as possible and lightly, to avoid the strain it throws on the rigging and bracing. In turning, one side should pull around very easily (always in time for the sake of practice), the other side having the oars flat on the water and never holding or backing while first side is rowing, as this strains the boat badly. In meeting a swell it should be taken full broadside with the boat riding and falling in trough. If taken at any angle the strain is tremendous, and will weaken the best boat.

It is well to have the coxswain give all orders for rowing, stopping, etc., the captain giving them to him. Emergency orders, as "hold," however, must not wait for repeating, and any order from the coxswain must be obeyed at once, for he is the pilot.

There is one part of the coach's and captain's duties about which the general public hears but little, and upon which practical knowledge is a most important component toward making a winning crew. That part is the "rigging," or, commonly speaking, the arrangement of each individual in the boat, so that he may by proper use of his seat, stretcher, outrigger, and oar, get the maximum power into his stroke at the minimum expenditure of strength, and so that the entire crew may act as a most harmonious whole. What the proper timing and the concerted action of men in a team play is to foot-ball, the rigging is to a boat crew. A poorly rigged crew make hard work of keeping time,— they may be rigged so badly as to make time almost impossible,— become quickly exhausted from being compelled to do their work in awkward positions, and, finally, that work is performed at a mechanical disadvantage.

To cover the detail of rigging exhaustively would be to take up measurements which could be multiplied almost indefinitely; but it is possible to give some general directions that will enable the captain of brains to adjust his crew satisfactorily by careful scrutiny and following out the principles. The rigging should be so arranged that when a man is on full reach he will get his oar into the water at about five to seven feet forward of the thole-pin, and bring it out at finish from four to five feet aft of the thole-pin. His outrigger should be high enough above the water, so that his hands comfortably clear his knees on the recover, with oar-blade four inches above the water, or about 7½ to 8½ inches above his seat. The seat is, according to the man, from six to nine inches from the bottom of the boat, and the slide from fifteen to twenty inches in length. This slide is on a pitch aft of one inch. In general, a short man must have a higher seat and must come farther aft of thole-pin, in order that he may get a longer reach. He is also forced to reach farther forward with his shoulders and swing back farther.

"The stroke," as commonly spoken of, means the entire action of the oarsmen of a crew in propelling the boat by the repetition of the motions connected with the repeated plunging of the oars into the water. This action is divided into two component parts—the stroke proper, and the recover. The stroke proper lasts from the time the oar is put into the water— "the catch"—until it leaves the water at "the finish." The "recover" is from the time the oar leaves the water until it again enters it. The stroke consists of three parts—the catch, the pull through, and the finish; while the recover consists of the feather, the carrying back over the water, and the turning up for the catch. During the stroke the oarsman swings up with his shoulders, kicks out his slide until his knees are nearly straight, and, finally, brings oar to body with his arms. During the recover he performs these movements in reverse order and manner, getting his hands out, his knees bent, and his shoulders forward, ready for the next stroke. The art of the oarsman lies in doing these things in the proper order and time, until the entire act is as smooth and rhythmic as the stroke of a bird's wing. The stroke may be subdivided indefinitely, many giving it over a score of component parts; but that is more for the theoretical study of it than for the novice or ordinary boating man.

In training crews a very important feature is understanding how much work they should be called upon to perform daily, and what the nature of that work should be. It is just as advisable that the preparation for a boat race should be gradual as it is that a man should learn to read before undertaking advanced studies. In many sports nature speaks out at once when a man is forced. For instance, if a man without training should undertake to run a mile at full speed, it is probable that he would sink exhausted or become afflicted with violent nausea before he had gone half the distance. But in boating there might not be so apparent an outcry against overtaxing the novice, and yet no good could come from it, and much harm might. Moreover, looking at it from the standpoint of the captain, overtraining means that his crew will lose the race. It is well, therefore, to follow the course of training adopted for a 'varsity crew or college. The English rowing men do not take so long a course as Americans; but boating is more general, and the material is usually well broken in before it reaches the hands of the president of the boat-club. A Harvard or Yale 'varsity crew, after what little work they may perform on the water in the fall, really settle down or go into training in midwinter, after the Christmas vacation. Their winter work consists of a bit of general exercise in the form of various movements, intended to increase the freedom of action and strength of the muscles used in rowing. This lasts, perhaps, fifteen minutes. Then the crew start out for a jaunt, mostly an easy run, broken up by occasional spurts and walks, which, beginning very moderately, lengthen out after a few weeks to a distance of several miles, returning to the gymnasium well blown. After a short rest they go down for tank work,—that is, to sit in a boat which is stationary, while they drive the water around through its channel with the oars. Of course the likeness to real rowing is decidedly crude; but there is enough similarity to make it possible and practicable to coach men for the later work upon the water. This tank work is not a long-continued pull, but broken up by frequent stops, while the coach explains to the crew in general or to the individual the faults and how to remedy them. After this work, lasting perhaps an hour, the men take their bath, and are well rubbed down. This winter work of the crew is usually performed in the afternoon, and gives a man a short time to rest before dinner. Until the water is clear and the weather a little less than bitterly cold, the tank or gymnasium work continues; but with the very earliest possible opening the captain takes his crew to the boat-house and gets them upon real water in a barge. As this is likely enough not until April, the men are in fair physical condition to stand work. When a crew gets upon the water, the judicious captain or coach knows that the work is not like that of the field sports, where the time occupied is, and should be, almost the same daily after the men settle down to mid-season work. Some days the coaching upon a particular fault may keep a crew out for hours and yet the actual labor not be excessive; and again at other times a straight, long pull may be advisable where the rowing is kept up every minute of the time the men are out. The duration of the practice, therefore, varies, say from one to two and a half hours. Short, hard pulls, with coaching, are necessary for the eradication of individual faults; while if a crew is "badly together" (that is, rowing each man for himself without regard for time), a long, easy pull of five or six miles "shakes them together" (that is, makes them row more alike and as a unit) the best of anything. Once or twice a week the distance to be pulled in the race should be rowed over on time. On these days only a little light work should be done, consisting of spurts and coaching pulls. During the week of the race there is no special modification, except very light work for the two days preceding the event. If a crew can row twice a day instead of once, two hours on the water in the morning—if not too hot—in coaching individual rowing, and the same in the afternoon, can be endured; but the captain and coach must watch his men very carefully, particularly the ones likely to become overtrained. Boating men speak of a man as "going fine," and mean by that that he is on the border-line of becoming overtrained or "stale." The indications are loss of appetite, general laziness and indisposition, with tired, aching feelings in the muscles and bones. There is a bad taste in the mouth and poor sleep, maybe persistent insomnia, and a failure to gain from day to day the weight rowed off. Ordinarily this loss and gain of weight should be from two to four pounds, although it often reaches six or even seven. The only treatment for this condition of fineness is rest, either partial or, if necessary, complete. A change from the diet of the training-table should be enjoyed if case be obstinate, and in worse cases a few days' change of residence will work a cure. Drugs are useless, and worse. Champagne and claret may be of use in case it is so late in the season that a rest cannot be afforded.

A freshman crew can in the main stand a similar course of work, although there may be instances occasionally where the youth of some individual member will make a little less desirable.

A school crew, where the boys are from fifteen to nineteen years old, should average from a half hour to an hour and a half of work a day, and pull the length of course to be rowed once or twice a week.

In regard to the time a crew should leave the barge and take to shell rowing, it may be said that in general the earlier the better, after they have mastered the rudiments. The change should never be made, however, till the barge is perfectly balanced, and the crew is able to row in good time, and no glaring faults are apparent.

While in the barge the stroke should vary from 22 to 26 to the minute. On entering the shell it should remain at that number till the boat runs well on an even keel, when it can be gradually raised to the top point at which the crew can row, this varying with different styles of rowing: the English crews and Harvard have even touched forty on spurts, while Yale is usually somewhat lower.

If, as is almost invariably the case, some man finds himself the possessor of an obstinate fault, the place for him is the pair-oar, no matter at what season of the year. Either with his coach or alone, he can often find and remedy the difficulty in a short time, whereas in the cranky and rapidly moving shell he is completely at a loss how to act.

Perhaps nothing is of more interest to the athlete than a study of past methods and deductions made by his predecessors in any sport, and the man who makes a study of these often has at hand explanations and suggestions in cases coming up in his own time, which are of great value to himself and his fellows in determining a course of action. To no branch of American athletics does this apply with greater force than to boating, because in that sport we still adhere in the principal points to almost the same general line as that prevailing in England for a long series of years. The Englishmen have little base-ball, cricket taking its place. In foot-ball we have wandered far from the original principles of Rugby Union; in track athletics there is little in the way of apparatus, and the questions of training simply differ for climatic reasons; but in boating, the general rigging, the stroke and methods have a peculiar interest for us, and I shall therefore go into some of the comments of English authors upon the rowing of the universities, giving some of the old as well as later ideas expressed by men thoroughly familiar with the sport. An English authority says, most properly, that training is "putting the body with extreme and exceptional care under the influence of all the agents which promote its health and strength, in order to enable it to meet extreme and exceptional demands upon its energies." And the best English authorities upon training insist upon the progressive system of very gradual development. But for all that, their university crews do not as a rule spend nearly as long a period of time in this progressive preparation as do American boating men. But in the selection of their men, they do lay particular stress upon the importance of selecting men of good build in the upper body and chest. They look for men whose lungs and heart have plenty of room, and one of their authorities gives the following measurements of a man who rowed number seven in one of the Oxford University boats as being those of one of the best specimens of both muscular and respiratory power he had ever seen: Age, 21 years; height, 5 feet 9½ inches; weight, 11 stone 6 pounds; chest, 40 inches; forearm, 12 inches; upper arm, 14 inches. As will be seen, this man was no giant, but his chest was of the kind that English boating men like to note in their candidates. In contradistinction to this, let me instance the case of a man who was advised particularly not to go into boating, but who was found rowing in one of the minor college boats. This man's measurements were as follows: Age, 19 years; height, 5 feet 9 inches; weight, 9 stone 3 pounds; chest, 32 inches; forearm, 9¼ inches; upper arm, 9¾ inches. As far as possible, they dislike to have any man take up rowing who at eighteen years of age has not a minimum chest development of thirty-six inches. In training, their diet is as liberal as ours, and with perhaps more freedom in the use of beer, or ale, as we call it. Not to too greatly alarm the friends and relatives of any man who may be selected for a coxswain in an American boat, let me instance the course of training for one of these much-abused candidates in an English boat. "For a week before and during the week of the race, pills and Turkish baths twice a week, running daily in heavy clothing, and food as little as would sustain life." But if a man is willing to pay for the pleasure of having eight magnificent fellows row him about for weeks, he must expect the bill to come rather high; and no one, I believe, has had the temerity to advance the sport of coxswaining as one that produces marked physical development. One of the most interesting studies of English boating men was that made some twenty years ago by Mr. Morgan of Oxford, in pursuance of the inquiry as to the number of university oars benefited or injured by the sport. He followed up every man who sat in the 'varsity crews from 1829 to 1869, during which period 26 races had been rowed. There were 294 of these men, of whom 255 were living, 39 having died, and his final conclusions were as follows:

Benefited by rowing 115
Uninjured 162
Injured.................................... 17

This was in the days before the more careful system of training and selection had been adopted. Some of the letters he received and some of his comments are of deep interest to oarsmen, and carry a pleasant sentiment in the lines.

From Bengal writes McQueen: "I am now a stout man weighing fifteen stone, but able to be in the saddle all day without fatigue, or, if necessary, walk my ten or fifteen miles without distress." I wonder if he still possesses the same hand-power that he had in his youth? He had simply the strongest hand and wrist I have ever known, and never did I place my own palm in his without setting my teeth close. His was the true Herculean build. Nind writes from Queensland: "Since taking my degree in 1855, my constitution has been put to the test in many climates, for I have lived in Canada, on the west coast of America, and in Australia, and I can safely aver that I have never, in trying circumstances, found any failure of physical power; and that when hard pressed by fatigue and want of food, the recollection of the endurance developed by rowing and other athletics gave me fresh spirit and encouragement." And yet Nind was not naturally a powerful man. His frame was 'the very antithesis to that of McQueen. Those who remember him as he first came to the university, will recall his exquisitely molded features, almost feminine in their softness and sweetness of expression. Schneider writes from New Zealand: "I may state that, so far as I am concerned, I am able to discover no particular symptoms, either good, bad, or indifferent, attributable to rowing." Then follow other letters, and these lines: "In the list of oarsmen, certain names are printed in italics,—not many, thank God!—a small percentage only. They have rowed out their life-race. They rise before my mind's eye as I first knew them. Brewster's magnificent form towering half a head above his stalwart shipmates. Invalided from his regiment, caught cold by returning wet from a Brighton Volunteer Review, died from its effects. Polehampton, the chivalrous, the gentle, the brave!. Decorated while at college with the Royal Humane Society's Medal, for saving a companion from drowning at his own imminent peril. Shot through the body at Lucknow.—and died of cholera while attending to his comrades stricken by the same malady. The very career he would have marked out for himself had it been left to his hand to trace it! Hughes, the accomplished, the frank, the manly,—the very nature that, speaking in our love and in our pride, we emphatically style the beau-ideal of an English gentleman,—died last year of inflammation of the lungs."

Who knows but that some one will write a list of the memorable names in our American sports, men who sat in our boats, and played upon our fields? And that list will contain names that mean as much to us as these do to the Englishman.

The Rev. T. H. T. Hopkins of Magdalen College, Oxford, wrote as follows of the sliding seat nearly twenty years ago. "The mechanism of the sliding seat consists of two runners or rails formed of glass, brass, hardwood, or other suitable material on which the rower's seat slides to and fro in a direction parallel to the keel of the boat. Friction is obviated by the introduction of friction wheels; the traverse fore and aft is limited by stops. The effect of this seat on the rowing work may be stated briefly as follows: In order to obtain the necessary traverse for the oar, we require a backward and forward motion of about three feet each way. This reach, as it is called when speaking of the motion forward, is attained on *fixed seats* by inclining the shoulders and trunk of the body from the hips as far forward as possible, and by extending the arms straight out to their fullest stretch, the knees being at the same time somewhat bent up; on the *sliding seats* the same, or, to speak more correctly, a longer reach is attained, partly by inclining the trunk of the body forward, but not to the same extent as with the fixed seat, partly by sliding the whole body forward on and with the seat, partly by extension of the arms as in the fixed seat, the knees, however, being considerably more bent. We shall probably be near the mark in stating that the body of a rower on a fixed seat moves through about 90 degrees; on a sliding seat through about 45 degrees."

One crew, when practising for the Henley regatta of 1872, adopted them and increased its speed, at its first row, by twenty seconds over the Henley course, though four oarsmen out of the eight had never rowed on sliders before.

Mr. Knollys of Magdalen College, Oxford, writes: "The difference of sliding and fixed seats is the same as if one were to try and raise a great weight off the floor between or over the knees. In fixed seats the muscles of the leg and those of the small of the back are used about equally, and in sliding seats the muscles of the leg, especially those just above the knee, are used about twice as much as those of the back. My idea of correct sliding is to row for about four inches in the ordinary way, and then kick as hard as one can."

Mr. Knollys thus sets forth what he considers the great advantage of the sliding seat: "I think they do not pump one so soon. Most men's wind gets exhausted before their muscles, and on a sliding seat one does not get blown so soon as on a fixed one. The reason for this I take to be, that all the work is done with the body in an almost upright position. There is not nearly so much movement of the body, and none of the pressure of the legs against the abdomen and ribs when forward." The above are nearly all collected from the opinions by Mr. McLaren, in his book upon training. He also gives the description of a practical test made by the Rev. Mr. Hopkins, and confirmed by the investigation followed by Professor Haughton, of the University of Dublin, to determine the actual force employed in the propulsion of an eight-oared shell at racing speed. Mr. Hopkins weighted an eight-oared shell with sand-bags, to match an average crew. This boat was then towed by a line upon which was a dynamometer, and the calculation showed that a force of 63 lbs. would be required to propel a boat at the rate of 9 miles an hour, or a mile in 7 minutes. He goes on to say, however, that the formula would prove true only within limits, and only approximately so at high speeds. Professor Haughton, working out the same problem, on the basis of a mile in 7 minutes, showed that the work done per man is 18.56 foot-tons in 7 minutes, or 2.65 foot-tons each minute, and also gives us the rule. "The work done per minute by a boat's crew varies as the cube of the velocity. Thus a double speed requires an eightfold work per minute." Comparing the work done in rowing a mile at racing speed, or in 7 minutes, with the work done by one of his eight-oared crew, weighing 11 stone 4 lbs.,—158 lbs.,—in racing costume, walking 1 mile, he has

        Rowing . . . . 18.56 foot-tons.
        Walking . . . . . . 18.62   "

If, then, one may take the Englishman's conclusions after many years of boating experience, the sport is far from dangerous, and one in which the man of sound body will always find pleasure and profit.

A REMARKABLE BOAT RACE

AS SEEN FROM THE REFEREE'S LAUNCH

IT was the day of the long-talked-of Atalanta-Yale race; and every one was on the tip-toe of expectancy at the thought of the question of boating supremacy to be settled between the champion amateur eight and the champion college eight. Experts in boating matters had expressed differing opinions as to the probable result, and every one at all interested in rowing had read of the merits of the rival crews. The general opinion was that the Atalantas would lead for at least two miles, and then would strain every nerve to hold that advantage to the end of the four miles which had been agreed upon as the distance. The race was to be rowed between the hours of ten and seven, at any time when the conditions of wind, tide, and water were most favorable. At nine o'clock the wind had sprung up; and the crews, referee, and judges, who were assembled at the Yale boat-house in preparation for the start, began to cast dubious looks at the flags as they stood out straight from the poles in the freshening breeze. The course had been laid out in the harbor, extending four miles direct from the outside breakwater to the end of Long Wharf. The boat-house stood a mile back from the long pier, and the boats of both crews were here housed until the referee should order them out for the race. The Long Wharf and boats and bridges were black with people by ten o'clock. Eleven o'clock, and still the wind whipped the water into waves, not high, but too rough for the low eight-oared shells to ride without danger of becoming filled before the four miles could be rowed. Now the only hope of the weather-wise was that on the turn of the tide, just after noon, the wind would slacken. This hope proved well founded, for by twelve o'clock the flags were drooping, and, the water becoming quieter, the referee ordered out the boats, and the crews hastened to bring the slender shells.

The Yale crew then jumped aboard the referee's steam-launch, which started down the harbor, towing the shell. A steam-tug performed the same offices for the Atalantas. As the two little steamers puffed down past the piers, the "Rah! rah!—Yale!" of the college sympathizers mingled with the cheers of the friends of the Atalantas. By the time they reached the starting-flag, the course was by no means bad except at a few exposed points. The two crews at once crept gingerly into their cranky shells, and paddled up to the line.

Soon the shells were in place; the referee called out, "Are you ready?" and then his "Go!" rang out like a pistol-shot. The sixteen oar-blades were buried, and the two boats sprang forward like unleashed hounds, the Yale bow a trifle to the fore. Now for the lead! The Yale crew have been told that they must not be alarmed if the Atalantas should at first succeed in obtaining the coveted lead, but they have also been instructed to "spurt" up to thirty-five strokes to the minute (which is two or three above their regular number) rather than let these sturdy rivals have their own way at this point. Both crews are putting forth all their strength; the Yale blades splash a little more than those of the Atalantas, but nevertheless the power of their stroke keeps them still a foot ahead. Almost stroke for stroke they row, but now the Yale boat is traveling more smoothly on her keel, and she begins to draw away. The half-mile flag is passed, and there is clear water between the boats. Down drops Yale's stroke to thirty-one, while the Atalantas' must remain at thirty-four.

On they go, the space between the boats slowly growing until, at the mile, Yale is three lengths ahead. At the mile and a half they have increased this lead to four lengths, and it begins to look as if it were "all over but the shouting." The Yale blades go more smoothly now, and there is hardly a splash in the rhythmic swing of the rising and falling oars when — what! stroke has ceased to row! See the spurting sheet of water rising over his motionless oar! Oh, Allen! — no one thought you'd fail! But why does he not recover? The water still leaps from the dragging blade; the cause is plain — he has broken his oar, and Yale's chances are gone! What a pity, after their fine work, and with such a lead! Allen is reaching out and unlocking his rowlock to set the oar free and stop its impeding drag upon the boat. The Yale oars go bravely on, not a stroke lost, although there are only seven oarsmen now. But the Atalantas are creeping up, and it is manifestly a hopeless task for those seven men to carry a "passenger" as heavy as Allen over the remaining two miles, and keep ahead of the eight in red, who are now steadily overhauling them. Allen has succeeded in freeing the broken oar, and drops the two treacherous bits into the water astern. Poor fellow, it will break his heart to watch the steady approach of that slender prow behind and be unable to help his men! See, he turns and says something to starboard-stroke, and now — he is certainly going to stand up! Just leaning forward, he rises as the seven oars make their catch and lift the boat firmly; and, almost without a splash, over he goes, clear of the boat, which shoots ahead as he turns in the water and calls cheerfully, "Go in and win!" A few strokes of his muscular arms, and he is reached by the launch, and swings himself up into her bows the hero of the hour! Now his crew still has a chance to win, for the loss of his oar is partly compensated by the decreased weight. A half mile will tell the story, for they have lost but a length or two of their lead. As they pass the next flag it is evident that the Atalantas are no longer gaining, and at the three miles they are surely dropping farther astern! Only a mile more, and if the plucky little coxswain can keep up the courage of his seven men, Allen will have no cause to mourn. We are near enough to hear the coxswain shout, "Only a half mile more, boys; keep it up and we'll beat them yet!" The boats at the finish begin to see them coming, and the whistles blow and the cheers come rolling over the water, encouraging them to hold that powerful swing just a little longer. Two minutes — and "bang!" goes the gun on the judge's boat, and the Yale crew shoots by, the winners of one of the most remarkable races ever rowed. And how the boys will make heroes of them all!—Allen for his coolness and pluck, the coxswain for his skill and courage, the starboard-stroke for his steady work, and all the crew for their endurance and nerve!

A BOAT RACE AT NEW LONDON

NOTE.—If in this race Yale wins, it is not to be taken that Yale wins an undue proportion of the races she rows with Harvard; but that, being a Yale man, my description, if I made Harvard win, would of necessity stop after the last stroke, or else be a most doleful tale of sad, disheartened home-coming without enlivening incident, and not conducive to the glamour I would throw over the sport.

IT is the end of June, and Commencement week is drawing to its close. The campus, with its canopy of old elms, has echoed with the annual shouts of class histories; the fence has again held the dangling limbs of the returning alumni, the chapel has been filled with the eloquence of orator and poet, and the white, stark old Center church has heard one more valedictory, and seen once again the giving of degrees.

To the graduating-class, the end of college days for the first time looms up as a reality. The excitement of class exercises has up to this time hidden the specter of farewell. Yet there remains one more event; once more may their blood be stirred, and their enthusiasm aroused, before they leave old Yale behind them for the more serious realities of life. The boat race is yet to come, and every one is going. The fair friends who have come on to see their brothers, and the brothers of other girls, graduate are in a flutter of excitement over the final event. They have crushed one and another of their pretty gowns at promenade, ball-match, and Commencement; but they appear at the depot as neat and trim and cool as one might wish, ready to set out for New London. The long excursion-train stands on the tracks, and from nearly every window flutters the blue of Yale. The cars are already crowded, and still they come. "Oh, I wish we'd start!" cries out a pretty girl, who is not alone in her impatience. At last the bell rings, and the train moves off on its two hours' trip to the Thames. Stories of last year's victory, rehearsals of the gaiety of the past week, gossip about the rival crews beguile the time away on the ride, and almost before we realize it the train draws into New London. Here we begin to find something beside the blue. Crimson ribbons dangle from parasols and encircle straw hats. Buttons of the same brilliant color are seen on coats, and before we have been in the town long it is evident that Harvard has plenty of supporters.

There is time but for a bite of luncheon, and then we all hurry over to the observation-train. How the sun beats down, and what a stew every one is in about seats. It is impossible for any one who has not secured seats in advance to get a place, and there are tales of fabulous sums asked by speculators for seats. Fortunately we purchased our seats several days ago, and we hurry about to find our car. Here it is at last, and—what a lark!—it is next to a Harvard car. See the red ribbons! Well, they'll make it pleasant for us if they win; but how we will glory over them if our boys only come in ahead! Is n't that a pretty girl just getting in, and what a stunning gown! The cars are full as far along the line as we can see, and it is time we started. There, there is the bell of the locomotive, and with a little jerk of the long train we are under way. Slowly, like a long serpent, the train twists along up the bank of the river to the starting-point, and every now and then we enliven its progress with a cheer, which is heartily answered by our Harvard rivals. At last, with a final jolt, this huge grand-stand of cars comes to a stop just beside the starting-line, where we see the diminutive steam-launches scurrying to and fro, bearing the instructions of the referee and starter. The two crews are not yet visible, and every one is craning his or her neck in vain attempts to catch the first glimpse of one or the other of the rivals. Presently there is a stir at the Harvard quarters over across the river, and the men from Cambridge are seen carrying their shell out on the float. Steadily they bear the fragile thing out to the side of the float, and we just catch a gleam from its shining side as the men turn it into the water. How daintily they step into her! But while we have been watching all this through a powerful glass, another shell has been put into the water, and, manned by eight fine fellows, comes pushing its slender nose along toward the starting-point. "Rah! rah! rah! Yale!" echo the cheers from car after car along the line. Almost before the cheers have passed the length of the train, the Harvard boat comes springing along under the impetus of the eight long sweeps which move like the legs of a great caterpillar walking the water. Now the red-ribboned spectators take their turn at cheering, and the cry of "Harvard!" rings out along the line.

The two boats are backed up to the starting-line,

the referee calls out his final instructions, and then, as the boats are held to await the word, there comes a sudden hush over the crowd, through which comes faintly over the water the "Are you ready?" and almost instantly the report of a pistol. How the two boats jump forward, and the oars flash, and the backs bend! See, the Harvard boat is drawing just a little ahead, but that little sends her adherents into a state of frenzied cheering, and as we pass behind the hill and lose sight of the boats, our last view shows a little clear water between Harvard's stern and Yale's bow. What a pause of anxiety it is while we drag along through this cut! Just as the first cars move slowly out into the open again a cheer goes up that certainly seems to end with "Yale." Can it be that Yale is picking up? In a moment our car emerges, and we, too, set up a most undignified, but very joyful, yell, as we see the two boats even once more and pulling almost stroke for stroke. The flash of the oars just before the catch, the clean finish, the sway of the bodies,— everything moves like clockwork in both boats as they shoot along side by side, neither gaining any advantage. But see, where there were eight swinging bodies a moment ago there are nine now, and—hurrah! it is the Yale bow-oar who makes the first one of the nine bodies. A few strokes more, and number two appears before the Harvard bow. Yale is unmistakably drawing ahead. Oh, what a relief to feel that they are really pulling away from that boat which hangs so persistently by their side! And what a satisfaction to see that though Harvard is now spurting they do not pull up, but simply hold their own. Now the Yale stroke quickens a little, and foot by foot they draw ahead, until clear water shows between their stern and Harvard's bow. It begins to look like Yale's race now, surely, for as they flash by the three-mile flag there is a gap of more than a boat's length. But the crimson crew has not yet given up. Their stroke calls upon them for another spurt, and one can almost feel the effort with which his men answer to it. Their bow is creeping up again, but they cannot hold it. See number two — how his head goes over as he yanks on his oar! Three and five are also in dire distress, while the blues are pulling like a machine, and increasing their lead again. Past the half-mile flag they go, and the race is virtually over. Nothing but an accident can now deprive Yale of the victory. They have again dropped their stroke, and are pulling almost leisurely. Harvard makes another effort, but without gaining a foot, and now the steam craft set up their shrill whistling. The cannon on the yachts puff out their flashes of smoke, but the sound of the report is hardly heard in the din, and Yale crosses the finish line a winner by five lengths. Now every cheer has "Yale" at the end, and blue flags wave, and Yale men are shaking hands with Yale men, while the Harvard colors trail along in the dust, and their sympathizers are dumb, and another race has been lost and won.

There is a rush for the bake-shops, and every one seizes what he may for himself and party, and in a short time we are all packed once more into the train for New Haven. One or two members of the crew are with us, and how they are cheered and hand-shaken and clapped on the back all the way home!

6*

Here is a man with his hat in his hand taking up a collection for fireworks. Nor does he have to do any begging. Bills and silver pile up rapidly in his straw hat, until he is obliged to make transfers to his pocket in order to have room for further collections.

As soon as we pull into the station every one hurries up to the campus and New Haven House, to make preparations to receive the victorious crew. A band is engaged, and a crowd starts back with the musicians to march up with the boys. We have hardly time to get a bite of supper before the fireworks begin. Trinity Church bells jangle out their chimes of "Here 's to good old Yale, drink her down, drink her down." The campus is a sea of fire, with burning barrels and boxes, cannon crackers, Roman candles, and sky-rockets, and in the midst of it all we hear the blare of the cornet, and the banging of the drum and cymbals, as the crew, led by the band and followed by a crowd of cheering men, turn the corner of Church Street and come marching up Chapel Street to the New Haven House. When they have reached this spot they stop, and one of the men, whose voice is already so hoarse as to be entirely unrecognizable, waves his hat for silence. As the noise lessens for an instant, he shouts out, "Three times three for Captain ——!" and the crowd responds most nobly. Then follows a cheer for each member of the victorious crew and the substitutes, and a final three times three for another victory over Harvard. Then the crew are taken into the New Haven House for a supper, while the crowd outside continue the fireworks and celebration. Almost without cessation the crackers snap and the candles flash out their liquid fire until long after twelve o'clock, and it is not till almost daybreak that the campus becomes deserted and the last smoldering embers are extinguished by the night-watchman. And when to-morrow comes not one of the many pretty girls will begrudge a burnt hole here and there in her gown, nor the torn gloves, nor any of the souvenirs left by the incidents or accidents of the day, but she will go off for the summer and tell how she saw the Yale crew win at New London, and the number of candles she herself set off in their honor on their return.

FOOT-BALL IN AMERICA

THE rules governing American foot-ball are an outgrowth or development of the English Rugby foot-ball game, the very name of which at once recalls to every reader the well-beloved "Tom Brown."

The credit of introducing these rules among our colleges belongs entirely to Harvard, who had learned them from the Canadians and were at the outset won by the superior opportunities offered by the new game for strategy and generalship as well as for clever individual playing. After Harvard had played for a year or two with our northern neighbors, Yale was persuaded to adopt these English rules, and in 1876 the first match between two American college teams under the Rugby Union rules was played. Since that time the code has undergone many changes, the greater number being made necessary by the absolute lack of any existing foot-ball lore or tradition on American soil. The English game was one of traditions. "What has been done can be done; what has not been done must be illegal," answered any question which was not fully foreseen in their laws of the game.

For the first few years our college players spent their time at conventions in adding rules to settle vexed problems continually arising, to which the English rules offered no solution. In this way the rules rapidly multiplied until the number was quite double that of the original code. Then followed the process of excision, and many of the old English rules which had become useless were dropped. During the last few years the foot-ball lawmakers have changed but two or three rules a year. The method of making alterations has also been perfected.

In order to avoid the petty dissensions incident to contests so recent that the wounds of defeat are yet tender, an Advisory Committee of graduates has been appointed, and all alteration of rules is in their hands. They meet once a year to propose any changes that appear to them necessary. They submit such propositions to the Intercollegiate Association for discussion and approval. Provided this association approve of them, they are then, by the secretary of the Advisory Committee, incorporated in the rules for the following season. In case the association take exception to any, they are returned to the Advisory Board, and if they then receive the votes of four out of the five members they become laws in spite of the disapproval of the association. This has never yet occurred, nor has there been anything to mar the harmony existing between the two bodies.

No change, then, is possible unless suggested by a body of men, not immediate participants in the sport, who have had the benefit of past experience. This most excellent state of affairs was the result of suggestions emanating from an informal conference held some years ago in New York, at which were present members of the faculties of Harvard, Princeton, and Yale. These gentlemen were at that time carefully watching the growth of the sport, and were prepared to kill or encourage it according to its deserts. Their suggestions have rendered most substantial aid to the game, and made its law-making the most conservative and thoroughly well considered of all rules governing college contests.

"How does the English game differ from the American?" is a very common question, and in answering it one should first state that there are two games in England—one "the Rugby," and the other "the Association." These differ radically, the Association being more like the old-fashioned sport that existed in this country previous to the introduction of the Rugby. In the Association game the players cannot run with the ball in their hands or arms, but move it rapidly along the ground with their feet—"dribble the ball," as their expression has it. Of course, then, a comparison between our game and the Association is out of the question. To the Rugby Union, however, our game still bears a striking resemblance, the vital point of difference being the outlet to the "scrimmage" or "down." In the English game, when the ball is held and put down for what they call a "scrummage," both sides gather about in a mass, and each endeavors by kicking the ball to drive it in the direction of the opponent's goal. Naturally, there is a deal of pushing and hacking and some clever work with the feet, but the exact exit of the ball from the "scrummage" cannot be predicted or anticipated. When it does roll out, the man who is nearest endeavors to get it and make a run or a kick. The American scrimmage, while coming directly from the English play, bears now no similarity to it. Instead of an indiscriminate kicking struggle we have the snap-back and quarter-back play. The snap-back rolls the ball back with his hand; the quarter seizes it and passes it to any man for whom the ball is destined in the plan of the play. In other respects, with the exception of greater liberties in assisting a runner, it would not be a very difficult task to harmonize our game with the British.

QUARTER-BACK TAKING THE BALL.

While the game has in the last ten years grown rapidly in popular favor, it would not be fair to suppose that all of the twenty or thirty thousand spectators who gather to witness one of the great matches have clearly defined ideas of the rules which govern the contest. Many of the technical terms they hear used are also Greek to them, and it would undoubtedly add to their enjoyment of the game to give a few clues to chief plays of interest.

While awaiting the advent of the players, one looks down on the field and sees a rectangular space a little over a hundred yards long and a trifle more than fifty yards wide, striped transversely with white lines, which give it the aspect of a huge gridiron. These lines are five yards apart, and their only purpose is to assist the referee in judging distances. There is a rule which says that in three attempts a side must advance the ball five or take it back twenty yards under penalty of surrendering it to the opponents. The field is therefore marked out with these five-yard lines, by means of which the referee can readily tell the distance made at each attempt. The gallows-like arrangements at the ends of the field are the goal-posts, and in order to score a goal the ball must be kicked over a cross-bar extending between the posts by any kind of a kick except a "punt." That is, it must be by a "drop kick," which is made by letting the ball fall from the hand and kicking it as it rises from the ground; by a "place kick," which is from a position of rest on the ground; or finally even from a rolling kick. A punt is a kick made by dropping the ball from the hand and kicking it before it strikes the ground, and such a kick can under no circumstances score a goal. Scoring is only possible at the ends of the field, and all the work one sees performed in the middle of the ground is only the struggle to get the ball to the goal.

There are two ways in which points may be made: by kicking the ball, as above described, over the goal, and by touching it down behind the goal line. A "safety" is made when a side are so sorely pressed that they carry the ball behind their *own goal line*, and not when it is kicked there by the enemy. In the latter case, it is called a "touchback," and does not

A TOUCH-DOWN.

score either for or against the side making it. A "touch-down" is made when a player carries the ball across his *opponent's goal line* and there has it down, *i. e.*, either cries "Down" or puts it on the ground; or if he secures the ball after it has crossed his opponents' goal line and then has it "down." Such a play entitles his side to a "try at goal," and if they succeed in kicking the ball over the bar, then the goal only scores and not the touch-down; but if they miss the try, they are still entitled to the credit of the touch-down. A goal can also be made without the intervention of a touch-down — that is, it may be kicked direct from the field, either from a drop kick or a place kick, or even when it is rolling or bounding along the ground. This latter, however, is very unusual. In the scoring, the value of a field-kick goal is only five, of a goal kicked from the touch-down, six; if the touch-down does not result in a goal it counts four, and a safety by the opponents' counts the other side two.

When the game begins, the ball is placed in the center of the field and put in play, or kicked off, as it is termed, by the side which has lost the choice of goal. From that time forward, during forty-five minutes of actual play, the two sides struggle to make goals and touch-downs against each other. Of the rules governing their attempts to carry the ball to the enemy's quarters, the most important are those of off side and on side. In a general way it may be said that "off side" means between the ball and the opponents' goal, while "on side" means between the ball and one's own goal. A player is barred from handling the ball when in the former predicament. When a ball has been kicked by a player, all those of his side who are ahead of him — that is, between him and his opponents' goal — are off side, and even though the ball go over their heads they are still off side until the ball has been touched by an opponent, or until the man who kicked it has run up ahead of them. Either of these two events puts them

A FAIR TACKLE.

on side again. Any player who is on side may run with and kick the ball, and his opponents may tackle him whenever he has the ball in his arms. It is fair for them to tackle him in any way except below the knees. They must not, however, throttle or choke him, nor can players use the closed fist. The runner may push his opponents off with his open hand or arm, in any way he pleases, and ability to do this well goes far toward making a successful runner.

When a player having the ball is tackled and fairly held so that his advance is checked, and he cannot pass the ball, the player tackling him cries out "Held!"

The runner must say "Down," and the ball is then put on the ground for a scrimmage. Any player of the side which had possession of the ball can then put it in play. Usually the "snap-back," as he is called, does this work. He places the ball on the ground, and then with his hand rolls the ball back, or kicks it forward or to one side, generally for a player of his own side to seize. When the ball is rolled or snapped back, the man who first received it is called the quarter-back, and he cannot run forward with it. When, however, it is kicked sideways or ahead, any one except the snap-back and the opposing player opposite him can run with it.

"Free kicks" are those where the opponents are restrained by rule from interfering with the ball or player until the kick is made. At the commencement of the game, the side which has lost the choice of goals has a free kick from the center of the field; and when a goal has been scored, the side which has lost it has a free kick from the same location. Any player who fairly catches the ball on the fly from an opponent's kick has a free kick, provided he makes a mark with his heel on the spot of the catch. A side which has made a touchdown has a free kick at the goal, and a side which has made a safety or a touchback has a free kick from any spot behind the twenty-five-yard line. This line is the fifth white line from their goal, and upon that mark the opponents may line up.

A violation of any rule is called a foul, and the other side has the privilege of putting the ball down where the foul was made. Certain fouls are punished by additional penalties. A player is immediately disqualified for striking with the closed fist or unnecessary roughness. A side loses twenty-five yards, or the opponents may have a free kick, as a penalty for throttling, tripping up, or tackling below the knees. For off-side play a side loses five yards. A player may pass or throw the ball in any direction except toward his opponents' goal. When the ball goes out of bounds at the side, it is "put in" at the spot where it crossed the line by a player of the side first securing the ball. He bounds or throws the ball in; or he may, if he prefers, walk out with it any distance not greater than fifteen paces, and put it down for a scrimmage.

Of the two individuals one sees on the field in citizen's dress, one is the umpire and the other the referee. These two gentlemen are selected to see that the rules are observed, and to settle any questions arising during the progress of the game. It is the duty of the umpire to decide all points directly connected with the players' conduct, while the referee decides questions of the position or progress of the ball. The original rules provided that the captains of the two sides should settle all disputes; but this, at the very outset, was so manifestly out of the question that a provision was made for a referee. Then, as the captains had their hands full in commanding their teams, two judges were appointed, and it was the duty of these judges to make all claims for their respective sides. These judges soon became so importunate with their innumerable claims as to harass the referee beyond all endurance. The next step, therefore, was to do away with the judges and leave the referee sole master of the field. Even then the referee found so much that it was impossible for him to watch, that it was decided to appoint a second man, called an umpire, to assist him. This umpire assumed the responsibility of seeing that players committed no fouls, thus leaving the referee's undivided attention to be devoted to following the course of the ball.

This has proved so wonderfully successful that the base-ball legislators have adopted a system of dividing the work between two umpires.

There are two general divisions of players — the "rushers" or "forwards," so called because they constitute the front rank of the foot-ball army; and the backs, called the quarter-back, the half-back or halves, and the full-back or goal-tend. The quarter has been already described. The halves, of whom there are two, play several yards behind the rushers, and do the kicking or artillery work. The goal-tend is really only a third half-back, his work being almost the same as that of the halves.

DEVELOPMENT OF THE NAMES OF THE VARIOUS POSITIONS

WHEN the sport of foot-ball was first introduced into our American colleges the players were called, according to their position, forwards, half-backs, and goal-tends. The forwards were also sometimes spoken of as rushers, and the goal-tends as backs. These latter names, apparently, were more suited to the tastes of the players, so they have become more usual, and the terms forward and goal-tend are seldom used. Beyond these general divisions there were neither distinctive names nor, in the early days, distinctive duties. One of the first rushers to receive a special name was the one who put down the ball in a scrimmage. Originally the man who happened to have the ball when the down was made, himself placed it on the ground. It soon became evident that certain men were unable to perform this duty so well as others, and it was not long before the duty was delegated to one man. As he usually stood in the middle, he was called the center-rusher. This name has since given place almost entirely to "snap-back," owing to the universal custom of playing the scrimmage by snapping the ball back with the hand.

As the game, after starting with eleven players, was then altered to fifteen, there was an opening made by these increased numbers for more positions. It was in the first days of fifteen men that the quarter-back play and position first acquired proper form. There was not only a quarter-back, but also a three-quarter-back — that is, a player who stood between the half-backs and the backs. With the return to eleven men the three-quarter-back disappeared, but the quarter-back, or man who first received the ball from the scrimmage, still remained.

The next position to assume prominence and a name was that of end-rusher. The two men who played on the ends of the forward line found unusual opportunities for the exercise of ingenuity in the sport, and their duties were more manifold than those of any of the other rushers. They found opportunities to make runs, opportunities to drop back a little and make fair catches of short kicks (for it was then quite in vogue to make a short kick at kick-off), opportunities of running along with a half-back and receiving the ball from him when he was likely to be stopped; in fact, to perform the duties of the position required so many qualities that the best all-round men were selected for the work, and it became quite a feather in a man's cap to be an end-rusher. After this there were but four men on the team who were not specifically classed and designated. These were the two next the ends and the two next the center. The latter took up the name of "guards," as they protected the quarter when the ball was snapped. The former were called "tackles," probably because, before the tricks in running were so highly developed as at present, a large share of the tackling did fall to them. This division of players is now universal, and each position has duties and responsibilities peculiar to itself.

The changes the game has undergone in its gradual development from the English Rugby are peculiarly interesting, showing as they do the inventive faculty of our college players. The way in which the quarter-back play was suggested and perfected illustrates this very strongly. Our players began exactly as the Englishmen, by putting the ball on the ground, closing around it, and then kicking until it rolled out somewhere. In the first season of this style of scrimmage play, they made the discovery that, far from being an advantage to kick the ball through, it often resulted in a great disadvantage, for it gave the opponents a chance to secure the ball and make a run. The players, therefore, would station a man a short distance behind the scrimmage, and the rushers in front would manage to so cleverly assist the kicking of the opponents as to let the ball come through directly to this player, who had then an opportunity to run around the mass of men before they realized that the ball had escaped.

Soon an adventurous spirit discovered that he could so place his foot upon the ball that by pressing suddenly downward and backward with his toe he would drag or snap the ball to the man behind him. At first, naturally, the snap-back was not sufficiently proficient to be always sure in his aim, but it did not take long to make the play a very accurate one, and in the games to-day, now that the hand is used instead of the foot, and the snap-back has undisturbed possession of the ball, it is unusual for the snap-back to fail in properly sending the ball to his quarter.

Originally the quarter was wont to run with or kick the ball, but now as a rule he passes it to one of the halves or to a rusher who has come behind him, instead of making the run himself. The quarter then directs the course of the play, so that scientific planning is possible; whereas in the old method the element of chance was far greater than that of skill.

One frequently hears old players speak of the "block game" and its attendant evils. This was a system of play by which an inferior team was enabled to escape defeat by keeping continual possession of the ball while actually making but a pretense of play. So great did the evil become, that in 1882 a rule was made, which has already been mentioned, to the effect that a side must make an advance of five yards or retreat ten[1] in three scrimmages. The penalty for not

[1] This was altered later to twenty yards.

doing this is the loss of the ball to the opponents. A kick is considered equivalent to an advance, even though the same side should, by some error of the opponents, regain the ball when it comes down. The natural working of this rule, as spectators of the game will readily see, is to cause a side to make one or two attempts to advance by the running style of play, and then, if they have not made the necessary five yards, to pass the ball back to a half for a kick. The wisdom of this play is evident. If they find they must lose the ball, they wish it to fall to their opponents as far down the field as possible, and so they send it by a long kick as near the enemy's goal as they can.

One other rule, besides this one, has had a development worthy of particular attention. It is the one regarding the value of the points scored. At first, goals only were scored. Then touch-downs were brought in, and a match was decided by a majority of these, while a goal received a certain equivalent value in touch-downs. Then the scoring of safeties was introduced; but only in this way, that in case no other point was scored a side making four less safeties than their opponents should win the match. A goal kicked from a touch-down had always been considered of greater value than a field-kick goal, but it was not until the scoring had reached the point of counting safeties, that it was decided to give numerical values to the various points in order that matches might be more surely and satisfactorily decided. From this eventually came the method of scoring as mentioned earlier in this article.

A few diagrams illustrative of the general position

of the players when executing various manœuvers will assist the reader in obtaining an insight into the plays.

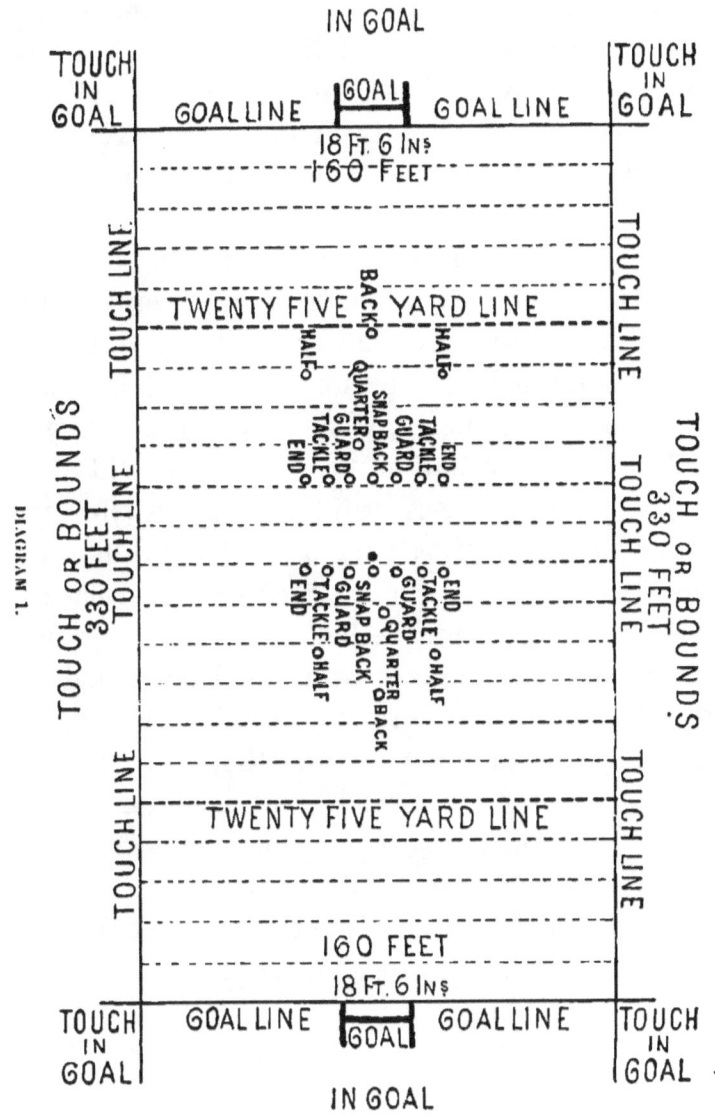

As there are no hard-and-fast rules for these positions, they are dependent upon the judgment of each individual captain; nevertheless, the diagrams indicate in a general way the formations most common.

The first diagram shows the measurements of the field as well as the names of the general positions of the two teams. While the front rank are all called forwards or rushers, distinctive names are given to the individual positions. These also are noted on this first diagram.

The forwards of the side which has the kick, "line up" even with the ball, while their opponents take up their positions ten yards away. They are not permitted to approach nearer until the ball is touched with the foot. Formerly, when it was the practice at kick-off to send the ball as far down the field as possible, the opponents were wont to drop two forwards, near the ends of the line, back a few feet; thus providing for a short kick. The quarter took his place in a straight line back from the ball some sixty or seventy feet, while the two halves and the back stood sufficiently distant to be sure of catching a long kick. The positions of the side kicking the ball were not so scattered. All their forwards and the quarter stood even with the ball, ready to dash down the field, while the halves and back stood only a short distance behind them, because as soon as the ball was sent down the field they would be in proper places to receive a return kick from the opponents.

The kick-off of the present day is more apt to be a "dribble," or a touching the ball with the foot and then passing or running with it. The result of this is that the opponents mass more compactly, the halves and quarter not playing far down the field, and the rushers at the ends not dropping back. The side having the kick, keeping in mind, of course, the particular play they intend to make, assume positions that shall the most readily deceive their opponents, if possible, and yet most favor the success of their manœuver.

For instance, the most common opening play is now the "wedge" or "V." In diagrams 2 and 3 are shown

DIAGRAM 2.   DIAGRAM 3.

the positions in this play. As the players "line out" they assume as nearly as possible the regular formation, in order that their opponents may not at once become too certain of their intention. As soon, however, as play has been called, one sees the rushers closing up to the center and the player who is to make the running dropping in close behind the man who is to play the ball. Diagram 2 illustrates the position at the moment of the kick-off. The kicker touches the ball with his foot, picks it up and hands it to the runner who is coming just behind him. The forwards at once dash forward, making a V-shaped mass of men, just within the angle of which trots the runner. Diagram 3 shows them at this point.

But this wedge no sooner meets the opposing line,

than the formation becomes more or less unsteady, exactly in proportion to the strength and skill of the opponents. Against untrained players the wedge moves without great difficulty, often making twenty or thirty yards before it is broken. Skilful opponents will tear it apart much more speedily.

Now comes the most scientific part of the play — namely, the outlet for the runner and ball. There are

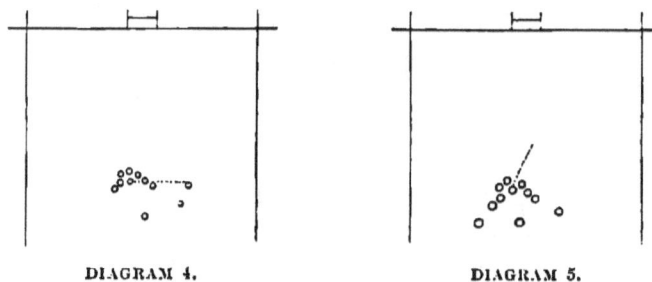

DIAGRAM 4.   DIAGRAM 5.

two ways of successfully making this outlet. One is to have a running half-back moving along outside the wedge, taking care to be a little behind the runner, so that the ball may be passed to him without committing the foul of passing it ahead. When the wedge begins to go to pieces, the ball is dexterously thrown out to him, and he has an excellent opportunity for a run, because the opposing rushers are so involved in breaking the wedge that they cannot get after him quickly. Diagram 4 illustrates this. The second, and by far the most successful when well played, is for two of the forwards in the wedge to suddenly separate and in their separation to push their opponents aside with their bodies, so that a pathway is opened for the runner, so he can dart out with the ball. Diagram 5 shows this.

The wedge formation is a good play from any free kick, because the opponents are so restrained by being obliged to keep behind a certain spot, that time is given for the wedge to form and acquire some headway before they can meet it.

The formation of the side which has the ball in a scrimmage, next occupies our attention. As stated before in this section, it is customary for them to make two attempts to advance the ball by a run before resorting to a kick. There is some slight difference in the ways they form for these two styles of play. Diagram 6 shows the formation just previous to the run. The forwards are lined out, blocking their respective opponents, while the halves and backs generally bunch somewhat in order to deceive the opponents as to

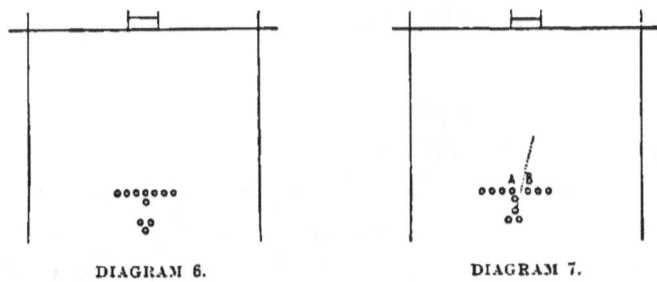

DIAGRAM 6.   DIAGRAM 7.

which man is to receive the ball, as well as to assist him, when he starts, by blocking off the first tacklers.

Diagram 7 shows the line of a half-back's run through the rushers. A and B endeavor, as he comes, to separate (by the use of their bodies, for they cannot use their hands or arms to assist their runner) the two rushers in front of them, that the runner may get through between them.

Diagram 8 shows still another phase of the running-game, where a rusher runs around behind the quarter, taking the ball from him on the run and making for an opening on the other side, or even on the very end.

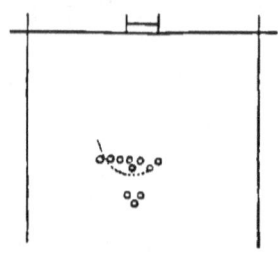

DIAGRAM 8.

Diagram 9 shows the formation when, having made two attempts and not having advanced the ball five nor lost twenty yards, the side prefers to take a kick rather than risk a third failure, which would give the ball to the opponents on the spot of the next "down." The formation is very like that for the run, except that the distance between the forward line and the halves is somewhat increased and the three men are strung out rather more.

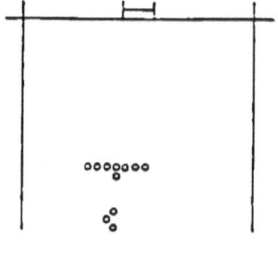

DIAGRAM 9.

Let us now consider the formation of the opposing side during these plays. There is but one formation for the opponents in facing the running-game, and that is according to diagram 10. Of course they alter this whenever they have the good fortune to discover where the run is to be made, but this is seldom so evident as to make much of an alteration in formation safe.

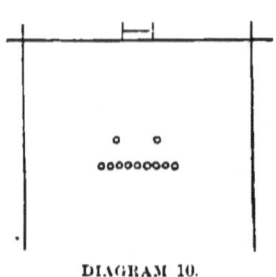

DIAGRAM 10.

Their forwards line up, and their quarter as well as one half goes into the rush line wherever he finds the best opening. Their half stands fairly close up behind, and their back only a little distance further toward the goal. The formation, after the two attempts to run have failed, is, however, quite different in respect to the half-backs and backs. They at once run rapidly back until they are all three at a considerable distance from the forwards. The back stands as far as he thinks it possible for the opposing half to kick, under the most favorable

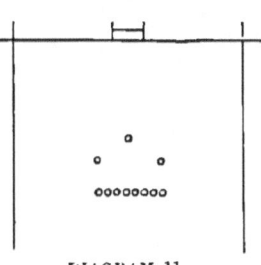

DIAGRAM 11.

circumstances, while the two halves stand perhaps forty or fifty feet in advance, ready to take the ball from a shorter kick. Some teams keep one half in the line and only two men back on this play. Diagram 11 illustrates this.

In a "fair," or putting the ball in from the touch (see diagram 12), the same general formation prevails as in the ordinary scrimmage, for it is really nothing more than a scrimmage on the side of the field instead of in the middle. It counts the same as an ordinary "down"

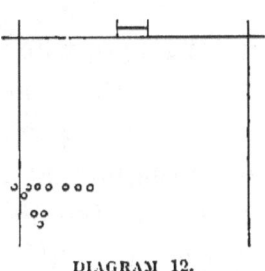

DIAGRAM 12.

in respect to the necessity of advancing five yards — that is, if a side has made one attempt, from a down, to advance, and has carried the ball out of bounds, and then makes another unsuccessful attempt to advance, but is obliged to have the ball down again, without accomplishing the five-yard gain, it must on the next attempt make the distance or surrender the ball.

After a touch-down has been made, if a try-at-goal is

attempted by a place-kick, the formation is somewhat similar to a kick-off. (See diagram 13.) The man who is to place the ball lies flat on his stomach with the ball in his hands, taking care that until the kicker is ready it does not touch the ground, as that permits the opponents to charge. The position of the opponents in this play is necessarily limited, for they are obliged to stand behind their goal until the ball is kicked. The same diagram (13) shows the position they assume. Their rushers undertake to run forward and stop the ball, while their halves and back are ready, in case it misses, to make a touchback.

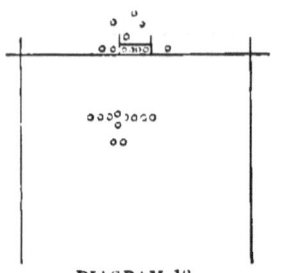

DIAGRAM 13.

These diagrams cover the most important plays of the game, and give one an insight into the general manipulation of the players during the match.

COACHING

THE time was, and that not so very long ago, when a captain could easily do all of the coaching that was expected, and if some of the older players came back for a few days, it was merely to look over the men and give a few words of advice as to the conduct of the important match. If one could give the rushers a little lecture stimulating them to hard work in the game, and a bit of encouragement to the halves, the duty of the coach was performed. To-day the available men — those who have served upon the best teams as players

—are as eagerly sought after for coaches as are experts in any branch of sport, and every team is put under the hands of a coach for at least part of the season. And it is this coaching by men who know the game thoroughly that has done so much for the sport. It has spread the knowledge of the finer points of the play — not alone the strategies, but the best methods — as no other system could have done. East, West, and South the skilled players have gone, not to play, but to teach the coming foot-ball player how to use his strength and skill to the best advantage.

The duties of the coach are manifold. He must know the most approved training, and must be able to direct the diet and amount of exercise to be taken. He must be able to handle a team without having any member get "too fine," or overtrained, and see that the men are in condition to stand the two three-quarter hours of a match. He must be able to preserve good discipline among the men, and, greatest perhaps of all, be able to make them work in perfect harmony. These are the duties of the captain as well, and the coach and the captain must always work together upon these points; but without any conflict of their powers, the captain should always remember that a coach ought to be positive. The suggestions I have endeavored to embody here are for captain, coach, and player; but they are intended for suggestions rather than absolute directions; and just as any one must meet special exigencies with special methods, so must the coach remember that if his governing principles be correct, he can often, to advantage, vary the application.

THE FIELD AND MATERIALS

As this book may fall into the hands of boys who have the wish and the spirit to become foot-ball players, but who do not enjoy the advantages of those in large preparatory schools or colleges, I shall take up the very beginning, and speak of the laying-out of the field, as well as the makeshifts sometimes rendered necessary. The ground for a field ought to be 400 feet long by 200 feet wide, although the field of play of regulation size is only 330 feet long and 160 feet wide. The additional distance at the ends is desirable to allow space for touch-downs and for kicks crossing the goal line. The space beyond the sides, or touch lines, is advisable in order that a player may not, when forced into touch, be pushed against a fence, and so run the risk of an injury. If it be impossible to get a field allowing space at the ends and sides, it is better to cut down a little from the regulation measurements in laying it out, so as to allow at least ten feet at the ends and eight feet at the sides. Having marked out the outer boundaries with plainly appearing lime lines, the marking of the transverse lines is next in order. These run across the field from side to side at every five yards, thus making 21 lines between the ends, or, counting the end lines, 23 in all. Of these the 25-yard lines—that is, the fifth one out from each goal—should be broader than the others, to distinguish the line of kick-out. Also the middle of the field—that is, the center of the eleventh five-yard line—should be marked with a broad white spot to indicate the place of kick-off. The easiest and most satisfactory way to do this marking is, after the outer boundary lines are made, to stretch the tape down each side line, and drive small stakes every five yards. Then let two boys hold a string from one stake to the opposite one while the marker is run over the string. The setting up of the goal-posts is the next undertaking, and is not an easy matter. To determine their position stretch the tape across the end of the field, and mark the middle of the end line—that is, 80 feet from each side. Then measure off each way a distance of 9 feet 3 inches, and the two points for the posts will be thus determined. The posts themselves may be of any material available, and of any size timber; but the best post is of cedar or chestnut,—although pine will answer,—tapering slightly, and about four inches by three inches at the base. The posts should be sufficiently long, so that, when set securely into the ground, they shall stand over 20 feet high. A cross-bar, sufficiently over 18 feet 6 inches long to allow for its lap, should be fastened across these posts ten feet from the ground-level—that is, so that when set up, the upright posts shall be exactly 18 feet 6 inches apart, and the cross-bar ten feet from the ground. I have given these measurements in this way because it will be found much more convenient to cut the posts to the proper height, and secure the cross-bars, before the posts are set up in the ground. The posts should have no braces attached to them, but be made firm by sinking them, and packing them well down into the ground. It is dangerous to put braces upon them, because the players may trip over them, or be forced against them, and so sustain serious injury. The field having been marked out, and the goal-posts erected, one at each end as above described, the ball must be next considered. This unfortunately cannot be of home manufacture to advantage. On account of the skill to be acquired in properly handling and kicking it, it is best that players should never use anything but the regulation ball. It is possible, however, to secure second-hand balls from almost any of the crack teams, and that too at a considerable reduction from the cost price. The regulation ball is of the size No. 5, and the quality known as the J. Lillywhite; but within the last year, the Intercollegiate Association has accepted an American ball made by Spalding.

This should bear the stamp, "Adopted by the Intercollegiate Foot-ball Association." I have elsewhere commented at length upon the clothing, but I want to add a word about the use of protecting material. There is no reason why a foot-ball player should subject himself to the needless ache of old scrapes and bruises, as he did some years ago. If it added anything to the value of the sport, he might continue to suffer; but it does not. Therefore I would say most emphatically that if a player receives a bruise or scrape on the shin, he had better put on a shin-guard at once, and continue to wear it at least until the need for it is past. If his knees are scraped or bruised he should have a few pieces of sponge sewed into the knees of his trousers, and he will find that the hurt will not trouble him further, and will speedily get well. Any severe bruise in the muscles of the leg should be protected until the soreness disappears. An injury to the nose or mouth can be protected by the use of a nose-guard, and bruises on the head by padding the cap. Similarly a pad is worn over a tender ear, and held in place by a band of surgeon's plaster over the forehead. All this may give the casual reader a false impression of the accidents of the game; but these bruises and scratches are not serious, and the reason for thus protecting the injured member is not that the injury itself is of any moment, but that the player may still enjoy his sport without the irritation caused by some of these slight mishaps.

A recent improvement in shoes has been the introduction of an ankle-supporter of leather, which, having been tried by the Yale team for several years, has proved almost a complete safeguard against sprained ankles. It consists simply of a thin anklet going about the ankle and under the instep, and lacing tightly. It may be attached to the shoe or not, but always goes inside. Another improvement has been in the form of leather or rubber spikes, supplanting the old-fashioned straight strip across the shoe. These offer a better hold for the runner, and do not require renewal any oftener than the old strip.

THE PLAYERS

As to the game itself, it often happens, not only at small towns, but even at schools,—and in my time I have known it to happen on the 'varsity field,—that there are not enough players to make up eleven on a side. Many times the sport is not undertaken because it is not possible to be sure of twenty-two men. Now, this is a great mistake; for even if short six men, almost all the plays can be effected, and the sport be just as enjoyable and equally good practice. If short one man on a side, drop out a half or a back, playing with but two men behind the quarter; if short two men on a side, drop the half or back and one rusher; if short three men on a side, drop the half or back and two rushers. The game can be played by still smaller numbers in like fashion; but less than eight on a side breaks up the method materially. To consider the other side of the question, which now is by far the more common in the large schools and colleges— namely, how to use more than twenty-two men. The side which opposes the 'varsity—the scrub side, as it is called—should always make up by numbers, in the days of early practice, what it lacks in physique and skill. The second eleven, as it is called, even though composed of more than eleven players, should be under the direction of a competent captain, who handles them as the captain or coach handles the 'varsity. The great value of the second eleven depends upon the ability of its captain, and a large proportion of the strength and skill of the 'varsity comes directly from the opposition which the second eleven can daily offer. In the early days of practice, as I say, the numbers of the second eleven can be almost unlimited—that is, the captain may play three, or even four, extra men in the line, and four, or even more, extra behind it. But after a time, when team play for the 'varsity begins, it is well not to give the second eleven more than two extra men in the line, although there may still be kept several extra men behind it, as halves and backs. With the last week or two of practice, only one extra man should be allowed in the line, and two extra halves or backs. Sometimes it is also advisable, particularly if the second eleven is exceptionally strong, to play half an hour each day of the last week or so with but eleven men, so that the 'varsity may make a fair test of all its trick plays and combinations, and learn what the difficulties may be in carrying them out against the regular number of players.

There is one other way of practising a 'varsity team; for instance, when, after mid-season, they have become so strong in their playing as to make it impossible to give them really hard work without adding to the number of players upon the scrub side. This method is one of the most effective I know of when there is a ground admitting of it. I refer to practising upon a field not level and having the 'varsity team play up hill. The great advantage of this is that it preserves the conditions existing in a match of an equal number of men and yet gives the scrub side the advantage in all pushing and mass plays. I have seen a team trained upon such a ground, and found that the advantage of it was marked.

GENERALSHIP

In another book I have gone into the detail of the individual positions, and here I shall pay more attention to giving captains and players some brief suggestions in the generalship of the game, and developing combinations that will enable them to get the most value out of the material they have. In the first place, there is no point upon which more depends than the absolute power of the captain. Upon this one of the best writers upon English Rugby Union foot-ball is thoroughly in accord with me. I refer to Mr. Harry Vassall. The captain should have sole power to select his team. He may take the advice of his coach, or of committees; but the putting of a man on or the dropping of him off should rest in his hands alone. In this way only can he properly fulfil the duties of his position and secure the thorough command over his men that such a position demands. He should be a masterful man, and so self-reliant in emergencies that his men will naturally stand by him and look to him for advice, help, and commands. His relations with his men should, however, be such that he is always ready to listen to suggestions,—never, or very seldom, on the field, but after the play is over.

One of the great secrets of good team play lies in adapting each play most carefully to the men taking part in it. If a team be a heavy team, but with no fast runners, the general study must be toward wedge and mass playing — that is, the team must be taught in every possible way to make use of their weight: not to attempt to outpace their opponents, but to crush them back. To begin with the subject as one would with green men, let us suppose the ball is in the center of the field for kick-off. Some light fast teams, with good runners and a swift passer at quarter, open with a long pass — that is, they make a pretended massing of men near one touch line, and only a smaller bunch at the other side, but nearer to the center. The ball is passed to a swift runner behind the smaller mass, which moves off sharply and endeavors to assist the speedy runner around the opposing end and tackle. A heavy team, on the other hand, will likely enough be best used by starting off with a solid wedge, or V, of men, with the runner inside, smashing a pathway as far into the opponents as possible, and then opening and crowding the runner out in front or to the side. Another play for a light-weight team, when there is a good kicker and fast ends and tackles, is for the man about to kick off to touch the ball with his foot, pass it back to the kicker, who punts it well down the field, while the ends and tackles, by starting the instant the man touches the ball, can easily be sure that the opponents do not return the ball, but have to have a fair catch or a down well within their 25-yard line. This, although no new play, is an effective one when it seems advisable to carry the ball early into the opponents' quarters. With a nervous and unsteady team the fact of being forced in this way is apt to make them very ragged in play, and early scoring may be the result of thus attacking them.

In making all team and combination plays in football there are several distinct points to be borne in mind, and from the very beginning of his foot-ball days the player and captain who wishes to succeed must study his play in relation to these points. To take these up in order, the first is to make use of a play, if possible, for which the opponents are the least prepared. This may be accomplished in two distinct ways. It may be done by masking or disguising the play, or it may be done by making the move and getting the ball in motion quickly before the opponents are ready for any play at all. The first method is by far the easiest, because it depends only upon a few easily learned tricks of formation. The latter is the more difficult, because it takes the greater part of a season's entire practice and coaching to make a team competent to play a fast game. But it is well worth while to combine the two, for they go admirably together, and a fast team is almost always a clever one, and usually a very reliable one. To disguise a play, the simplest method is to study out an arrangement of men of such a nature that the resulting move—the final outlet for the runner—may be varied without alteration in the first formation. Thus a wedge may be formed which shall start forward with the runner in the center and yet let him out either directly in front or at one side or the other. The signal given when the wedge is forming indicates to the runner and his assistants which outlet will be used, and the opponents are utterly unable from the position of the men to tell which the outlet will be. This prevents them from massing their men, and so renders the success of the play far greater. Similarly an occasional pretended kick altering into a run may prove very successful, as well as being demoralizing to the opponents. In such a case the ball is passed back as for a kick, and the man who receives it instead of kicking it dodges his man and runs for the end; or the ball may be passed to some one else who has escaped observation and who darts through the line from close quarters.

This play serves still another purpose in that it alarms the opponents and prevents their coming down so rapidly and freely at the kicker in future plays, because they remember the pretended kick and endeavor to guard against it. The criss-cross or double pass is another excellent example of a disguised play, the ball being passed by the quarter to one of the backs, who starts rapidly for one end of the line, but after going a few steps hands, or tosses, the ball to his companion who is going in the opposite direction and who carries the ball to the other end, which has probably been more or less weakened by the efforts of the men on that side to cross over and protect the end they fancied was to be assailed. One of the most remarkable of these disguised plays was the opening wedge practised by the Harvard team in 1892. This play was made by dividing the team into two parts, one consisting of the heavier men, the other of the lighter, but faster, ones. These two parts were placed the former some ten and the latter some fifteen yards behind the ball, and out two thirds of the way toward touch on each side. A runner was placed behind the heavier mass, a pretending, or "fake," runner nearer the middle, and a man at the ball to put it in play. At a given signal the two bodies of men started converging toward the ball, which was not put in play until all were close upon it. Then, while the ball was being played and handed to the runner, the two bodies united and, turning toward the side of the lighter and faster men, moved diagonally up the field. The play was susceptible of a complete change in direction by sending the combined masses to either the right or the left, as well as by using the fake runner, and was therefore a capital development of the masked play.

Working along the lines as suggested by these examples, the player and captain can bring out plenty of original plays, for the possibilities of the game in that direction are by no means exhausted.

As to the use of his men in combination plays, the

captain must consider that, while disguising plays is advisable, there are extremes. For instance, the methods that require hard work of each member of the team while only half enter into the real play, should not be resorted to too frequently, because it exhausts the men without compensating gain; and when the opponents secure the ball, the defensive play is found materially weakened by the condition of the men.

But besides the various advantages to be gained by taking the opponents at unexpected points, or by rapidity of play attacking them when unprepared, one should also consider the value of a persistent assault upon a known weak point, or upon a portion of the team already materially weakened by repeated assaults. As examples of the first, one may consider the case of a team whose halves and backs are poor catchers. In this case a judicious use of long high punts of a twisting variety, well followed up by the forwards, will often result in securing touch-downs, or repeated long gains, from their muffing. Here it is not material that the play be disguised; in fact, sometimes the very knowledge that the kick is coming, will render a poor catcher all the more unsteady and nervous. Again it may be well known that the center of the line of the opponents has proved in former matches essentially weak, and in that case undisguised forcing of that point may give repeated gains, besides discouraging the balance of the team, who are powerless to prevent the advance. Or one end may be weak, and grow even weaker when forced to continual effort.

In the second case, that more especially of tiring out a part of the line, more care should be used. The plays should not be all alike, but all directed at this one point, and played in as rapid succession as possible. The same man should not be made the runner by the assaulting team, but kept fresh by the variation of their action, and throwing the hardest work successively upon different men, while the same two or three men of the opponents are forced to meet it. The more men that are given a chance in these plays the better, because their combined force results in materially adding to the strength of the play.

There is one other vital point which should be always borne in mind by the captain when using his plays in a game, and that is the possibility of an accidental loss of the ball. This caution applies more particularly to trick plays and passing than to mass plays, because in the latter the loss of the ball seldom means a serious matter. In a trick play, however, the very formation of the men is likely to operate disastrously, by giving the opponent who secures the ball a chance for a long run. In passing, also, especially long passing, the same caution must be observed, and the cardinal rule, therefore, in both cases is not to venture such plays when within one's own 25-yard line, on account of the risk of the opponents securing a touch-down if a fluke be made.

KICKING, CATCHING, AND PASSING

The especially skilful features of foot-ball outside of team play are the kicking, catching, and passing. It is in these that the novice finds himself immediately inferior to the expert, and it is upon these that individual practice is essential. Of the three, passing belongs more particularly to the province of one player only— the quarter-back; for it is he who must receive the ball from the snap-back and deliver it to some other player. His passes vary, being sometimes long,— nearly across the field, perhaps,— and at other times consisting merely of handing the ball to a man, or even holding it to be taken out of his hands by the man as he goes by. All this requires practice; for there is a right and a wrong way. In the short passing, the wrong way upsets the man who receives the ball; and in the long passing, the quarter may not be able to throw the ball swiftly enough to have it reach the recipient safely. The best way to make a long pass is to place the ball in the hand so that the end rests upon the point where the fingers join the palm. The fingers are curled up so that the ball if held in the hand rests as though in a cup at its base, and lies against the fore-arm with its side. In throwing it, a side-arm swing is used, and the ball is whirled through the air turning upon its short axis, the fingers giving it an additional snap as it leaves them. The ball should be sent as nearly on a line as possible. In short passing, not so much force is needed, and when handed to another player it should be held by the quarter by the ends, one hand on each end and the arms a little extended, so that the runner may grasp it securely without striking the quarter's body.

Catching is something to be learned only after days of constant practice, and it is one of the most important points in the play of the two half-backs and the back. As a punt may traverse a distance of fifty yards, a muff may mean a loss of that distance, plus whatever the lucky man securing the ball may afterward gain in an almost clear field. A muff is the most serious mistake that a player behind the line can make. To be a good catcher, a man must have the natural qualities of coolness and pluck, and he must perform the act properly. The ball should not be caught as a base-ball is,—in the hands only,—but the arms should assist, while the body—and even the upper part of the leg—may add to the absolute security of the catch. There is one spot where the ball must not be caught, and that is on the chest. More backs are guilty of this error than any other one on the list. A man who catches the ball high, or takes it on his chest, is never a sure catcher, and almost always gets into difficulties before a game is over. The ball should be caught low,—"in the stomach," as the boys express it,—that is, below the chest, and where, by bending the body forward and stooping perhaps a trifle just as the ball settles into the hands and arms, it renders it almost impossible for the ball to escape, even though the player be tumbled over. The best catchers make this kind of a pocket for the ball, using the hands and arms to catch it, and also the body to make it sure, sometimes even drawing up the leg a trifle; but this last is hardly necessary.

Kicking is divided into three kinds—place-kicking, punting, and drop-kicking. No one of these varieties has been sufficiently developed by American players. It is only necessary to state that men have place-kicked goals from the middle of the field, to demonstrate the fact that we are not up to the highest mark. We have brought out but one side of place-kicking,—namely, the goal-kicking from touch-downs,—and even that imperfectly. Long place-kicking from fair catches is seldom seen, and mainly because there are no men who can perform the part. A fair catch, when there is no wind, or a favoring wind, should yield a goal from as far back as the forty-yard line with moderate frequency, and be a "fighting chance" from ten yards back of that.

To place-kick, the ball should be pointed, for short kicks, nearly upright, and then lowered as the distance to be kicked increases, but the point never brought so low that the force is not in a line with the long axis of the ball. The placer of the ball should hold it with the lacing up, and the kicker should sight along the upper seam. The placer should hold the ball with both hands, just off the ground, resting his elbow; the lower hand should be well under, but not upon the lower tip, and the fingers of the upper hand steadying the ball just above the lacing. As he sets the ball down, he turns his under hand flat on the ground so that it does not interfere with the ball, and steadies the ball with one or two fingers of the upper hand as it is kicked out from under by the kicker. He does not let go of the ball. The kicker should "cock up" the toes of his foot well, so that the foot is firm and the toe of the shoe catches the ball just below the lower point.

In punting, the ball is kicked with the instep and not with the toe. The ball should be dropped—not tossed; merely dropped—from the hand to the foot as the swing is being made, and should be struck upon the point by the top of the instep. The swing may be a straight one or somewhat of a side swing, but the foot strikes the ball squarely in either case. The ball should not be too near the ground; something over a foot in the clear is the proper height, except for special kicks, and the full weight of leg and body put into it, as hereafter described, for the drop-kick. Accuracy should be an aim of the punter as much as distance. He should practise daily at some kind of a mark, and steadily increase his distance from that mark. A little felt padding over the top of the foot and instep, so that the shoe laces snugly, is conducive to good punting as well as good kicking of all kinds.

There are three distinct styles of drop-kicking, and all of them good: first, the drop-kick, using but one hand to hold and drop the ball, the point being toward the goal, and taking a good, slightly side, swing in the kick; second, holding the ball in a similar position, but by the use of both hands; and third, holding the ball in both hands, but with the point tilted backward, or away from the goal. In all three cases the dropping of the ball and the kicking are similar. The ball is dropped directly to the ground, falling so that it strikes the turf not exactly upon the point, but leaning off the perpendicular some twenty degrees or so. Just as it strikes, or rather just as it rises off the ground, the foot swinging forward catches it squarely with the toe and drives it as it does in a place-kick. Good drop-kickers send the ball forty yards and over, although few of them are dangerous in a game unless they get nearer than that. Drop-kicking as well as punting should be practised with men coming down at the kicker in order to accustom him to the conditions which he will find always prevailing in a game. It is the duty of the captain to determine when in a game a drop should be tried, and his decision must depend upon the accuracy and reliability of his kicker, the score and time of the game, and, finally, the condition of his team as to their ability to reach the line without losing the ball if the drop be given up.

The above suggestions can hardly be called directions, for to make them as extended as one would like would take up an almost indefinite number of pages. They are merely suggestions that even the novice can begin his work upon and be sure that if he will supplement them with ideas of his own and unremitting practice he will be able to make himself a player of value to any team. The sport is farthest of all college sports from the limit of its development, and the boys now in the lower forms of the preparatory schools will play better foot-ball in their college teams than that we are seeing now, if they will but put the same interest in it that their predecessors have. Play strictly under the rules, but never be afraid of a play because it is a new or unheard-of one, is the best advice I can give to the coming players.

GENERAL STRATEGY OF THE GAME

It would be to leave the subject of foot-ball but half completed, did one fail to touch upon the larger strategies of a campaign, and to show how the almost unlimited lesser plays, when properly grouped, prove irresistible in advancing the ball. The first thing to be considered is the material at the captain's command. The foot-ball player can never be educated to a pitch of machine-like perfection, nor will any amount of training make him absolutely untiring. It is therefore necessary to start with the premise that no one

This picture shows the finally successful tackle of a runner who has evidently made a dashing run, throwing off the men until several have tackled him together, and, by throwing themselves upon him, at last brought him to a standstill.

or two men can do all the work. The object must be to use each man to the full extent of his capacity without exhausting any. To do this scientifically involves placing the men in such positions on the field that each may perform the work for which he is best fitted, and yet not be forced to do any of the work toward which his qualifications and training do not point. From this necessity grew the special divisions of players as indicated in another paragraph. It might seem that this division of players would take all responsibility from the captain's shoulders; but it does not do this by any means. It only insures some sort of regularity of work for each individual. For instance, a rusher will never be called upon to drop-kick a goal, nor will a half be forced to snap-back the ball.

There still remains the possibility of giving any one of these men so much work of his own special kind to perform as will exhaust him, and thus make it impracticable to call upon him when he is most needed. Here is an element quite dissimilar to any entering into our other popular sport, base-ball. If one might suppose that it were possible in that game to let the most rapid base runner do as much of the running for the rest of the nine as the captain chose, we should have a temptation similar to that which assails the foot-ball captain. It would not be improbable that this chosen runner would become exhausted under certain circumstances; and should he happen to be the pitcher as well, the results would prove fatal to the success of his nine. It seems as if no amount of calm reasoning can convince the average foot-ball captain of this fundamental principle. Year after year has the "one man" game been attempted, and year after year it has brought to grief the team attempting it. Nor is it enough for a captain merely to transfer the play

---

The picture on the opposite page shows a try-at-goal by a place-kick. The forwards are lined out across the field, each one careful to be behind the ball when it is kicked. The man lying on the ground is pointing the ball at the goal under the direction of the half-back. This man stands back several yards, as the kick is evidently to be a long one.

from one player to another in order not to exhaust any. He must do this at the proper time, and not at haphazard. His best runner will be needed at some critical moment, and at just that moment must he be used. Forwards must not be given too much running to do early in a game, or their tackling and getting through will suffer. It is a serious mistake to take the edge off their strength until one is certain of the style and force of the adversary's running. As a policy which, while not infallible, will be most uniformly successful, the following may be laid down:

Save the rushers as much as possible until the enemy have had an opportunity to send two or three of their (presumably) best runners up against them; then, if the line holds these men without difficulty, the rushers can be used more freely for general play.

The halves and back should not be given any tackling to do in the beginning of the game. Insist upon the rushers attending to their business so thoroughly as to avoid all possibility of a runner coming through.

Early in the game, give the halves an opportunity to run once or twice, as it warms them up, and puts them in better shape for catching the ball. Nothing is more unpleasant for a poor shivering half, who has n't had the ball in his hands, than to be forced to make, as his first play, a fair catch.

These ideas regarding the use of material will suggest the details to any thoughtful captain.

The next point to be considered is the adversary. In the great games, a captain usually has some knowledge of his rivals' strength and resources before he faces them on the field. Even though he may not have this knowledge, fifteen minutes of play ought to give him a fairly accurate idea of the weaknesses and strong points of his adversary. It then remains for him to take advantage of this knowledge. It is well nigh a rule, so common is it, that a team has a strong side and a weak one. Without intention, this state of affairs comes to exist toward the end of a season. At this weak side of the opponents, then, must the early efforts of a team be directed. When a punt becomes necessary, let the ball be driven over on that side. When an opposing runner comes, force him in that direction. Keep a steady press upon the weak side, and before the game is half over the result will be most marked.

Next, if the opponents prove to be high tacklers, a captain should make constant use of his low runners and reserve his high steppers for other work. If the opposing halves are new or green men, he should see that they have plenty of kicks to catch.

Another important point is to make the most of any natural advantages, existing at the moment, in the force and direction of the wind, the slant and condition of the ground, and the position of the sun. These are elements of success which no team can afford to ignore. The writer has seen a team start out with a strong wind and the sun at their backs, and actually throw away half an hour of the first three quarters by a running game without score. Then, evidently realizing their mistake, they began to kick, and succeeded in making two goals in the remaining fifteen minutes. Whenever a favorable wind is anything more than moderate, a captain is inexcusable who exhausts his men by holding too closely to his running game, no matter if his runners be excellent. A wind which blows diagonally across the field is by no means to be despised; for if a captain will work the ball to the windward side, on his runs and passes, his kicking will be greatly assisted. The sun, too, plays an important part, particularly when it is low in the horizon

The picture on p. 135 illustrates the typical feature of the American game in distinction from the English; namely, the open scrimmage. The ball is placed on the ground, and the snap-back stands (usually with his hand instead of his foot) upon it, and when his quarter-back gives him the signal that all are ready he snaps it backward. The quarter receives it and passes it to another of his own side for a kick or run. The position of the players in this picture is excellent, showing, as it does, the points of play as one can see them only in an actual game. Beginning at the left of the picture, we see the end-rusher of the side which has not the ball. With his eyes fixed upon the center with the keenest attention, he awaits the first movement of the ball to dash through at the man who is likely to receive it. His opponent stands watching him with equal intensity, ready to block him at the moment he starts. Next stands the tackle, apparently perfectly oblivious of the man facing him, and there is a confidence expressed in his attitude which assures one that this man, at least, will get through like a flash when the ball goes. Then there are two men, both stooping forward so that one sees but a leg of each. Of these two one is the guard and the other the quarter-back, who, seeing a chance of getting through, has run up into this opening. The opposing guard is straightening himself up, in order to cover, if possible, both these opponents. If one may judge from appearances, however, he will be tumbled over most unceremoniously by the onslaught of the guard and quarter. The center-rush is braced for a charge, and with mouth open for breath awaits the first movement of his opponent. He, the snap-back, has just placed his foot upon the ball, and is ready to send it back as soon as the quarter, whose back and leg are just visible, shall give him the signal. The two men in the foreground are opposing guards, one of whom is ready to dash forward, and the other to block. The man who is about to block has his hands clasped, in order that he may be sure not to use them to hold his opponent, as that is an infringement of the rule. The other men in the rush-line we cannot see, but one can rest assured that they are as wide awake to their duties as the eager ones in view. Behind the group stands the referee with his arms folded and eyes intent upon the ball.

so that a low punt, driven hard at the half-back, forces him to face directly at the sun in making the catch.

Regarding the general conduct of a final game, or the one upon which depends the championship:

From the less important minor games, and from the daily practice, the captain has learned not only the caliber of his team, but also their strongest and weakest plays. Now comes a most difficult act for any captain, namely, the elimination of all plays that are not sufficiently well executed by his men to be classed on the average as successful plays. Many plays that are peculiarly successful against weaker teams are, from their very nature, useless against well-disciplined opponents. Such plays must be classed with the unsuccessful ones, and must not be used in the critical game. The object of eliminating all these plays is twofold. Certain ones of them must be given up because they would risk the loss of the ball; and others because they would needlessly exhaust the men. As an illustration, let us take the play of short passes along the line when running. This has always been a tempting play. It appears scientific and skilful. It gains distance rapidly, and against a weak team gives the team practising it an appearance of superiority not to be denied. The reason for this is that a weak or undisciplined team take it for granted that they must all make for the man who has the ball, and there is, therefore, a rush of several men at the runner. He passes the ball and they all dash after it again. This work quickly tells upon them, and they become tired out and discouraged, so that the runners have everything their own way. With a thoroughly disciplined team all this is changed. One or two men may tackle together, but the line as a whole remains steady, and when the runner passes the ball the man receiving it has a tackler upon him almost at once, so that he too is compelled to pass the ball to still another, who may expect a similar fate. As all this passing must be at least on a line, and generally backward, nothing is gained, but, on the contrary, some ground is lost. In addition to this, there is always the chance — and by no means a small one — of losing the ball in this quick passing.

Another illustration is the case of long end throwing, or passing the ball to a runner stationed well out on the side of the field. This play is unquestionably strong against rushers who bunch toward the ball, and in the smaller games it has resulted in many a touchdown. Against veterans, however, the play fails, because both the end and tackle are on the alert and carefully guarding any player who is stationed at the end. By the time the ball reaches him one or the other of these men is so close to him that he fails to get a fair start and is usually downed in his tracks. Then, too, it will sometimes happen that an unusually watchful and agile tackle will jump through and actually catch the pass before it reaches the runner. Such a catastrophe has too severe consequences to make the risking of it otherwise than an extremely doubtful venture. A man who thus gets the ball is in a fair way to realize a touch-down from it, for the only player who has a good chance at him is the back, and the best tackler on a field must have an unequal chance against a runner who has the entire breadth of the field in which to dodge him. Yet again, the runner to whom the pass is made may muff the ball. This, although not nearly so serious as an intercepted pass, always results in loss of ground and sometimes loss of the ball as well.

The consideration of such plays as the two mentioned gives one a fair insight into the methods by which the captain must weigh each play before entering a game of importance with rivals who in skill, strength, and strategy are presumably the equal of his team.

"WHAT makes a good foot-ball player?" is a question asked over and over again. Many are the answers given, but no answer is correct that does not contain the word "pluck." The same elements that go to make up excellence in any of the other field sports are requisite in foot-ball; but while in certain of the others that peculiar type of courage called pluck is required only in a moderate degree, in foot-ball it is absolutely indispensable. Many a man has said: "Oh! I am too small to play foot-ball; I could n't get on the team." Such a man makes a mistake. Look at the records of our players, and see how full they are of the names of small men. Withington, Cushing, Harding, Hodge, Beecher, and twenty others, have played weighing under a hundred and forty! Nor has it been that their deeds have been remembered because performed by such small men. These men made points as well as reputations. There is a place on the foot-ball field for a man, no matter what he weighs; and that brings to mind a remarkable pair of boys and what they did for a Yale team at one time. One was the son of a United States senator from Massachusetts, and the other a younger brother of a well-known Brooklyn lawyer. They were classmates at Yale, and had done more or less foot-ball work during the course. These two men weighed about a hundred and twenty-five pounds apiece, or together a little over the weight of the 'varsity snap-back. In that year the 'varsity team was suffering from a combination of two disorders — over-confidence and lack of strong practice. None knew this better than these two little chaps, for they understood the game thoroughly. One day, then, they appeared at the field in their foot-ball toggery, and without assistance from the 'varsity captain set at once to work upon organizing the "scrub side," as the outside or irregular players are called. One of them played center and the other quarter, and it was not many days before the scrub side began to have a game and a way of its own. The overfed, underworked university players began to find that they could n't have things all their own way. Such tricks were played upon them that they were forced to awake from their apathy. These two boys began to show them the way to make use of brains against weight and strength, and the scrub side, that a week or two before had been unable to hold the 'varsity even enough to make the contest interesting, actually had the audacity to score against them once or twice every afternoon. How those two ever got such work out of the rabble they had to handle, no one knows to this day; but it was the making of the 'varsity team, for it speedily developed under this experience into one of Yale's strongest teams, and I have often heard one of that team remark since that he 'd rather play against any team in the Association than against the "scrubs" led by "Pop" Jenks and "Timmy" Dawes.

This brings us to another quality: the *brains* of a team. That team is the best which has the most brains. Foot-ball is, even now, an undeveloped sport. There is room for an almost infinite number of as yet unthought-of plays. Every season brings forward many new ones. If a player wishes to devote a little of his spare time to a fascinating amusement, let him take pencil and paper and plan out combinations in the evening, and try them the next day. He will soon find that he is bringing out not only new but successful plays. Some think that the captain of the 'varsity team is the only one who has an opportunity to try this; but if two or three on the scrub side will make the attempt they will find that a 'varsity team is no more proof against a new scheme than the veriest scrub team in existence. In fact, oftentimes the 'varsity players are so sublime in their own consciousness of superiority that they are the simplest men on the field to lead into traps and defeat by a little exercise of ingenuity. If a boy at school is n't on the first team, he can get together a few men of the second team and have the satisfaction of actually showing his betters how to play.

"Play not for gain but sport," is thoroughly sound; but it means play honestly and hard, not listlessly and carelessly, and make it your sport to win. Then if you lose, put a good face on it; but go home and think out a way to win next time. Brains will beat brute strength every time if you give them fair play.

Endurance is another element of success. Plenty of dash when it is necessary, but behind it there must be the steady, even, staying qualities. For these, good training is chiefly responsible; because, although natural endurance does exist in some men, it is not common, while the endurance of well-trained men is a thing that can be relied upon with confidence.

A direct case in point was a victory of Princeton over Yale in 1878. Upon the Yale team were some three or four men — upper-class men — who thought that they had done enough training in former years, and they therefore made but a pretense of following out the rules of strict training. The example of these men affected several of the other players to such an extent that there was great laxity. Up to the time of the final contest, this team had performed well, and it was generally believed that they would have no great difficulty in defeating Princeton.

In the first half of the game they pressed the Orange men hard, and several times all but scored. In the dressing-room at intermission there was a general impression that, with the wind, which would be in Yale's favor the second half, they must surely win. The second half began, and it was not many minutes before the Yale men found themselves steadily losing ground. There was in the Princeton runners a resistless force that kept Yale retreating nearer and nearer to her own goal. At last, by a brilliant play, Princeton succeeded in making a touch-down from which a goal was kicked. During the remainder of the game, Princeton, although making no further score, held Yale fast down inside the twenty-five-yard line, and the Blue went back to New Haven with a very salutary lesson on the evil of neglecting the laws of training.

These are laws which no foot-ball player can afford to ignore.

LAMAR'S RUN

One of the most magnificent dashes ever made on an American foot-ball field was the run made by Lamar, of Princeton, in the game with Yale which was played upon the Yale field, November 21, 1885. The game had been an unusual one in many respects. Princeton had come to New Haven after a long wrangle about the place of playing, and had brought a team supposed by experts throughout the country to be sure winners. The Yale team was a green one, and none of her partizans hoped for more than a respectable showing against the Princeton veterans. But Peters, the Yale

LAMAR DODGING THE YALE TACKLERS.

captain, had done wonders with his recruits, as the game soon showed. His team opened with a rush, and actually forced the fight for the entire first half. They scored a goal from the field upon the astonished Princetonians, and, in spite of the valiant efforts put forth against them, seemed certain of victory. The feeling of the Princeton team and her sympathizers can easily be imagined. The sun was low in the horizon, nearly forty minutes of the second half were gone, and no one dared to hope such failing fortunes could be retrieved in the few remaining minutes. The ball was in Yale's hands, half way down the field, and on the northern edge. For a moment Captain Peters hesitated, and consulted with another of his players as to whether he should continue the running game and thus make scoring against him impossible and victory certain, or send the ball by a kick down in front of his enemy's goal and trust to a fumble to increase his score. Perhaps not a dozen men knew what was in his mind. A kick was surely the more generous play in the eyes of the crowd. He settled the ball under his foot, gave the signal, and shot it back. The quarter sent it to Watkinson, who drove it with a low, swinging punt across the twenty-five-yard line and toward the farther goal post. It was a perfect kick for Yale's purposes, difficult to catch and about to land close to the enemy's posts. A Princeton man attempted to catch it, but it shot off his breast toward the southern touch-line. Lamar, who had been slightly behind this man, was just starting up to his assistance from that particular spot. As the ball slid off with its force hardly diminished, he made a most difficult short-bound catch of it on the run, and sped away along the southern boundary. The Yale forwards had all gone past the ball, in their expectation of getting it, as they saw the missed catch. Lamar, therefore, went straight along toward the half-back and back. Watkinson, the kicker, had hardly stirred from his tracks, as the entire play had occupied but a few seconds, and he was therefore too near the northern side of the field to have even a chance to cut off the runner. Lamar, with the true instinct of the born

LAMAR AFTER PASSING YALE'S TWENTY-FIVE-YARD LINE.

runner, saw in a moment his opportunity, and ran straight along the southern edge as if he intended to get by there. Bull and his comrade (who then were inexperienced tacklers) were the two men in his pathway, and they both bunched over by the line as the

Princeton runner came flying down upon them. Just as he was almost upon them, Lamar made a swerve to the right, and was by them like lightning before either could recover. By this time two or three of the Yale forwards, Peters among them, had turned, and were desperately speeding up the field after Lamar, who was but a few yards in advance, having given up several yards of his advantage to the well-executed manœuver by which he had cleared his field of the half-back and back. Then began the race for victory. Lamar had nearly forty yards to go, and, while he was running well, had had a sharp "breather" already, not only in his run thus far, but in his superb dodging of the backs. Peters, a strong, untiring, thoroughly trained runner, was but a few yards behind him, and in addition to this he was the captain of a team which but a moment before had been sure of victory. How he ran! But Lamar — did he not too know full well what the beat of those footsteps behind him meant? The white five-yard lines fairly flew under his feet; past the broad twenty-five-yard line he goes, still with three or four yards to spare. Now he throws his head back with that familiar motion of the sprinter who is almost to the tape, and who will run his heart out in the last few strides, and, almost before one can breathe, he is over the white goal-line and panting on the ground, with the ball under him, a touch-down made, from which a goal was kicked, and the day saved for Princeton. Poor Lamar! He was drowned a few years after graduation, but no name will be better remembered among the foot-ball players of that day than will his.

BULL'S KICK

The season of 1888 had opened with a veritable foot-ball boom. The previous season had ended with a close contest between Harvard and Yale, while Princeton, although occupying third place, had had by no means a weak team. Reports of the preliminary work of the three great teams, while conflicting, pointed in a general way to an increased strength at each university. The Boston papers were lauding the work of the Harvard team, and the New York papers returning the compliment with tales of large scores by the Princeton men. Advices from New Haven showed that Yale had a far greater wealth of material from which to draw players than either of the others, so that although the actual strength of the team could not be learned, it was certain that the lugubrious reports from the City of Elms had little foundation. In this state of affairs, the first game, which was scheduled to be between the Crimson and the Orange and Black, was eagerly awaited. The game was played at Princeton, and an enormous crowd assembled to witness the match. Both sides were confident of victory, and Princeton was also determined to avenge the defeat of the former season. The day was perfect, and the game a thoroughly scientific one. Although Harvard battled manfully up to the very last moment, she could not overcome the lead which Princeton had obtained early in the game, and was at last forced to return to Cambridge defeated. The hopes of Princeton soared up that afternoon to the highest pitch, and those who were well posted on the relative merits of foot-ball players agreed with them that their prospects were indeed of the brightest. Had it not been for news which came over the wires that evening from New

BULL, OF YALE.

Haven, it would have been concluded that Princeton would find an easy prey in Yale. But that news was something startling. It seems that the Yale-Wesleyan championship game had been played that same day. Harvard and Princeton had each already met Wesleyan, but neither had scored over fifty points against that team. The astonishment of all foot-ball men was great, then, when the news came that Yale had made the almost unprecedented score of 105 against the Middletown men. This, then, was the state of affairs previous to the Yale-Princeton match. Harvard was now out of the question, owing to her defeat by Princeton, and all interest centered in this final contest. The day, while not very promising in its morning aspect, turned out propitious toward noon, and fully fifteen thousand people crowded the Polo Grounds before the players stepped out on the field. A perfect roar of applause greeted the entrance of the rival teams, and as they lined out facing one another, not even the most indifferent could help feeling the thrill of suppressed excitement that trembled through the vast throng. The game began, and for twenty-five minutes first one side gained a slight advantage, then the other, but neither had been able to score. The Yale men had a slight advantage in position, having forced the ball into Princeton's territory. So manfully were they held from advancing closer to the coveted goal, that people were beginning to think that the game might result in a draw, neither side scoring. At this point Yale had possession of the ball. That slight change in position,—that massing of the forwards toward the center and the closing up of the back,—that surely means something! Yes, Princeton sees it too, and eagerly her forwards press up in the line with their eyes all centered on the back, for it is evident he is to try a drop-kick for goal. This bright-faced, boyish-looking fellow, with a rather jaunty air, is Bull, Yale's famous drop-kicker. He seems calm and quiet enough as he gives a look of direction to the quarter, and with a smile steps up to the spot where he wishes the ball thrown. There is a moment of expectancy, and then the whole forward line seems torn asunder, and through the gap comes a mass of Princeton rushers with a furious dash; but just ahead of them flies the ball, from the quarter, straight and sure into Bull's outstretched hands. It hardly seems to touch them, so quickly does he turn the ball and drop it before him, as with a swing of his body he brings himself into kicking attitude, and catching the ball with his toe, as it rises from the ground, shoots it like a bolt just over the heads of the Princeton forwards, and — down he goes in the rush! The ball, however, sails smoothly on, high in the air, just missing by a few feet the wished-for goal.

A sigh of relief escapes from the troubled breasts of Princeton sympathizers as they realize that for a time, at least, the danger is past. The Orange and Black bring the ball out for a kick-out, and work desperately to force it up the field, having had too vivid a realization of danger to desire a repetition. Again, however, they are driven steadily back until the Yale captain thinks he is near enough to give Bull a second opportunity, and at a signal the formation for a kick is again made. Bull, a little less smiling, a trifle less jaunty in his air, again takes his position. Again Princeton opens up the line and drives her forwards down upon him, but again that deadly drop sails over their heads; this time a foot nearer the black cross-bar. Another kick-out by Princeton follows, and another desperate attempt to force the Blue back to the center of the field; but with a maddening persistency, and with a steady plunging not to be checked, the gray and blue line fights its way, yard by yard, down upon the Princeton territory. Captain Corbin glances once more at the goal, sees that his line is near enough, and again gives the signal. Bull steps up for the third time, and his smile has flown. He realizes that twice have his ten men carried the ball for him up to the very door of victory, only to see him close that door in their faces. His lips are firmly set as his resolve shows itself in every line of his well-knit frame. He settles himself firmly on his feet and gives the signal for the ball to come. For the third time the little quarter hurls it from under the very feet of the plunging mass, and this time Bull sends it true as a bullet straight over the cross-bar between the posts. With a yell of delight the Yale men rush madly over the ropes and seize the successful kicker. In the second half Bull has but one opportunity; but he takes advantage of that one to score another goal, and when the game is over is borne off in triumph by the rejoicing Yalensians, the hero of the day.

If there be anything that might make a momentary ripple upon the steady, resistless stream of New York life, it should certainly be one of these foot-ball games. While there are plenty of base-ball enthusiasts, they possess their souls and their enthusiasm in patience before they reach, and after they leave, the grounds. But the collegian has no sense of repression, and his enthusiasm annually stirs up the sober, sedate dignity of Fifth Avenue from the Brunswick to the Park. A few years ago the wiseacres said: "No one will come to a game on Thanksgiving Day. New-Yorkers will never give up their annual dinner for anything under the sun." At the latest game played on that day thirty thousand people postponed their annual dinner to see the Yale-Princeton match. Perhaps nothing will better illustrate the pitch to which the interest has attained than to take the ride to the grounds, first with the spectators, then with the team. Coaches have been bringing as high as a hundred and twenty-five dollars apiece for the day, and even at that price are engaged weeks before the contest. Stages are resorted to. The old 'bus appears in rejuvenated habiliments, bedecked with great streamers of partizan colors, and freighted with the eager sympathizers of the Orange or the Blue. Long before noon, tally-hos draw up before the up-town hotels, and are soon bearing jolly parties out to the grounds, in order to make sure of a place close to the ropes. The corridors of the Fifth Avenue, Hoffman, and Windsor have for twelve hours been crowded by college boys eagerly discussing the prospects of the rival teams. Any word from the fortunate ones who are permitted to visit the teams is seized and passed from mouth to mouth as eagerly as if upon the outcome of the match hung the fate of nations. The condition of Jones's ankle is fraught with the utmost interest, and all the boys heave sighs of relief at hearing that he will be able to play.

Having talked over the state of affairs all the evening, and until noon of the momentous day, each boy is thoroughly primed to tell his sister (and particularly his chum's sister) all about every individual member of his own team, as well as to throw in the latest gossip concerning the opponents. He is frequently inter-

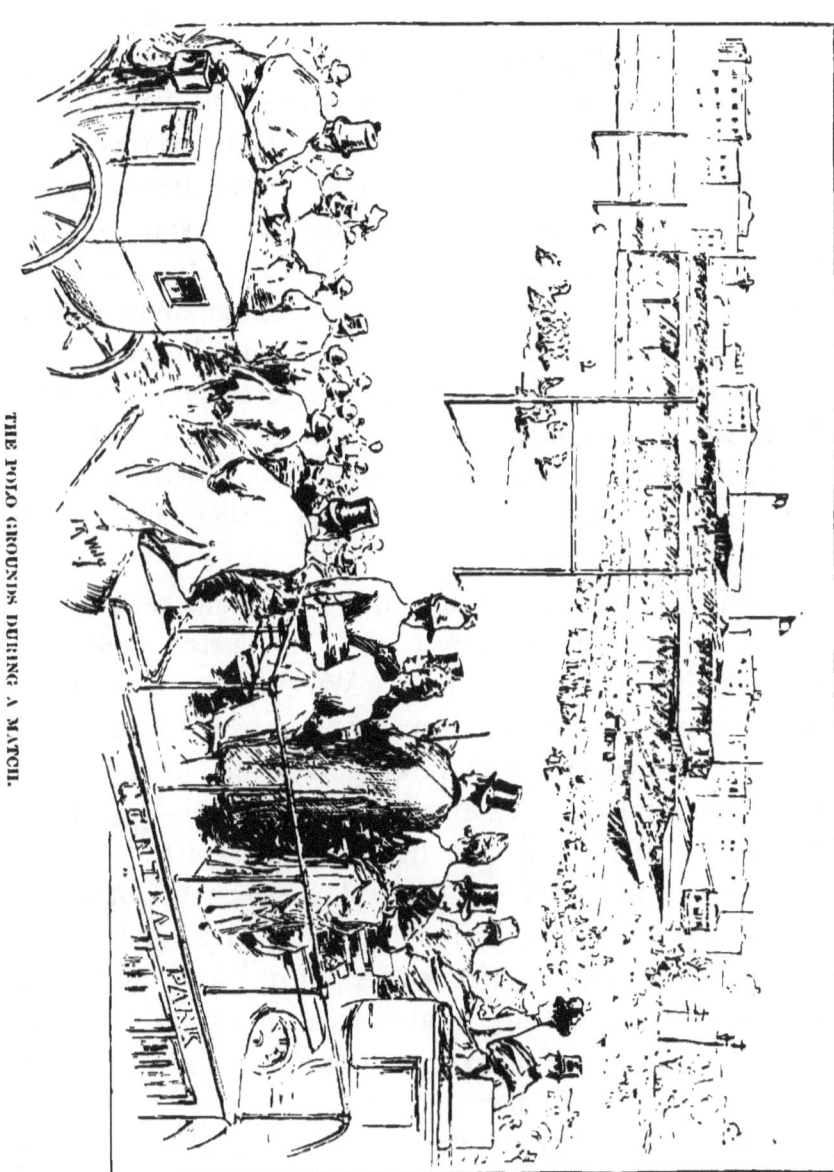

THE POLO GROUNDS DURING A MATCH.

rupted in this conversation, held on the top of the coach, by the necessity of stopping to cheer some house where his colors are displayed in the windows, or to salute some passing tally-ho from which the similarly colored ribbons dangle and banners wave.

Arrived on the grounds, the coaches are drawn up in line, and while anxiously awaiting the advent of the two teams, the appearance of each Princeton or Yale flag becomes an excuse for another three times three. And how smartly the boys execute their cheers! The Yale cry is sharper and more aggressive, but the Princeton boys get more force and volume into theirs. The fair faces of the girls are as flushed with excitement as are those of the men, and their hearts no less in the cheering.

Having followed the spectators out, and seen them safely and advantageously placed, let us ride back and return with one of the teams. We find the men (who have been confined all the morning between four walls in order to prevent their talking over the chances, and thus becoming anxious and excited) just finishing their luncheon. They eat but little, as, in spite of their assumed coolness, there is no player who is not more or less nervous over the result. Hurriedly leaving the table, they go to their rooms and put on their uniforms. One after another they assemble in the captain's room, and, if one might judge from the appearance of their canvas jackets and begrimed trousers, they are not a set of men to fear a few tumbles. Finally, they all have appeared, the last stragglers still engaged in lacing up their jackets. The captain then says a few words of caution or encouragement to them, as he

THE FOOT-BALL TEAM STARTING FOR THE POLO GROUNDS.

thinks best. He is evidently in dead earnest, and so are they, for you might hear a pin drop as he talks in a low voice of the necessity of each man's rendering a good account of himself. Thoughtfully they file out of the room, troop down the stairs, and out through the side entrance, where the coach is waiting for them. Then the drive to the grounds,— very different from the noisy, boisterous one we have just taken with the admirers of these same men. Hardly a word is spoken after the first few moments, and one fairly feels the atmosphere of determination settling down upon them as they bowl along through the Park. Every man has his own thoughts, and keeps them to himself; for they have long ago discussed their rivals, and each man has mentally made a comparison between himself and the man he is to face, until there is little left to say. Now they leave the Park and rumble up to the big north gate of the Polo Grounds. As they crawl leisurely through the press of carriages, everything makes way for them, and the people in line for tickets stare at the coach for a glimpse of the players. They are soon in, and, jumping out at the dressing-rooms, run in and throw off outside coats, still keeping on the heavy sweaters. Now comes a slight uneasy delay, as it is not yet quite time to go out on the field lest their rivals keep them waiting there too long in the chill air. This is in truth the *mauvais quart d'heure* of the foot-ball player, for the men's nerves are strung to a high pitch. Perhaps some one begins to discuss a play or the signals, and in a few minutes the players are in a fair way to become thoroughly mixed, when the captain utters a brief but expressive, "Shut up there, will you?" and growls out something about all knowing the signals well enough if they'll quit discussing them. A short silence follows, and then they receive the word to come out. As they approach the great black mass of people and carriages surrounding the ground, they feel the pleasant stimulus of the crisp fresh air, and their hearts begin to swell within them as they really scent the battle. Just as they break through the crowd into the open field, a tremendous cheer goes up from the throats of their friends, and the eager desire seizes them to dash in and perform some unusual deed of skill and strength.

The Polo Grounds have fallen before the advance of city streets. That old inclosure, the scene of some most exciting college contests, will never again resound with the mad cheer of enthusiastic spectators; but there will be handed down to boys coming after, the memory and story of some grand old games, and there will always be a touch in common among the old players who saw service on those grounds.

THE COSTUME AND TRAINING

The old-fashioned woolen jersey has given place, in great measure, to the less comfortable but more serviceable canvas jacket. This change was first made by a team of Trinity College, of Hartford. There had been a few rumors afloat to the effect that there was a new foot-ball garment, made of canvas, which rendered it almost impossible to catch or hold the wearer. No one at the other colleges had paid much attention to this report, and it was not until the Trinity team stepped out of their dressing-rooms at Hamilton Park, that the Yale men first saw the new canvas jackets. Strange enough they appeared in those early days, too, as the Trinity eleven marched out on the field in their white jackets laced up in front. It gave them quite a military air, for the jackets were cut in the bobtail fashion of the cadets'. The men in blue looked contemptuously down on the innovation upon the regulation jersey, and it was not until they had played for nearly half an hour, and had had many Trinity players slip through their fingers, that they were ready to admit that there was some virtue in the jacket. The Trinity men, bound to give the new costume a fair trial, had brought some grease out with them, and each jacket had been thoroughly besmeared. They were therefore as difficult to grasp as eels, and it was not until the Yale men had counteracted this by grasping great handfuls of sand that they were able to do anything like successful tackling. This, then, was the beginning of the canvas jacket, and although the greasing process was not continued (in fact, it was stopped by the insertion of a rule forbidding it), the jacket itself was a true improvement, and it was not

THE OLD WOOLEN COSTUME.

long before all the teams were wearing them. The superiority of the canvas jacket over the jersey lies in the fact that it gives much less hold for the fingers of the tackler, and also that it does not keep stretching until it offers an easy grasp, as does the jersey.

The next article of the foot-baller's costume which demanded particular attention was the shoe. Probably, in spite of all the trials and the great exercise of inventive faculty bestowed upon the sole of a foot-ball man's shoe, there is to-day no better device for all fields and all weathers than the straight cross-leather strips which were used in the first year of the sport. They are shown in diagram I of the accompanying cut. One of the earliest plans was to lay out these strips in various different lines across the sole, in order to present an edge no matter in what direction the foot was turned. This gave rise to as many styles as there were men on a team. The cuts show a few of these (diagrams II, III, IV, V).

I II III IV V

Rubber soles were also tried, but they proved heavy, and when the ground was wet they did not catch as well as the leather strips. We have not yet seen a trial made of the felt soles which are now used in tennis, but these probably would not answer for kicking, as they would not be sufficiently stiff.

The trousers also have quite a history. At first, several of the teams wore woven knickerbockers made of the same material as the jersey. These fitted them tight to the skin, and although they offered very little obstruction to the freedom of a man's gait, they neither were things of beauty nor did they prove much of a joy to the wearers; for when a hole was once started, it spread most amazingly. Another serious feature was, that when a game was played on frozen ground every tumble and slide left its mark not only on the trousers, but also on the player's skin beneath, as these trunks offered almost no protection. The next remove from these "tights," as they were expressively called, was to flannel knickerbockers. These prevailed for a season, but they were not stout enough for the rough work of the game, and many a youth has needlessly enlisted the sympathy of the tender hearts in the audience, when his comrades gathered about him and bore him from the field, only, however, to reappear again — such a plucky young man! — in a few moments. Some of the more knowing ones noticed that the trousers worn by the young man on his second appearance were not the same as those in which he began the game. Corduroy was tried with no better results than flannel. The most approved cloth now in use among the players is a sort of heavy fustian, and even these are thickly padded at the knees and along the sides of the thighs.

The caps ran through a series of changes from a little skull-cap to the long-tasseled affair called a toboggan toque. The only really serviceable innovation was a cap with a broad visor, to be worn by the backs and half-backs when facing the sun. The stockings are thicker than they used to be, but otherwise there has been no change. The foot-ball player of to-day puts on a suit of flannels underneath his uniform, and if his canvas jacket is a little loose or the day cold, he wears a jersey next the jacket on the inside.

His shoes are of stout leather with straight strips across the soles; and, if they have become a little stretched from constant use, an extra pair of socks underneath the woolen ones gives his feet a more comfortable feeling.

He is better dressed to avoid bruises than the old-time player, but the canvas jacket is hard to play in, and such men as the quarter-back, who have little opportunity to make runs, but much stooping to do, still cling to the jersey. The back also can dispense with the canvas jacket if he finds it very irksome, but as a rule every one but the quarter is better dressed for service if in canvas rather than a jersey.

To come to the more particular points of the diet and exercise suitable for a foot-ball player. Long experience has shown that men who are training for this sport must not be brought down too fine. They should be undertrained rather than overtrained. The reason for this is that an overtrained man becomes too delicate for the rough, hard work, and perceptibly loses his vigor after a few sharp struggles. The season of the year is favorable to good work, and it is not difficult to keep men in shape. They should be given a hearty breakfast of the regulation steaks, chops, stale bread; nor will a cup of coffee hurt a man who has always been in the habit of having it. Fruit also can be had in the early part of the season, and it is an excellent thing to begin the breakfast. About ten or eleven o'clock the men should practise for a half-hour or so. The rushers should be made to pass the ball, fall on it when it is rolling along the ground, and catch short

A TACKLE.

high kicks. They should also be put through some of their plays by signal. The half-backs and back should practise punting and drop-kicking, not failing to do some place-kicking as well. The quarter-back should pass the ball for them, and also do some passing on his own account in order to increase the rapidity of his throwing as well as the distance to which he can pass the ball. The half-backs and back should be made to take all the fly-catching they have time for, and it is best to have some one running toward them while they are performing the catch, that they may become accustomed to it. A very light lunch should be served at about one o'clock. It should consist of cold meats, toast, warm potatoes, eggs if agreeable; in fact, no great restriction should be placed upon the appetite of the men at any of the meals, except where certain things manifestly disagree with certain individuals. Nothing very hearty should be given them at noon, however. At half-past two — or, better, at three — they should start for the grounds, and then play against a scrub team for an hour and a half. When they have had their baths, and been well rubbed down, it is about five o'clock, and in an hour from that time they will eat more dinner than any other set of men in training. No alcoholic beverages are permissible except for particular cases — as for a man who is getting too "fine" a little ale is not out of the way and may give him a better appetite and better night's rest. Plenty of sleep is indispensable. One other feature should be mentioned, which is, that as the rule for foot-ball games is "play, rain or shine," a team must practise in bad weather. Notwithstanding the fact that one would naturally predict colds for the men from practice in the rain, experience teaches quite the opposite. A cold is almost unheard of, and when it does occur is always traceable directly to some foolish exposure after the playing is over; as, for instance, remaining in the wet clothes. This must on no account be allowed. If the men are put into their baths, and dressed immediately after in warm, dry clothes, they will never take cold.

The above points are the vital ones in foot-ball training, and give a general view of the course to be pursued. The smaller technicalities every captain must discover for himself.

BASE-BALL—FOR THE SPECTATOR

THE next generation of Americans will be as thoroughly educated in the technicalities of base-ball as our English cousins are in the intricacies of cricket. Many a man to-day has felt a little defrauded by the increasing space his morning paper gives to the game, and has been inclined to look with disapproval upon the devotion of his boy at school to something apart from his studies. As the present generation of boys become men, however, there will be a softer spot in their hearts for a pastime whose ways they know and whose fascinations they remember. Putting aside for a moment its professional questions, base-ball is for every boy a good, wholesome sport. It brings him out of the close confinement of the school-room. It takes the stoop from his shoulders, and puts hard, honest muscle all over his frame. It rests his eyes, strengthens his lungs, and teaches him self-reliance and courage. Every mother ought to rejoice when her boy says he is on his school or college nine. And she would if she knew what he means when he says he is "in training." It means that he is following, with the closest observation, the laws of health. He is free from the taint of dissipation, and is making of himself a clean, strong young man. This training has been made a study, and the results have been handed down through college and school, until every boy now enjoys the advantages. The enforcement, too, of these laws of training is more strict than that of any rules of teacher or faculty; for, instead of surveillance, the boy is bound by his honor to his captain and his fellows.

The history of the game is an interesting record of progress and development. Away back in the fifties we find it assuming its first stage as a well-defined sport. Previous to that time there were certain games played with bat and ball, but there were not enough points of similarity to warrant one in attempting to prove or disprove conclusively where the game of base-ball originated. In this early stage the game was chiefly confined to local nines, with here and there a sporadic outbreak of it at the colleges. There were occasional attempts at organization; but while these had existed here and there, an association or league of men making base-ball a profession was unthought of. Men who played ball for a financial consideration had other means of livelihood, and there were no players whose efforts could accumulate a fund sufficient to last through the winter. As the game grew in popular favor it became possible for men to turn it into a money-making venture, and this they did not hesitate to do. The sport had not at that time acquired sufficient strength to withstand the evils dragged into it by those whose sympathies were only with the gambling and pool-selling classes, so that in the sixties the evil of betting had crept into the sport so much as seriously to compromise its prospects and give it a bad odor among respectable communities. Sold games were a common thing, and many of the journals of that day predicted its speedy downfall. As a notable effort to reinstate the game in popular favor, and scotch the betting and selling evil, stands out most prominently the convention held in Philadelphia in December, 1867. An idea of the thoroughness of the effort can be gained from the fact that five hundred clubs were represented.

The leading ball clubs during the next year or two were, in the East, the Atlantics of Brooklyn, Athletics of Philadelphia, Unions of Morrisania, and the Mutuals; while the Red Stockings of Cincinnati bore the palm in the West. This latter club made a most successful trip east in 1869, winning all of the twenty-one games played. Such was the enthusiasm produced by these victories that on the return of the club it was met by a perfect ovation, tendered a banquet, and presented with a champion bat. This rather remarkable testimonial was twenty-seven feet long and nine inches in diameter. The same nine made another Eastern trip the following season, and met with almost equal success, suffering but one defeat, and that by the Atlantics on the Capitoline grounds. A crowd of ten thousand people assembled to witness this match, and so lost their heads in the excitement as to give the Western men a very unfair reception. The game was not decided at the end of the ninth inning, each club having five runs. The tenth inning was played in a pause of breathless excitement, neither club scoring; but in the eleventh inning, in a perfect bedlam of noise, the Atlantics succeeded in making three runs, while the Red Stockings scored but two.

In 1874 American base-ball men made their first foreign trip. The ex-champion Athletics and the champion Bostons crossed the water and played several exhibition games. Their first game was played at Lord's, on Bank Holiday, August 3.

Fifteen years later, in 1889, two nines of representative American ball-players, after carrying the sport

THE CATCHER.

through almost every civilized quarter of the globe, completed their tour by a game at Lord's.

The comments of the English papers upon the sport at that time are very amusing. Speaking of the practice before the game, they say: "The larking indulged in by the Americans for ten minutes before the match showed great precision, but after the game commenced returns were not so accurate." Comparing the game with cricket, they admit that the fielding is far better, but ascribe it to the difference in the ball used. By this time the American game had also made a fair stand in Canada, the Maple Leaf Club of Guelph, Ontario, being the most prominent in that region.

In 1876 the National League was formed of eight clubs, containing the very pick and flower of the ball-playing fraternity. This selection was so small when compared with the large number of people anxious to be spectators of ball games that in 1881 the American Association was organized. Until time had demonstrated that there was plenty of room for both, there was bitter rivalry between the two. This was not long-lived, and what is known as the National Agreement then united the two in respectful and harmonious tolerance. Their united power became quite sufficient to govern, with their black-lists, reservations, and contracts, the entire professional ball-playing community. Their rule provoked much hard feeling and occasionally open rebellion, but not a revolt sufficient to overthrow their authority.

During the twenty years from 1870 to 1890 the Boston Ball Club won more than a third of the annual championships, bearing off the honors in seven years. The Chicago Club stands next, with five championships to its credit. The only other club to win more than once was the Providence nine, which was successful twice. A study of the records of the League and the Association shows that the contest was closer in the latter—that there was not so great a difference between the records of the first and last clubs.

Another feature of the records is of interest, as showing the tendency of men to drift in and out of this rather nomadic profession. There were but seven men in the books of 1888 who had played through the twelve years upon one or the other of the League nines. These seven men stood, however, with but one exception, high in the profession, and exhibited the same superiority that tenacity of purpose and experience produce in any calling.

The history of college baseball follows the line of the professional game very closely. At times the college men have been rather more conservative, and have clung to certain rules for a season or two after their abandonment by the professionals. In the end, however,

AN "OUT-CURVE"—THE BEGINNING.

in nearly every instance, they have realized the advantage of the change, and followed the lead set them. In the early days of the sport the collegians coped successfully with the majority of the semi-professionals; but even then, when they were pitted against the strongest, the college nines met with defeat. The first game of note between a college nine and professionals was in the spring of 1868, between Yale and the Unions of Morrisania. The Unions were at that time the champions of the country. The game was intensely exciting. At the end of the fifth inning Yale led 8 to 4, but by the end of the ninth

AN "OUT-CURVE"—THE END.

inning the Unions had tied the score, and eventually won the game, 16 to 14. Frequently the score-sheets of college nines show excellent fielding; but when these same men are brought to face the sharp, hard hitting of the professional batsmen, their errors begin to multiply, and, in an inverse ratio, their hits diminish. The increase of errors is due to the difficulty they find in handling the fast drives of the trained batsmen, and also to the nervousness produced by the knowledge that they must play a quicker game. A professional gets away to first base far more rapidly than a college player, and the first sensation of a college in-field on meeting a professional nine is one of hurry. A short-stop or third baseman finds that he has no time to "juggle" the ball and then throw the man out, as he often can do with college runners. The ordinary college pitcher is no match for League batters, and they find an easy prey in him. On the other hand, the skill of the professional pitcher readily balks the attempts of the college batsmen to find the ball, and only the best men handle the stick with any effect. The rest of the nine become nervous over their failure to judge the delivery, and before the end of the game apparently dread to come to the plate for their turn.

Perhaps the host of people who understand the game of base-ball thoroughly will forgive a few words of explanation for the sake of those who have never witnessed a match. It may not be uninteresting to try to realize how the game appears for the first time to an outsider. Any comparatively level piece of ground over a hundred yards square will serve for a base-ball field. Upon this field is laid out a diamond whose sides measure thirty yards, and whose nearest corner is distant about ninety feet from one end of the field. This corner is marked by a white marble plate a foot square, sunk level with the ground, and called the home base. At the other three corners are canvas bags fifteen inches square, and called, beginning at the right as one looks into the field from the home plate, the first, second, and third bases respectively. The lines from home to first and home to third, indefinitely prolonged, are called the foul lines.

PITCHING A "DROP" BALL.

The game is played by two sides of nine men each, one of these sides taking its turn at the bat while the other side is in the field endeavoring, as provided by certain rules, to retire or put out the side at bat. Each side has nine turns at the bat. The arrangement of the men in the field, with the exception of pitcher and catcher, is in the form of two arcs facing the home plate, whose radii are, roughly speaking, thirty and sixty yards. Forming the arc with the lesser radius are four men called the in-fielders, and named the first, second, and third basemen,

STOPPING A GROUNDER.

and the short-stop. The latter player stands midway between the second and third basemen. The other arc is composed of the out-fielders, and they are named right, center, and left fielders. Inside the diamond, and distant in a straight line in front of the home plate some fifty-five feet, is the pitcher's position, or box, as it is called. This is a plate upon which the pitcher is obliged to have his foot when performing the duty which devolves upon him of delivering the ball to the batsman. The catcher's position is not thus defined, but according as necessity requires he stands either close behind the batsman, or, when no runner is on the bases, and the batsman has not reached his last strike, some seventy feet back of the plate. When standing thus he simply performs the duty of returning the ball to the pitcher, as it is unnecessary for him to catch it under these circumstances. The players of the side at the bat take their turn in regular rotation, and continue until three of them have been put out by the opponents. This retires the side to the field, and the others come in to the bat. The batsman has a certain space marked off, in which he must stand when striking at the ball. The batsman becomes a base-runner immediately when he has made a "fair hit" (that is, knocked the ball so that it will fall in front of the foul lines); or when he has had "three strikes" (that is, three fair opportunities of hitting the ball); or, finally, when the pitcher has delivered "four balls," none of which have been struck at by the batsman or have passed over the plate at the proper height. In this latter case he is entitled to occupy first base without being put out; in the other cases he is the legitimate prey of the opponents, and his only havens of refuge are the bases, which he must take in regular order, first, second, third, and home. When he completes this circuit, and crosses the plate without being put out, he scores a run; and the number of runs thus scored in nine innings decides the match.

A batsman is put out if he hits the ball and the ball be caught by an opponent before touching the ground. A base-runner may be put out in any one of the following ways: if, having made a fair hit, the ball be caught by an opponent before touching the ground, or, having touched the ground, be held by a fielder any part of whose person is touching the first base before the runner reaches that base; if, after three strikes, the ball be caught before it touches the ground, or, having touched the ground, be held at first base as above described; and, finally, if he be touched by the ball in the hands of a fielder at any time during his circuit of the bases when he is not touching the base to which he is legally entitled. To provide for the satisfactory conduct of the game, an umpire is agreed upon by the contesting nines, and it is his duty to see that all the provisions of the rules are observed. He is also the judge of good and bad balls, put outs, and runs. Any other point liable to become a point of dispute comes under his jurisdiction. Sometimes two umpires act at the same time, one at the plate and the other on the bases.

Such, in general, are the laws by which the modern game of base-ball is governed. These laws or rules are the growth of many years, and it is to them and to their annual revision and improvement that the game owes in a large measure its success. There are many technical terms, and a knowledge of these is necessary to a perfect understanding of the game. Every ball that the pitcher delivers to the batsman, and which he does not hit with his bat, is called by the umpire either

RUNNING TO FIRST BASE.

"a strike" or "a ball." If the batsman attempts to hit it and misses it, it is a strike, whether it passed over the plate at the proper height or not. If the batsman makes no attempt to hit it, and it passes over the plate at a height not greater than his shoulder nor below his knee, the umpire calls it a strike. If it fails to meet these requirements and the batsman makes no attempt to hit it, the umpire calls it a ball.

As above described, four of these called balls make the batsman a base-runner and entitle him to his base; and at the third strike, whether called or attempted, he becomes a base-runner and must reach first or be put out. A base-runner cannot run out of the direct line in order to avoid a player with the ball, nor can he interfere with any of his opponents legitimately attempting to handle the ball. It often happens in a game that a base-runner is obliged to vacate his base by the occupancy of that base by a following runner. This is called being "forced," and when it happens that runner may be put out by being touched with the ball, or by its being held by a fielder on the base to which this succeeding runner forces him, before he can reach it. There is only one base which a runner may overrun without liability of being touched out, and that is first base. "A balk" is any motion made by the pitcher toward delivering the ball to the batsman without so delivering it, and every base-runner is entitled to the next base on such offense. Within the province of the umpire comes the duty of deciding regarding the weather and darkness. In the case of

SLIDING TO BASE.

the former, the rule is laid down for him that the rain is sufficiently severe to stop the game when the spectators seek shelter. If the rain then continues for a half-hour, he "calls" the game; and if five complete innings or over have been played, it stands as a game, otherwise not. The same result holds in the case of darkness.

In the scoring of the game there are also technical terms, and a slight knowledge of these enables one to glean from the tabulated forms in the newspapers a fairly good idea of what each man has accomplished. The columns are headed by the initials of these technical terms. The first column is headed R., and indicates the number of runs he has made. The column headed B. H. or 1 B. indicates the character of his batting, and the letters stand for the term "base hits," or 1st base hits. A batsman makes a base hit when he strikes a fair ball in such a direction that it is impossible for his opponents either to catch it on the fly or to field it to first base before he crosses that base. Following this column is sometimes one headed S. B., which means "stolen bases." These are bases gained by good running or by strategy, without the assistance of a hit. In addition to these columns, which indicate what each man of the side has accomplished while at the bat, are three columns devoted to the record of the fielding. These are headed P. O., A., and E. The first stands for "put outs," and indicates how many of the opponents he has individually retired. It will be noticed that the first baseman and the catcher usually succeed in taking the lion's share of this column. The next letter stands for "assists," and any player who handles a ball during a play which might or does eventually result in the putting out of an opponent receives for every such assistance a credit of one in this column. The last column indicates the number of missed opportunities, or "errors." A player is accredited with an error for every chance he has failed to accept in a manner to result directly or indirectly in the putting out of an opponent. It will be seen, then, that the sum of these three columns shows just how many opportunities each fielder has had; and the relative ratio of the sum of the put outs and assists to the errors indicates his fielding record.

Other special phrases and terms are almost self-explanatory. An "earned run" is one that is made without the assistance of fielding errors—that is, in spite of the most perfect playing of the opponents. From the nature of things, a ball so knocked that it cannot be caught or fielded to the plate before the man can make the entire circuit of the bases yields an earned, or, as it is in such instances more generally called, a "home run." A "passed ball" is a pitched ball which by an error of the catcher is allowed to go behind him so that a runner is advanced a base. A "wild pitch" is a ball delivered by the pitcher so wide of the mark that the catcher cannot recover it before the runner has advanced a base. A "sacrifice hit" is a ball so batted as to advance a base-runner while it gives an opportunity of putting out the man batting it.

There are certain strategic plays which go to make up the finer points of the game. One of the most common of these is throwing first to one base, then quickly to another, in order to put out more than one man. For instance, when there is a runner on first base and a ball is batted near second, if the second baseman merely threw the ball to first he would put out the man who hit it, but the man on first would hold his base or go to second when the ball was thrown. Whereas, if the second baseman seizes the ball and touches his bag, the man on first is forced out at second, and by quick work the second baseman can throw the ball to first before the runner who struck the ball can reach that point. In this way he makes what is called a double play, putting out both men. Triple plays are also possible, although seldom made. Another point which shows the brains of the game is in attempting to put out the man who is nearest home in his circuit of the bases. Thus, whenever there is an opportunity of putting out either a runner who is coming from third or one who is going to first, the preference is given to the former, unless the chances of putting him out are unusually slender. Still another fine point is the race of man against the ball, as shown in the case of a man on third base when a long fly is batted into the out-field. According to the rule, the runner must touch the base after the fly is caught before he can run, but the distance from the fielder making the catch to the home plate is so great that there is a very fair chance of his getting home before the ball. He therefore stands with his foot touching the bag, and leaning forward for a start. Just as the ball settles into the fielder's hands off he goes. The fielder, too, is prepared for this, and recovering himself almost instantly, he drives the ball in on its long journey toward the plate, often reaching it just as the runner crosses it, but too late for the catcher to touch him.

FIELDER CATCHING A FLY.

Of all the positions on the field, the two that command the most attention are those of pitcher and catcher, or battery, as they are called. Upon them are pinned the hopes of every other man. If the pitcher succeeds in deceiving the opposing batsmen and the catcher gives him good support, all will be well; but if the curves and strategies of the pitcher are readily solved, or if the catcher fails to hold him well, the field will have some sorry work to do before the nine innings are finished. Successful batteries are in great demand, and receive the highest salaries among professional ball-players. In valuing a battery the first points of consideration are their effectiveness and endurance, and then their ability to get on well with the rest of the nine.

A pitcher to-day is not a strong pitcher unless he has good command of the curves, a fair amount of speed, and ordinary accuracy. These are only the average recommendations. The crack men have these, combined with excellent judgment and unusual endurance. A pitcher who can pitch more than two games a week successfully through a season can boast of his record. Nor is a catcher much better off. His hands are liable to slight injuries which may keep him off a day or two, or, if he persists in playing, result so badly as to incapacitate him for weeks. The constant strain when under the bat is too great for him to endure more than two or three games a week. The rest of the men can, if necessary, play their four or five games a week without serious inconvenience, but the battery requires constant care and frequent relief.

Probably no point in the game has been more developed in the last twenty years than the pitching. The old method was to deliver the ball by a perfectly straight swing, the arm passing close to the side of the body, and the ball being sent from a point below the pitcher's hip. This style of delivery would meet with such a reception from the trained batsmen of to-day that an inning would last longer than the ordinary game. The first step from this old-time true pitching was to the use of the wrist in the delivery, making what was known as an underhand throw. At just about the same time the discovery was made that a ball could be so pitched or thrown as to cause it to curve slightly from the straight line. Many were the skeptics regarding the possibility of such a thing. For a long time men versed in physical science and phenomena pooh-poohed at this, saying that it was impossible, and that it was simply an optical delusion. But the ball did curve, and the first pitchers to acquire the art proved problems to the best of batsmen. The "out-curve" was the one first discovered, as it is easiest to effect. This is a delivery by a right-handed pitcher which causes the ball to curve away from a right-handed batsman. Slowly after this came the "in-curve," or reverse of this. This curve is so slight as to be but little more effective than a straight ball. The "rise" and "drop," which had probably existed for some time previous, then took on definite names and became combined with the other curves. The most logical explanation of the curvature of a ball depends upon the supposition of the compression of the air just in front of the ball and a corresponding rarefaction immediately behind it, so that the ball by its friction is deflected from its true course. When the curves were mastered, the tendency of the pitchers was to bring the hand up above the hip in order to give more of a twist to the ball, and thereby assist the curve. The difficulty experienced by umpires in controlling this tendency led to the adoption of a rule allowing the pitcher to deliver the ball from any point below the shoulder. This rule prevailed for a time, but no sooner were the pitchers allowed this leeway than they began to make the umpire's task equally difficult again by getting their delivery just a trifle higher than the law allowed. In order to put an end to the eternal field discussions upon this point, a rule was passed permitting the pitcher to throw the ball in any way he saw fit, and this rule has met with comparatively good success. The pitcher, who had formerly been placed forty-five feet from the batsman, was relegated to a fifty-foot distance. Even then, by taking advantage of a step or two behind his line, he acquired so much speed that it became necessary to fix his position more definitely, and to-day he is even bound to the extent of the exact position of his feet when delivering the ball. In spite of all these restrictions, such is the growing skill of pitchers that the problem is constantly under discussion how to legislate in favor of the batsman.

FIRST BASEMAN CATCHING A HIGH BALL.

The rest of the fielding has kept some measure of progress with the pitching, the catcher's position exhibiting the highest development. This development is fortunately accompanied by numerous safeguards against the shocks of the increased speed of the ball. The first catchers who came up under the bat were wont to wear a small piece of rubber in the mouth as a protection to the teeth from foul tips. It was not long before an inventive genius designed a wire mask which buckled about the head, and, while allowing perfect freedom and sight, rendered the catcher safe from any chance ball striking his face. The next was the use of a large breastplate extending quite to the legs. This is made of rubber, and inflated so as to make a yielding cushion. The gloves which the catchers have worn ever since the days of the rubber mouthpiece have also undergone radical changes, and are to-day so heavily made as thoroughly to protect both hands, leaving free only the fingers of the right hand.

Outside the battery, in these days of almost perfect fielding, the strongest factor is team play. Plenty of men can be found who can perform the ordinary duty of basemen and fielders, but the problem is to secure men for these positions who are strong batsmen and who harmonize well with one another. The usual merits for the individual players are: in a first baseman, ability to catch bad throwing; in a second baseman, an especial capacity for covering a large amount of ground; in a third baseman, rapidity in fielding ground balls over to first. A third baseman must recover himself quickly and have a strong throw. A short-stop should be an accurate thrower, and a man of brains sufficient to take advantage of opportunities for double plays and fielding out advanced runners. The out-fielders must be fast, not only in covering ground, but also in returning balls to the diamond.

Base-ball is a game for the people. The materials are inexpensive, and all that is wanted is a field. If one may judge from what one sees by the way, it is more difficult to say what will not answer for a ball-field than what will; for, in spite of carts, cabs, and police, no street is too small or too crowded for Young America to make a ball-field of it. With its eager young followers everywhere, and with many men now growing into the prime of life who have enjoyed it most heartily in their younger days, it is safe to say that as a sport, and as, par excellence, the American sport, it is sure of a long life.

BASE-BALL—FOR THE PLAYER

THE GROUND AND THE OUTFIT

WHILE laying out a base-ball ground is quite a task, it is not more difficult than marking tennis-courts, and the result is much more lasting. The nature of the ground, and its surroundings, practically determine the general position of the field; and on this account it is usually convenient to take what is technically known as the "back-stop" for a starting-point. The back-stop is usually the front of the "grand stand," or a convenient fence; and the rules provide that the back-stop must be at least ninety feet behind the home plate. There is no advantage in making that distance greater, so measuring ninety feet directly into the field from what is to be the catcher's back-stop locates the home plate. By fastening a tape at the home plate, and carrying it out 127 feet 4 inches in a straight line into the field, the position of the second base is found. Taking a line 180 feet long, fasten one end at the home plate and the other at second base. Then, seizing the line in the middle, carry it out first at one side, and then on the other, and where it is taut the locations of the first and third bases are determined. To determine the location of the pitcher's box, under college rules, measure 50 feet on the line from home to second; this point will be the center of the front line of his position. The principal points having been thus located, lay out the pitcher's box 5 feet 6 inches long by 4 feet wide, then the two batsmen's positions, one for left-handed men and one for right-handed men. These batsmen's lines inclose two rectangular spaces, each 6 feet long and 4 feet wide, the nearest line being 6 inches distant from the home plate, and extending 3 feet in front and 3 feet behind the center of that plate.

Having thus laid out the field, we proceed to further mark the various points. In doing this, if the field is to be a permanent one, it is best to make use of the most improved apparatus; but if the field is only a temporary one, there are various devices which save expense, and which answer the purpose quite satisfactorily. The home plate is, by the rules, a whitened piece of rubber a foot square, sunk flush with the ground, its outer edges being within the lines to first and third bases. An excellent substitute for rubber is a piece of board painted white, or a bit of marble such as can be readily obtained at any marble-yard. The first, second, and third bases are canvas bags, 15 inches square, stuffed with any soft material, and so fastened as to have their centers at the corners of the diamond which we have already marked out. They will thus extend several inches outside the diamond. The customary method of fastening the bag is by means of a leather strap passing through loops upon the bag and directly around the center. This strap is slipped through an iron staple in the top of a post driven firmly into the ground at the corner of the diamond, and the strap is then buckled on the under side of the bag. The wooden post and the iron staples can be easily obtained, and it is quite worth while to have them rather than let the base be movable, or to use a stone, which may be the cause of some serious injury to a runner. As for the bags, they can be home-made by procuring pieces of canvas (or old heavy carpet) and stuffing them with excelsior or rags, or, best, hair from an old chair, lounge, or mattress. If nothing better offers, shavings from any carpenter's shop will answer. The straps may be obtained at a harness-maker's, or a piece of stout clothes-line can be substituted.

Next, the pitcher's box must be permanently marked. This is done by flat iron plates or stones six inches square, sunk even with the surface at each corner. Wooden posts of smaller dimensions will answer equally well.

It is customary to have the in-field well turfed, and this turf should extend behind the lines from second base to first and third for quite a distance, in order that the short-stop and second baseman may play well behind these lines. The turf of the out-field is not of so much importance. The turf of the in-field is cut out from the pitcher's box to the back-stop to the width of about nine feet. It is also cut out along the base lines, about one third that width. After the turf has been thus cut out, the spaces are filled with hard, well-packed earth until level with the field. All this turfing and cutting out of lines is intended, of course, for a permanent field, and where expense is of minor consideration. As a matter of fact, the players will very soon make the base-lines and batting-crease quite

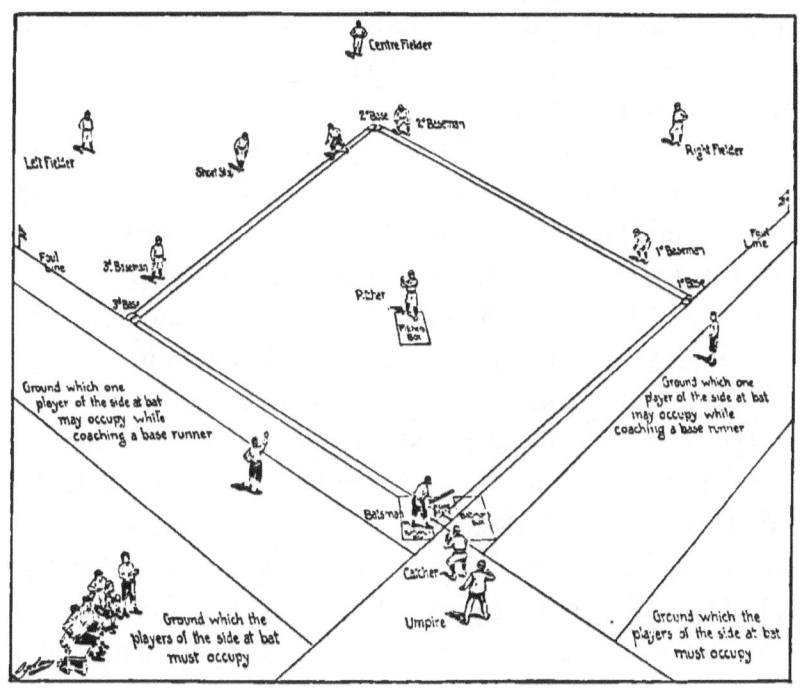

DIAGRAM OF THE FIELD.

marked on any field. Many a good in-field has no turf on it, and is called a "scalped" field. The batted balls travel faster and lower on such a field, but with greater regularity.

To make a fair division of labor in laying out a field for immediate use, let three boys agree to furnish the iron staples, and posts (preferably of cedar) for the bases and pitcher's position, seven in all. The four for the pitcher's box may be anywhere from three to six inches square at the top, and two feet long; those for the bases being three inches in diameter; and all of these sharpened to drive in like stakes. The staples, three in number, should be two inches wide. Let three others agree to furnish the bases: one boy to provide the six pieces of canvas or carpet cut about sixteen inches square; another boy to furnish three two-inch straps with buckles, or else sufficient rope to answer the purpose. These straps must be at least three feet long. Let the third boy see that the bags are looped for the straps, stuffed, and securely sewn. Let three others agree to furnish the home plate and to bring to the ground the following implements, to be used in laying out the positions and marking: a tape line 200 feet long, a supply of cord, a sharp spade, a sledge-hammer to drive stakes, a small hammer to drive in staples, some lime to mark out the lines, and a pail to wet it in. If any boy has a tennis-marker, let him bring it; it will save labor. In marking out the field for a match, there are a few lines to be made which are omitted in the above description, as they are only necessary at an important game. For instance, in ordinary games, the imaginary line from home to third is enough to show the "foul" ground, as the base-line worn by runners makes a fair guide. As a matter of actual law, however, the foul-lines are lines drawn along the outer edges of the home plate and passing through the outer edge of the first and third bags. The foul-line thus does not run exactly along the base-line which we originally marked out, but, starting with it, is $7\frac{1}{2}$ inches from it at third and first. It is, of course, wholly within the cut of three feet where the turf has been taken out. These foul-lines should extend to the boundaries of the ground, and should then be prolonged back of the home plate to the end of the field, forming the "catcher's lines," as they are called.

The "coacher's" or "captain's lines" are determined

by taking two points fifteen feet from a foul-line and seventy-five feet from the catcher's line, then drawing two lines on each side, one parallel to the foul-line, the other parallel to the catcher's line.

The "player's lines" are drawn from the catcher's lines, fifty feet from the foul-lines, and parallel to

LAYING OUT AN AMATEUR FIELD.

them. As both these coacher's and player's lines are drawn merely to keep the men in their proper places, where they will not interfere with the game, and as the catcher's lines are in turn drawn as points of measurement for the other lines, it is hardly worth while to go to all this trouble except for an important match.

For the benefit of those players whose club treasury is in such a prosperous condition as to make unnecessary the home-made devices described above, it is well to say that a set of base bags with straps and spikes can be purchased at any base-ball outfitter's for $4, $5, or $7, according to quality, while a rubber home-plate costs $7, a marble one $3, and an iron one $1.

The next articles for our consideration are the implements for the players. The best ball to purchase is the regular "league" ball. These balls are the most uniform in manufacture and quality, and give the best satisfaction in the long run. They can be purchased for $1.50, with a discount for quantity. It is worth while to purchase more than one, because it often happens that wet grass ruins the cover of the ball. For this reason, when a base-ball has been used in wet weather it should be put aside, and the next time the nine wish to practise on a wet day this ball, which will be as hard as a rock, should be brought out. As soon as it is wet it softens again, and it is just as useful as a new one would be after fifteen minutes' wetting. This constant wetting rots the covers, but a harness-maker will re-cover the balls, and they may be used for practice. In the kinds of bats there is far more variety. A special bat is said to be made of wagon-tongue, but the more commonly favored is of ash, second-growth, and thoroughly seasoned. These can be purchased for from twenty-five cents to one dollar each, according to the quality of the wood. Lighter bats are made of willow; and the cheapest, of basswood. These do not last so well as ash, however. The rules specify that the bat shall not be over $2\frac{1}{2}$ inches in diameter, nor more than 42 inches in length. In selecting a bat, individual taste is the best guide as to matters of weight and balance, but the grain should be examined carefully, in order that one may not choose a stick that will leave him in the lurch by breaking just as he becomes accustomed to it. The grain should run lengthwise, and not cross sharply, particularly over the handle. A knot in the handle will often lead to a break, but one farther down toward the end is not of any moment. If a bat is varnished highly, the handle should be scraped, so that it will not turn easily in the hands. The first baseman and catcher should each wear gloves to protect the hands from the constant pounding of the ball which playing these positions involves. Any one can make a very serviceable pair of base-ball gloves out of a stout pair of buckskins. The fingers and thumbs should be cut off at the first joint for the basemen, and if any extra padding is needed, pieces of felt can be sewn on. The catcher's gloves can be made in a similar way, except that the left-hand glove is kept whole and the ends of the fingers reinforced by heavy leather tips. A shoemaker will put on these tips, and they should be about an inch and a half long. Both gloves should have padding in the palm and over the ball of the thumb. This padding can be made of as many layers of felt as are desired, sewn in when the glove is turned wrong side out. Many of the best catchers prefer to do their own padding. The pads should be so cut that they run up into the finger a little way, and thus form a protection for the base of the fingers. By those who wish to purchase gloves, and thus save the trouble of making them, the catcher's gloves can be purchased for $3.50 and $5. The basemen's gloves cost about $2.50. Every man who intends playing behind the bat should wear a mask, and it is best to purchase a good one, as the cheap ones are likely to be fragile, not well made, and may perhaps be broken by a foul tip. While an acci-

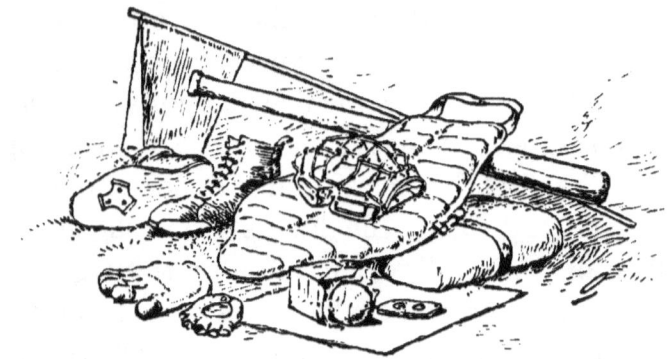

ARTICLES OF A BASE-BALL OUTFIT.

dent from a broken mask is very unusual, as the wires are so bent as to spring outward when broken, still it is not well, for the sake of a slight saving, to run any risks of this kind. A good mask will cost from $2 to $4.

A body protector is also an admirable invention, and saves many a bruise. The cheaper ones are made of leather and canvas, and cost about $5. The best are made of rubber, and can be inflated so as to form a kind of air pillow. These cost from $6 to $10.

Individual uniforms next attract our attention. A tennis or cricket suit, or any set of flannels, will answer nicely. A flannel shirt and an old pair of long trousers tied or strapped in at the ankles was an old-fashioned uniform, and it is just as serviceable to-day. The most convenient trousers, however, are of the knicker-bocker pattern, and it is well to pad them heavily at the knees and along the side of the leg and thigh, particularly if one is to do any sliding to bases. This padding can be made by quilting in any heavy pieces of cloth. The long stockings should be heavy and stout, and extend well above the knee. The shoes should be broad and easy, with low heels, and may be of canvas or leather, the latter being the most lasting. A triangular spike is placed on the sole of each shoe in order to prevent slipping, and of these spikes, the broad ones are the easiest and best. Sometimes a smaller plate is worn on the heel as well. The pitcher should have upon the toe of his right shoe a metal plate, to prevent the speedy wearing out of the shoe in pitching. This plate is a sort of cap, and covers the inside corner of the shoe. Any shoemaker can put one on. A cap with a visor is the most convenient form of headgear, and interferes least with the player's comfort. Complete uniforms can be purchased from the outfitters for from $5 to $30. Below is a list of the separate articles, showing the range in prices: Shirts, $2.00 to $5.00; trousers, $1.75 to $4.50; stockings, 50c. to $1.50; caps, 50c. to $1.00; belts, 25c. to 30c.; shoes, $2.00 to $7.00; spikes, 15c. to 75c.; toe-plate, 50c.

Base-ball is a game so entirely dependent upon the condition of the ground and weather, that it never can become, in our climate, an all-the-year-round pastime. No one can play base-ball when the fingers are numb with cold, nor can there be any play upon a ground covered with snow. But the sport has become so scientific, and practice is so essential to its highest development, that quite a proportion of the players have now taken up some systematic winter practice.

Particularly is this the case among college and school nines. Professionals, making a business of following the game, can travel to Southern cities, where they may anticipate the Northern season by several weeks of outdoor practice; but those who seek it merely as a pastime cannot enjoy any such means of attaining additional skill. College and school boys, therefore, have recourse to gymnasiums, where, by a judicious use of certain apparatus, they prepare themselves for the regular field work. Some of the best equipped of these gymnasiums have long, low alleys, completely bounded by two walls and a wire netting, in which throwing and batting can be practised. These are known as "cages." The irregular and indiscriminate use of the apparatus, or even of the cage, results in little good to the player, but a systematic and well-directed use of both tends to put a nine into the field in a superior condition for the work required. In addition to this, the benefit to the general health of regular exercise during the winter and early spring is not to be disregarded as a factor in the problem of developing successful nines. The use of the apparatus should be directed toward the development and strengthening of the various muscles which are to bear the brunt of the labor when on the field.

Many of the exercises really need no equipment such as a gymnasium affords, and one can take advantage of any room at home. A pair of dumb-bells, the Indian-clubs, a rope fastened to the ceiling or a beam, an old foot-ball hung as a "punching-bag," another rope, on which a heavy "spool" slides freely, stretched from a point about the height of a man's shoulder up to the opposite wall, where it joins the ceiling—such an amount of apparatus will give full opportunity for the best kind of exercise. The only part needing any explanation is, perhaps, the sliding-spool. This is an admirable device for cultivating the muscles used in throwing. The point at which the spool

THE BODY PROTECTOR AND CATCHER'S MASK.

would come in contact with the ceiling should be well padded with some rather inelastic substance, in order that the spool may not rebound too severely. By throwing the spool along the rope a number of times daily, any man can acquire a powerful throw.

The winter work of a college nine will give a good idea of the methods practised in indoor preparation. There are usually at least twenty candidates for positions, and, as it is impossible that all should practise the same work at the same time, these candidates are usually divided into squads of perhaps four men each. The times are so arranged as to give to each squad an allotted hour in which they can have the use of the cage and other apparatus. These squads are still further subdivided into pairs, and, while two of them occupy the cage, the other two make use of the running-track and apparatus. In the use of the cage the men do not attempt to practise violently, but rather to acquire good form, both in batting and fielding. One of the men pitches for the other to bat, and the batter endeavors to meet the ball squarely, with the bat moving on a line. He also is particular to accustom himself to meet the ball at any height, and to stand firmly on his feet when striking. In fielding practice one of the men bats grounders for his comrade, who stands at the other end of the cage, and, picking up the ball, throws it at a spot marked on the end wall at about the height of a man's chest. The batter does not drive the ball as hard as possible at his companion, but at a medium rate of speed. In picking up and throwing, the first thing to acquire is quickness and freedom of movement. Accuracy and force come very rapidly in this daily practice, so that a player soon finds it simple enough to take the ball cleanly and get it easily down to the mark. On the running-track, the men take a few turns to limber up, and then practise quick starting, and short, sharp spurts at full speed, rather than the more leisurely, long-continued run of the men who are training for boating honors.

In connection with the running-track one should mention a device for practising sliding to bases which has proved of the greatest practical advantage to players. One of the college nines, by making use

PITCHER AT PRACTICE IN THE "CAGE."

of this sliding-bag during their winter practice, acquired such dexterity as to have for that year a record in stealing bases more than three times that of any other nine in the association. This sliding apparatus may be rigged up in a variety of ways, the only object to be attained being the arrangement of a yielding cushion upon which a man may practise sliding until he acquires sufficient confidence and dexterity to make it no effort of will for him to plunge headforemost at the base. The first one of these cushions consisted of a frame, about fifteen feet long and three or four feet wide, upon which was tightly stretched a piece of carpet.

The work with the boxing-gloves is designed to improve the man's general muscular development, make him quick and firm upon his feet, and rapid in judgment and action. The men usually devote most of the time to going through a certain set of exercises, rather than to indulging in "slugging" matches. The dumb-bells, Indian-clubs, and other general apparatus in a gymnasium are used with a view to acquiring a uniform development as well as a considerable range of muscular action. Whenever any player is inordinately or unevenly developed in any set of muscles (particularly if he has over-developed the shoulders), he is not encouraged to strengthen the already too powerful muscles, but is so trained as to give them flexibility and freedom of action. Exercise that toughens the hands—such as swinging on the flying-rings, or rope-climbing—is found to be useful.

After the men have gone through their round of exercise, they take a shower-bath, are thoroughly "rubbed down," and then their training is over for the day. The amount of time required is probably not more than an hour or an hour and a half, and yet the effect upon the condition of the men is quite noticeable before the end of the month. In no respect is the result of this gymnasium work more evident than in the improvement in throwing. Not only is it the exception to find men who have undergone this winter work suffering from lame arms when they begin practice on the field, but the accuracy and strength of their throwing is also greatly increased. One of the reasons for this is, that in throwing in the cage the player is compelled to throw the ball low, because of the low ceiling, which continually operates to improve the player's ability to shoot the ball along on a line rather than "up and over."

The winter training outside of this regular gymnasium practice, is not considered to be of any very great importance. The men pay no special attention to their diet, but avoid every kind of excess. An outdoor cage is sometimes erected, in which the men may have outdoor practice in pleasant weather. The chief advantage of this cage is the better light for batting. It is also possible by its use to get a little real practice on taking grounders. The outdoor cage is usually a very crude affair, and consists of netting so strung on posts as to encompass an alley about seventy feet long by twenty wide.

With the first warm sunshine that comes after the frost is out of the ground, there stirs in the heart of the base-ball player an intense desire to get into the field and begin playing. I remember a young man who used to work in clock factories in Connecticut. Although an excellent workman, he never seemed to secure any permanent position, but drifted from one town to another. Early one fall he applied to me for a position, and as he showed that he knew his trade he obtained employment. He worked admirably and well, through the winter and even into the spring. One day — and it was a beautiful day, everything just turning green and the sun shining as bright and warm as in midsummer — I missed him, and asked the foreman of the room what had become of him. "Oh, he's

PRACTISING THROWING WITH THE SPOOL.

off," was the reply; "he'll get his kit to-morrow, and you won't see him again till next fall." I took pains to meet the young man the next morning, when he came to take away his traps. "What's the matter?" I inquired. "Nothing," said he, "'cept yesterday I heard a blue-bird singin', and I don't do any work in shops after that." A similar yearning to be out of doors tempts the ball-player. Many times the fine weather is treacherous, and premature practice is cut short, or even rendered detrimental to the welfare of a nine, by damp, chilly winds. As a rule, it is wise to take advantage of only the very warmest days, practising in the early afternoon, until the weather is fairly settled. The New York nine were once obliged to take a vacation, after a few weeks of practice in a cold spring, because so many of the men had lamenesses of one kind or another from exposure in inclement weather. When a college nine goes on the field for the first time, there is usually a superfluity of enthusiasm, which leads players to practise too long or too violently. Captains have learned this, and, unless they are carried away with the same tendency, do not encourage any long practice during the first weeks. After that, as the men become "broken in" and the weather improves, the players are allowed to do more work. All the men playing in the out-field can practise together, as the work of the three fielders is much the same. These men take positions in the out-field in something of a cluster (not so near, however, as to interfere with one another), while a batter knocks fly-balls out to them which they take turns in catching. A most important preliminary to this practice is the selection of an experienced man to bat the ball. There are many men who may be good players, but to whom knocking flies to an out-field is an utter impossibility. Such men may have to hit the ball a half-dozen times before sending a fly-ball near any of the fielders. Again, it is not advisable to select a man who knocks only the simplest kind of flies every time,—although such a man is to be preferred to the wild hitter who sends the men chasing a half-dozen failures in order to receive one catch. The batter should be able to knock high flies, line hits, long flies, and occasionally a sharp, hot grounder. His object is to give the fielders as much practice of every kind as possible, and a good man will gauge the ground the fielders can cover, and, while avoiding "running them to death," will occasionally give each man an opportunity to make a brilliant catch. Nothing encourages and improves the candidates so much as keeping their ambition thoroughly aroused during the entire time of practice.

FIELDING, THROWING, AND GENERAL PRACTICE

CANDIDATES for in-field positions are usually too numerous to admit of their all practising together, as would-be out-fielders may do. On this account it is customary for them to take turns, in parties of perhaps four at a time. The others, who are obliged to wait their turn, make themselves useful as batsmen to the rest; or they may stand about half-way between the out-fielders and the man batting to them, and thereby get an occasional ball, besides returning the ball to the batter for the out-fielders. To those who take the bases balls are sent in turn, or occasionally at random, which they field over to the first-base man. He usually practises throwing to third base. The batsman contrives to give each man a variety of balls, mostly grounders, such as each would be called upon to take in a game. An occasional short high fly is knocked, and once in a while a sharp liner. While the ball is sometimes batted directly at the fielder, the best practice for him is to have it sent frequently upon one side or the other of the place upon

BATTING FOR THE FIELDERS' PRACTICE.

which he stands. Thus, in the case of the third baseman, whose position is a few feet inside the line to the home plate and a little behind the line from second to third, balls should be batted not only along the front line occasionally, but very often several feet toward the short-stop. One of the best arrangements between a short-stop and a third baseman is for the latter to take all slow hits coming where he can run in and handle them, while the short-stop plays what is known as a "deep-field,"— that is, considerably back of the base line,— and takes whatever balls the third baseman cannot reach on account of their speed or direction. In this way much more ground can be satisfactorily covered by these two men. When men are practising these plays, the batter should send some slow, bounding balls directed toward the short-stop, and the third baseman should run in on them and handle them. Then a sharp drive should be sent, which the short-stop will receive, as the other could not reach it in time. It is not a difficult matter for two men to acquire this style of play, and when once it is learned it makes a very strong fielding combination.

The second baseman plays about on a line with his base, but away from it toward first some twenty feet or so. The batter should send the balls on both sides of him, extending his field as much as possible. In batting over the second-base bag, however, the batter should not drive the ball too fast, or it will be practically a base-hit, and too many such drives tend to discourage the player who zealously tries for each. A slow hit is one of the most difficult for a second baseman to handle, particularly if he plays well back in order to cover ground. It is not so much that he cannot run up rapidly on it, but that it usually comes to him just about the spot most cut up by the base line, and where an irregular bound puts it out of the question for him to field it cleanly. On this account the batter should give the second baseman plenty of this very kind to take, in order that he may acquire the habit of rapid judgment as to how far in he should meet the ball. A fly should be occasionally batted almost over the first baseman's head, just a little too high for that player to reach. The second baseman can take many of these, and practice soon shows him that he can cover a deal of ground there.

In batting to the first baseman, balls should be knocked that force him to use good judgment as to whether he should go after them or let the second baseman take them. These and slow grounders along the base line are the ones upon which he will need the most practice.

While the in-field and out-field are thus getting their general practice, the batteries are usually "limbering up," although the pitcher should be careful not to indulge in a severe delivery until he faces a batsman, as it is too great a strain upon him for nothing. He should strive merely to get the muscles of his arm working easily and freely, while the catcher also warms himself up gradually to the work.

Batting practice can be had in two ways: first, by placing the batter at the plate and stopping the ordinary practice in the in-field; second, by stationing him out to one side, where he will not materially interfere with the practice. The latter is preferable, as accomplishing more work in the same time.

The regular pitchers ought not to be obliged to do all the pitching for this batting practice. In fact, it is best to have them do only as much of it as they can do without getting at all tired or listless. Two or three men who throw well and have a moderate control of the curves should be brought out to do a greater part of this rather tedious work. Nothing is more demoralizing to a good pitcher than to keep him pitching for batting practice, until he becomes tired and careless. Each man should be given a certain number of hits, until all have had a turn. After this it is wise to select the most promising nine men, and arranging them in their positions, to place a tenth man at the bat and one or two substitutes on the bases. Then let the playing be as if it were a regular game. This gives a new and added interest just at the time when the men are perhaps becoming a little tired. After fifteen minutes of this work, the captain, or (if he be not a successful batter for the practice) some other player, takes the bat and ball and, standing on the home plate, knocks the ball to the in-field or out-field, as he chooses, calling out at the same time what play to make with the ball. In this he should give every man some difficult play to execute; such, for instance, as stationing a runner on third with instructions to try to come in on a fly after the ball is caught, and then knocking a fly to the outfielder and having him send the ball in to the plate to intercept the man. A few double plays in the in-field, some practice in catching a runner between bases, a little throwing to second by the catcher, and some fielding home by the in-field should complete the work of the day.

Now, a few words regarding the objects to be aimed at in this general practice. First, as regards throwing. Every one has what may be called a natural way of throwing the ball, but this so-called "natural way" usually means a perverted method acquired through carelessness, or attempts to throw too hard before the arm is sufficiently accustomed to the work. As a result of this, there are few boys or college men who may not learn a great deal in the matter of throwing by careful attention for a few weeks to one or two points. The first man to whom attention should be called is the man who takes a hop, skip, and jump before he lets the ball go. No man can run fast enough to beat a thrown ball, and consequently it takes longer to carry the ball part way and throw it the rest, than it does to throw it all the way. Therefore the first thing for the man who has acquired this trick to do, is to stand still when he gets the ball, and then throw it. The opposite fault to this is that of leaning away when throwing. A man gets a sharp grounder, and throws the ball before he has recovered his balance, and the force of his throw is thereby greatly diminished. While this is not nearly so common as the other fault, it is quite as difficult to correct. The happy medium between the two is the man who receives the ball and, quickly straightening himself, drives it while leaning forward; and, as it leaves his hand, takes his single step in the direction of his throw.

So much for the feet and body, now for the arm, hand, and wrist.

The best and most accurate throwers are those who continually practise what is termed a short-arm throw. To get an idea of the first steps toward the acquisition of this method, let the player take the ball in his hand, and bringing it back just level with his ear, planting both feet firmly, attempt to throw the ball without using the legs or body. At first the throw is awkward and feeble, but constant practice speedily results in moderate speed and peculiar accuracy. After steady practice at this until quite a pace is acquired, the man may be allowed to use his legs and body to increase the speed, still, however, sticking to the straight, forward motion of the hand, wrist, and the arm. The secret of the throw is, of course, keeping the hand in a line with the arm and not swinging it out to the side and away from the head, where much of the accuracy and some of the quickness is lost. Certain catchers have brought this style of throw to such a pitch of perfection as to get the ball away toward second almost on the instant it strikes the hands. They aid the throwing by a slight twist of the body.

SHORT-ARM THROW,
THE BEGINNING.

The quickness of this method of throwing is due to the fact that there is no delay caused by drawing back the arm past the head or by turning the body around, which lose so much valuable time. Its accuracy is due to the fact that it is easier to aim at an object with a hand in front of the eyes than when it is out beyond the shoulder. One can easily ascertain this by comparing the ease of pointing the index finger at any object when the hand is in front of the face, with the difficulty of doing so when the arm is extended out sideways from the body. Still further, in the almost round-arm throwing, which many players use, the hand describes an arc, and the ball must be let go at the proper point to go true. If let go at any other point in the swing, the throw is certain to be wild. In the other method, that of straight-arm throwing, any variation is far more likely to be a variation in height only, and in that respect the variation may be greater without serious error. A straight-arm throw sends a ball much easier to handle than the side-arm style. The latter is likely to curve, bound irregularly, and be more inconvenient for the baseman. In-field throwing should be on a line, as much as possible, and there are few distances to be covered there that require any "up and over" throwing. In getting a ball in from a deep out-field, the distance is sometimes so great that none but professionals or exceptionally strong throwers can drive the ball in except by giving it quite an upward direction; even then, however, one should be careful to keep the ball fairly well down, as it is far better to have it reach the catcher on the bound than to go sailing over his head. "Keep it down" is a cardinal rule when fielding to the home plate from the field. If a low ball be thrown, it is easier for the catcher to touch the runner, who in a tight place will invariably slide as close to the ground as possible. A high throw gives the catcher

SHORT-ARM THROW, THE END.

almost no chance to recover and put the ball on the man, whereas a low throw brings his hands in the most advantageous position for touching the runner.

FIRST BASEMAN THROWING TO SECOND FOR A DOUBLE-PLAY.

The same is, of course, true in the case of the catcher's throws to the second or the other bases, to put out the runner.

The position of the fingers when throwing a ball is a point upon which there are individual differences of opinion; but the majority of the best throwers in the country use principally the fore-finger and middle-finger in giving direction to the ball. Further particulars regarding special throwing will be noted in commenting upon the individual positions.

Handling the ball well is quite as important an element in the game as throwing. By the non-playing spectator there is little difference noted between the various ways of catching a fly or picking up a grounder. Muffs and fumbles are the only errors of this kind which excite their adverse comment; but, in point of fact, there are errors almost as serious which entirely escape their observation. A player may hang back from a slow hit so long that even though he pick it up well and throw it accurately the runner will nevertheless reach his base. Indeed, the scorer may give it as a base-hit, and the fielder escape a deserved error. Again, a fielder may, by not starting quickly enough, be obliged to turn and run with a fly so that he catches it while facing away from the plate, and is thus unable to field the ball in, in time to intercept a runner who starts from third after the catch. Sometimes it is necessary to catch the ball in this way, but it should be the last resort; not only because it is very difficult, but also because this method makes it impossible to get a quick return of the ball when required. An in-fielder should always take the ball while coming forward if possible. This does not mean that he should dash madly into the ball, but that his weight should be moving in an advantageous direction when he takes it. It is best to bring the heels together just as the player stoops for the ball, if it be a low one, and hug the ground closely. The knees should bend, and the hands and arms, as they go down, will make, with the legs, an almost impassable barrier, so that even should the player fail to get the ball cleanly in his hands, he will stop it, and perhaps still have time to field it. The end to be aimed at is, of course, to always take the ball on a good bound; but no one can rely upon doing this invariably, as irregularities of the ground and the peculiarities of batting render exact results impossible. The fielder must also bear in mind the fact that he should take the ball on the *earliest* good bound, and not, by waiting or backing away, make his throw necessarily a hurried one. There are times when good judgment leads a player to take the ball a little late; as, for instance, when he has an opportunity for a double-play with the ball coming directly at the base he wishes to cover. By a step backward he can take the ball while his foot is touching the bag, and then instantly throw to the other base; whereas by meeting the ball early, he would have to run back a step or two to touch the base before throwing.

Rapidity of judgment is more valuable in base-ball than in almost any other sport, and it is only this quick thinking which will enable a player to take every advantage that offers. Wherever it is practicable, a fielder should endeavor to take the ball in the most convenient position for immediate throwing to the quarter where the ball is most needed. For instance, a right-handed player should, as far as possible, avoid taking the ball while turned to the left, when, by a little extra effort, he can bring himself squarely in front of it. The out-fielders will profit by the same advice as has been given for the in-fielders, and in addition they should remember that they have far more distance to cover. When a ball is pitched, every out-fielder should be ready for an instant start, and if a fly be batted each should be off toward the spot where it will probably fall. Of course, if the ball is falling in left-field, the right-fielder after a step or two may stop; but the center-fielder should go on, not to take the fly, but to be ready to assist if the ball goes through the left-fielder's hands. An out-fielder should bear in mind one cardinal principle, namely, that he should run as fast as possible until he nears the spot

MAKING SURE OF A CATCH.—LEFT-FIELDER CATCHING, CENTER-FIELDER BACKING HIM UP.

where the ball is coming. Then he can slow up, but his fast running should begin as he starts, and not after he has gone half way, and finds that he is likely to be late. A moderate runner who starts instantly for the right spot makes a far better fielder than a more speedy man who gets off slowly, and whose judgment of the spot where the ball will probably land is not so good. A fly should always be handled in front of a man if possible, as he is then in a better position to throw it if caught, as well as to stop and return it if a muff is made. In taking a grounder, an out-fielder should sacrifice rapidity of handling to security. A ground hit which goes by an out-fielder is so disastrous that no chance of missing it should be taken. He must stop it, even though, as the expression has it, he has to "lie down before it." The out-field is usually rougher and more irregular than the in-field, and hence the player must be more careful to put himself directly in the pathway of the ball. In catching a fly, the hands should be used cup-fashion, the thumbs up and the lower edges of the hands brought close together. Line-hits can not, of course, be handled in this way, but must be taken like thrown balls, with the little fingers in front and the thumbs forming the back of the cup; a low ball, with the thumbs forward and the edges of the hands forming the back. It is occasionally necessary to take a ball directly over the head, owing to a sudden change in its direction due to the wind carrying it over the player. Such balls must be taken with the little fingers up and the thumbs making the bottom of the cup.

The base-running practice of a nine consists for the most part of quick starting and bold sliding. The gymnasium work will have added greatly to the abilities of the men in these directions, but this must be reinforced by daily work on the field. The point most neglected, and yet the most vital to success, is a quick start for first after hitting the ball. Many a slow hit is turned into a base-hit by the speed and

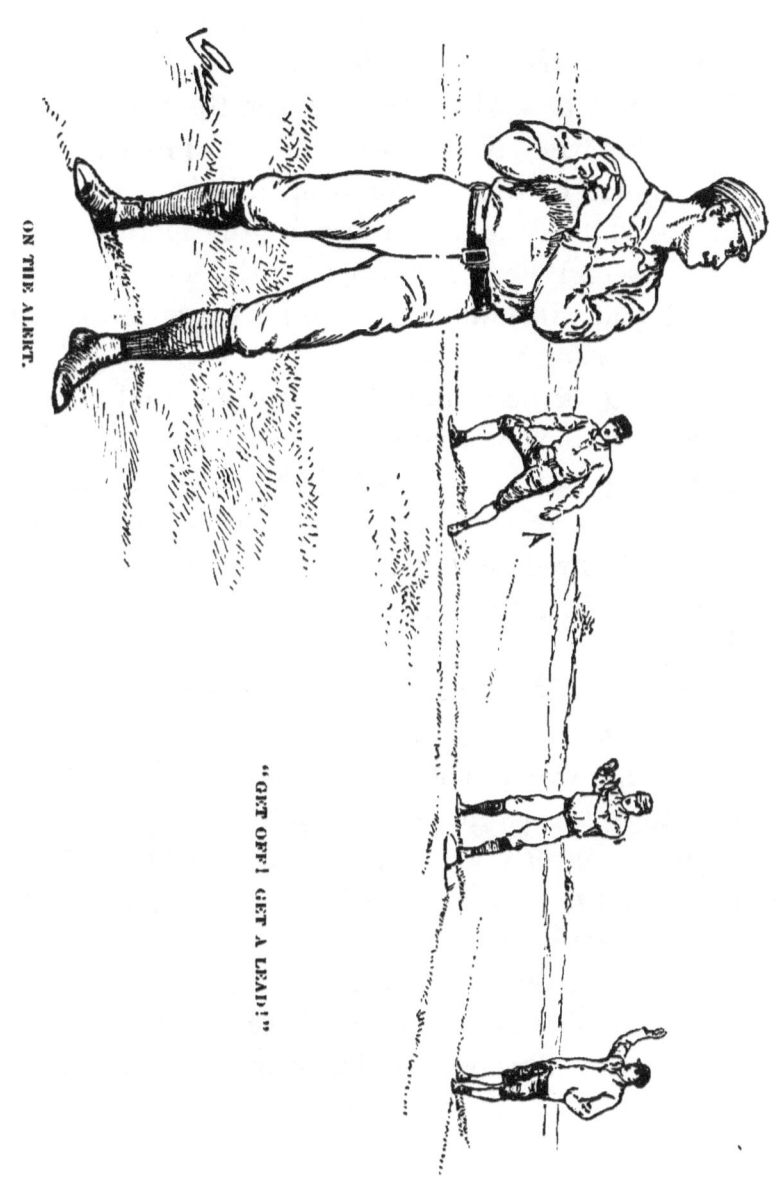

ON THE ALERT.

"GET OFF! GET A LEAD!"

quickness of the runner. Many an error is saved an in-fielder by the slowness of the batter in getting under way. Every man should be made to practise this start until he springs toward first the instant the ball leaves his bat. If a player can be impressed with the importance of this, by showing him how often it is that the ball beats the runner by the merest fraction of a second, he will appreciate the advantage to be gained, and will himself use all his energies toward the acquisition of this quick start.

Such points of play must be made habitual to the player by constant practice, because, no matter how much he may desire to make them at certain times, as, for instance, in the ninth inning, with perhaps his single run required to win, he is not capable of doing so unless his former work has been directed toward acquiring them.

The next practice is in "stealing second." The battery should be placed in their places, and the runner on first base. The pitcher should hold the runner as close to the base as he can by motions and an occasional throw, exactly as he would in a game, and the runner should be sent down when a good opportunity offers. He should be coached to take as great a lead as he can with security, always bearing in mind, however, that he should not lead off so far as to make it necessary for him to be off his balance in the wrong direction, for a good start is worth two or three feet of lead. In taking his lead he should be willing to go far enough at times to make it necessary for him to go back for first with his hands if the pitcher throws to the bag, for by getting back in that way

A WILD THROW AND A SAFE SLIDE TO SECOND.

he is enabled to take a little longer lead. When he starts for second, it should be with his whole heart and as if his life depended upon it. Here again, if necessary, he must slide for it, going head first at the base, and taking it with his hand. When the baseman is in the way it is sometimes necessary to slide feet first in order to avoid injury.

There are two cautions to be remembered in this play. One is to slide as far behind the baseman as it is possible to do, and yet catch the bag; the other, not to begin to slide so early as to lose the advantage of the last step or two of the run. This last caution is by no means a needless one, as men who are expert at sliding are very likely to fall into the habit of "sliding up to the bag"; beginning the slide so early as to lose headway and valuable speed, and thus be so slow as to be touched by the baseman before the hand reaches the bag.

THE BASEMEN AND THE SHORT-STOP

During all the general training involved in the practice mentioned in the former paragraphs, there must also be particular coaching for each individual position; and it is in this position-work that the players improve most rapidly, later in the season, when each has been assigned to his own place.

The in-fielders are the first to exhibit the good effects of practice, and the methods of perfecting their play are most interesting. For instance, the third baseman usually begins his season by very slow playing He finds that from third base to first is a considerable distance, and that he has to make an effort in order to get the ball over. As a result of this feeling, it takes him longer to throw than it should, and any ball batted sharply and rather close to his base is a safe hit; because, even if he stop it, the runner will reach the base before the baseman can field it.

The first coaching, then, for the third baseman should be with the object of acquiring a sharp, strong throw. He must therefore practise steadily the short-arm throw already described — the hand being brought back and close to the ear, and nearly level with it, instead of swinging at arm's-length, away from the body. For some time it will perhaps seem almost impossible to get the ball over to first by means of this throw, but in a week's practice that result is achieved satisfactorily, and thenceforth the third baseman will be little troubled about his throwing. His speed and accuracy will be increased by every day of his practice, and he will seldom disgrace himself by anything like a wild throw.

Of all the in-fielders, it especially belongs to this player to throw swiftly, and also to get the ball away quickly. To acquire this latter skill should not be nearly so difficult as most amateurs find it. The reason for their difficulty lies in the fact that the ordinary player does not analyze the play sufficiently in his own mind to discover in just what part of it he is deficient. The result is, that the entire play becomes hurried and inaccurate; and once careless, instead of improving the player is likely to retrograde.

Just to illustrate this, let us analyze the play: Suppose a ball be batted parallel to the third-base line two feet inside that line. The ordinary amateur third baseman, by failing to make a sharp start, is obliged to take such a ball just as it goes by the bag, and as a result he is turned partially away from first base, and is running from that point as well. This makes it necessary for him first to stop his run and then to turn about, so as to face the base before throwing. All this preparation takes so much time that there is seldom much use in his throwing the ball over at all; but as he is too hurried to realize this, over it goes,— not infrequently with a wild throw into the bargain.

Now let us watch a good professional, and note the difference. I remember seeing Denny, at one time a noted third baseman, execute this play once on a "scorching drive" just inside the line. The instant the bat hit the ball, I saw Denny jump for the third-base line. So quick was the spring and so clever the intuition by which, from the direction of the stroke, he realized where the ball was coming, that he and the ball met in front of third base; and Denny was actually throwing the ball to first before the runner had taken a half-dozen steps. Of course, all third basemen are not so quick and clever as Denny, but every amateur who fills that position can by an instant start, instead of a

"JUMP IN FRONT OF THE BALL."

slow one, meet the majority of batted balls before they can go so far past him as to turn him away from first. To turn away from first is the great fault, and to its correction the coach must give his attention, and the player must direct his labor. "Jump in front of the ball," is the best coaching order that can be given any in-fielder, but it is particularly good for the third baseman.

Picking up the ball is the next step of the play. If possible it should be taken cleanly in the hands, of course; but that is not of nearly so much moment as to get in front of it early, and thus stop it. If a third baseman gets a sharp hit anywhere in front of the line from second to third, and he is a swift thrower, he can stop the ball by letting it strike him, and, picking it up, get it to first base before the runner. But if the fielder takes the ball a few feet behind that line and while running toward foul ground, the best handling will seldom enable him to catch the runner.

Finally comes the execution of the throw itself. He should use the short-arm throw and lean toward first. This latter suggestion is an important one, and should be continually in the player's mind during his daily practice. Whenever he gets the ball he should recover speedily, and with what becomes almost a second nature, should lean toward the point to which he is to throw. The entire action in detail, then, should be: instantly jump in front of the ball; while picking it up, recover a steady position, and leaning toward first, throw as nearly on a line as possible. Of these, the particular part of the play which can be hurried to least advantage, and yet the part which the inexperienced fielder oftenest endeavors to hurry, is picking up the ball. It is never good policy to snatch at the ball instead of picking it up.

The tenor of this advice is applicable as well to all the in-fielders, but the third baseman's position is one in which the desirability of thoroughly steady and sharp play is especially marked. In handling balls which must be fielded elsewhere than to first base, second and home are usually the objective points for the third baseman; and it may be laid down as a rule particularly applicable to the amateur, that he should take very few chances in these throws. Unless the hit be a sharp one, and he receive the ball without a fumble, there is little likelihood of his getting the ball to second or home in time to intercept a runner. When the runner is "forced," so that the catcher or the baseman is not obliged to touch him in order to put him out, there is a little better chance, and under such circumstances the play is of course more advisable.

As illustrating the foolishness of ill-judged attempts to catch the man at the home plate, I recall a championship game between Harvard and Yale, in which, up to the ninth inning, Yale had led. In fact, Yale was then three runs ahead.

Singularly enough, on the afternoon before this game, there had occurred a discussion among members of the Yale nine as to the advisability of the practice (then common among all college nines) of always fielding to the home plate, when there was but one man out and a runner was on third. In order to make a fair test of this question on its merits, a runner was placed on third and the in-fielders came closer up, as they were accustomed to do under such circumstances. The pitcher then would toss the ball, and the batsman hit it sharply anywhere in the in-field, the runner at the same time trying to come home. Out of twenty trials the runner was put out but five times — getting home safely the other fifteen.

In spite of this experiment, however, when Harvard was at the bat for the last inning, there being one man out, a man on second, and one on third, with three runs to tie and four to win, the Yale in-fielders came further in and tried to throw the man out at the plate. Three of these attempts and one single hit gave Harvard four runs and the game; whereas, had the Yale men thrown to first they would almost to a certainty have put out the side at the sacrifice of but one run, and would have won by two runs.

It is not a difficult matter to see the reasons why a third baseman should seldom attempt to field to the plate, unless the ball comes fast and on a clean bound. If the hit be a very slow one, and the base-runner have anything like the lead he should take, there is no chance to run up on the ball and throw it to the plate in season. The ball must be fielded to the catcher in such a manner as to enable him to touch the runner; and to field the ball thus from third base is no easy matter, as it often involves throwing the ball almost over the runner's shoulder. Under similar circumstances I have seen Hankinson, in attempting this throw, hit the runner squarely between the shoulders; and although fortunately the blow did not injure the runner in the least, unfortunately it was impossible for the catcher to put him out.

In fielding to first the ball may be thrown quite wide, and yet, by leaning out, the first baseman will be able to catch it while one foot remains on the base. If, however, the first baseman were obliged to touch the runner, as the catcher must do, fully one half the throws he receives would not be sufficiently accurate to enable him to execute the play. Moreover, a runner from third has an advantage of several yards over a runner to first. If a player wishes to convince himself of this fact, let him note the exact positions, under these circumstances, of the batsman who starts for first base and a good base-runner who is trying to come home. At the moment the ball leaves the bat, he will find that while the batsman is just starting, the runner from third is nearly half-way home, and besides has a "flying start."

In practising putting the ball on a runner, the third baseman should accustom himself to receiving the ball from first, second, short, home, and pitcher; and it

THIRD BASEMAN INTERCEPTING THE SLIDE OF A RUNNER FROM SECOND.

is no easy matter to acquire the proper way to receive the ball thrown from each of these positions. Any man who thinks the same motion will answer for all these different cases makes a serious mistake.

In deciding upon the proper method of receiving the ball, the third baseman will find that much depends upon the position of the runner. If the runner be coming back from home, because the pitcher, having caught him leading off too far, has thrown to third, the third baseman should step almost into his base line as he receives the ball, and, swinging his right hand low, should bring the ball against the runner.

The pitcher, if he understands the play, will throw into the line rather than at the base. If the runner be coming from second, and the first baseman be fielding the ball over, there is little likelihood of the throw being sufficiently accurate to allow the play in the method just described, and the baseman must therefore be prepared to use either hand, according to the position of the runner at the moment when the ball is received. Suppose, for instance, that the ball be thrown five or six feet toward second: the baseman can tell by sight or hearing just where the runner is, and if the runner has not reached him he should turn to the left with the ball in his left hand. If, however, the runner is just passing him, he should swing to the right with the ball in the right hand. In either case, he need not swing so low as he does when the ball is thrown nearer the base. In the latter case he should always almost sweep the ground in his swing, as the runner is sure to slide. Of course, catching the ball *on* the man is the perfect method; but unfortunately the ball so seldom comes to the proper point that these other methods of touching the runner must be practised faithfully.

In the matter of one player assisting another, the third baseman is more often to be "backed up" than be called upon to perform that office for some one else.

The short-stop needs the same coaching as the third baseman, in the way of urging him to jump in front of the ball, and to start quickly. The combination method of play, which was mentioned in a previous paragraph as an excellent one to bring out all the possible advantages of playing the two positions of short-stop and third base, requires plenty of practice. Particularly must the two players thoroughly understand each other. A very good way to begin practice upon this method is to station the third baseman where he can, by an effort, just cover the ground to his base, and to tell him to "take everything he can get, out in the

PLAYING A TRICK ON THE BASE-RUNNER. THE BALL IS PURPOSELY THROWN BY THE CATCHER OVER THE THIRD BASEMAN'S HEAD INTO THE SHORT-STOP'S HANDS.

diamond." The short-stop is then placed well back of the base line, as far as he can be and yet be sure of throwing to first in time to catch the ordinary runner on a hard hit. He must be instructed to "come in on" the ball as soon as it is hit and he knows its direction.

Irwin was one of the first of the professionals to develop this "deep field" play by a short-stop, and I remember how very strange it appeared to the collegians to see this little fellow station himself almost half-way out to left field; but before the game was ended he had shown himself fully able to cover all the space he had taken.

A short-stop has to make one peculiar class of plays in which he should endeavor to become thoroughly expert, and that is, taking short flies that go just outside the in-field but are too low for the out-fielders to get under. There are also occasional flies near the foul line, ten or a dozen yards behind third base, which

FIRST BASEMAN TAKING A LOW THROW BY REACHING FORWARD.

an agile short-stop may take. No player has ever been more expert in this line of play than John Ward, so well known for his advancement of the game. Many a short fly that the scorers were just putting down as a base-hit has found a resting-place in his outstretched hands, simply because he has made a practice of starting instantly, and of never believing any fly too far away for him to get.

"Backing up" is a special feature of the short-stop's duties. Any ball fielded from the other side of the diamond to the third or second baseman should find the short-stop behind the man who is to take it. This player should be particularly on the alert to back up the third baseman, when the ball is thrown to that point by the catcher, in order to put out an adventurous runner. This precaution is necessary, because any wild throw of the catcher's which the baseman fails to get will surely admit of the runner's going home unless the short-stop secures the ball. Sometimes a very good trick is played upon the runner in this way: The short-stop and third baseman are both advised by a preconcerted signal from the catcher that he will throw to third; and then the short-stop springs out behind the baseman, and the catcher sends the ball, but apparently throws it too high—in fact, throws the ball over the head of the baseman to the short-stop, and thus deceives the runner into the belief that he can run home, which, if the short-stop makes an ordinarily accurate throw, is of course impossible.

A short-stop must also always back up third when any of the out-fielders are throwing to that point. He should likewise make himself useful whenever a man is caught between bases and is being "run down."

It is occasionally the duty of this player to cover second base when a left-handed batter is at the plate and a runner is on first. This is in order that the second baseman may be left freer to run after balls toward right field than he would be if obliged to come back to the second base when the ball is thrown there. In the execution of this play, the short-stop stands a few yards nearer second, and runs to that base if

FIRST BASEMAN TAKING A LOW THROW ON THE LONG BOUND.

the ball be thrown. In attempting to intercept a runner at the home plate, the same remarks apply to the short-stop as to the third baseman, except that, being away from the base line, he is not obliged to throw over or by the runner, and so has a slightly better opportunity. This advantage, however, is partially compensated for by the greater distance which the ball has to travel. If the short-stop tries to throw to the home plate to intercept a runner, he should come up sharply on the ball, taking it at the earliest possible bound, and throwing hard. Should he fumble the ball, let him instantly give up his purpose of throwing to the plate, and field to first instead, as the chance of catching that runner is the better.

The second baseman has the shortest distances to throw of any of the in-fielders; but, on that very account, he should be able to cover more ground than any of the rest. He has more time after a hit, for the distance from the batsman to the position of the second baseman is the greatest. The player in this position should be impressed with these advantages in order that he may develop great activity in the way of covering ground. In no position is a desire to make one's self useful so important; for a sleepy short-stop or third baseman has so many balls batted directly at him that he must "play ball" whether inclined to be active or not; whereas a second baseman may stand like a post and escape being hit with the ball through the entire nine innings. A man who means to play second for all it is worth, must determine that no ball shall go by him between the pitcher and first baseman. It will, however, sometimes hap-

A RUNNER CAUGHT BETWEEN THIRD BASE AND THE HOME PLATE.

pen that a ball will be driven past the pitcher and nearly over the second base. The player at the latter point may reach it, but cannot handle it in time to put out the runner. This particular hit he should regard as his limit, and anything inside of that he should consider it his bounden duty to take and field to first in time. Many amateur second basemen, otherwise excellent, take as their limit a much narrower field, and hence, while they do not make many errors, their opponents enjoy many little-deserved "safe" hits.

It is well for the second baseman occasionally to practise underhand throwing to first, as it often happens in a game that he runs so far over toward first to receive the ball that he has not time to straighten up and throw the ball overhand, and a quick underhand throw will get the ball into the first baseman's hands in time. Throwing of every conceivable fashion is on this account permissible for a second baseman, and I have seen one of the best professional players almost scoop the ball, with one motion of his hand, from the ground into the first baseman's hands.

When a runner is coming down from first, the second baseman in covering his own base should not be so eager to start over to the bag as to put it out of the question for him to handle a ball batted in his immediate vicinity; for he should bear it in mind that he cannot be of any service standing on the second base if the ball is going along the ground toward right field. When the runner from first is fairly off, and the catcher is throwing the ball to second, the baseman should endeavor to take up such a position in receiving the throw as to be just in front of the base line and a little toward first. Here he must follow the same instructions relative to touching the runner as those given the third baseman. He must swing low and quickly, taking every advantage of the position of the runner and making the attempt cleanly and in but one motion. There is very little use in running after a man and "jabbing" at him with the ball; for even if the runner were touched the first time, the umpire naturally judges from the baseman's repeated efforts that he must have failed in the first attempt, and so declares the runner "safe."

It is sometimes possible for a good combination of catcher, pitcher, and second baseman to put out a runner who takes a long lead from second toward third when the ball is pitched, or who comes back slowly or carelessly. Burdock on second used to do this very cleverly. He had a signal (consisting of extending his left arm out in a straight line from his body, an action not noticeable to the runner, but very evident to the catcher) by which he instructed the catcher to perform the play on the next ball pitched. The method was as follows: The catcher, instantly upon receiving the ball, returned it with as swift a throw as the pitcher could well handle, and he in turn swung around and sent the ball at second just a little toward third. Burdock, who had started as soon as the catcher had the ball, would have reached this spot in the line, and it was a very lively undertaking for any runner who was not expecting the trick to get back to the bag in time. This play, as executed by these men, had little in common with the ordinary attempt of amateurs to execute it —

where there is enough shouting and calling to betray the plan long before the ball comes. It must, of course, be done in perfect silence, and the runner should have no warning until the ball comes flying back.

The second baseman occasionally has an opportunity of backing up first base, although the pitcher is able to do a large share of this work.

The first baseman's most regular work is catching thrown balls; but he has other duties by no means unimportant, chief among which is handling ground-hits. Like the third baseman, he stands as far from his base as he can and yet be able to stop any ball sent between him and the bag. Unlike the third baseman, however, he cannot be allowed to take everything he can get in the in-field; for, as a rule, he must not go farther from his base than to a point from which he can return to the bag in time to intercept the runner. Occasionally a ball is batted in such a manner that the play can be made to greater advantage by the pitcher's covering the base, while the baseman himself gets the ball and throws it to the pitcher. This is sufficiently unusual not to be counted on as a regular play, and a first baseman should attempt it only at a call from the pitcher. His best general rule is to "cover the base." In catching balls thrown to him, he should make a point of acquiring the habit of stepping from the base with either foot, keeping the other always on the bag. Many amateurs fall into the trick of always keeping the same foot on the base and twisting themselves about in correspondingly awkward ways. More than this, the man who plays first should never make the mistake of "putting the cart before the horse," by keeping his foot on the bag when to do so he must miss the ball. This is the commonest fault of all first basemen. I remember hearing Joe Start, one of the old pioneer base-ball players, who has stood on first base until his hair is white, say contemptuously of many a man playing first base, "Humph!—tied to the bag!" It is the duty of the first baseman to catch or stop the ball *any way*. If he can do it with his foot on the base, well and good; if he cannot, then he must leave the base for the purpose. A moment's consideration of the length of time a first baseman has in which to move, while the ball is traversing the entire distance from third, or short, to his base, will give one some idea of how wild any throw (except a high one) must be to be out of his reach, provided he dare to leave the base when necessary.

In the handling of a low throw, there is the greatest opportunity for the exercise of judgment. If a first baseman will keep one foot upon the bag and step forward with the other, bending the knee, he will see how far he can reach out with his hands into the diamond. Then if he steps backward, and notes how far behind the base he can take the ball, he will have an idea of the field of choice he has on a low throw. He should therefore always endeavor to take a low throw either on the "pick up" or the "long bound," and avoid that most disagreeable point of a ball's progress known as a "short bound." The best of players cannot be sure of taking a short bound,—there is always an element of luck in it,—while taking a pick-up, or a long bound, is far more a question of skill.

Another thing to be remembered by the first baseman in his practice, as well as in games, is to help the thrower. For example, when the ball and the runner seem about to reach the base at the same time, the baseman, by leaning forward into the diamond and toward the thrower, can gain just that almost inappreciable fraction of time that will put the runner out.

The "tied to the bag" fault is apparent sometimes in the player who seems unable to take a high ball. His trouble is usually found to lie in the fact that, while he does reach up after the ball, he feels that his foot must not leave the bag. If the ball be going too high to be reached in that way, he must jump for it. A good illustration of how a first baseman should take a high ball, is shown in an instantaneous photograph of McBride, a well-known first baseman of Yale. The player should jump so as to alight on the bag; for, if in time, he will put out the man: but he must sacrifice *everything* to stopping the ball. In touching the runner with a ball thrown from the pitcher, the first baseman, likewise, should follow the instructions given the third baseman. All players, however, are far more proficient—owing to greater practice—in sliding back to first than to third. A first baseman must therefore be even quicker in putting the ball on the man.

THE BATTERY

More than the professional nine, the amateur nine is dependent for its success upon the work of the battery. For this reason it is that so much time and attention are devoted to the men composing the battery, throughout the season as well as in preliminary training. The greatest cause of poor work by pitcher and catcher at the outset may be said to be lame arms. A pitcher whose arm is lame will go on exhausting himself, punishing the catcher, and breaking down the nerve of his nine from inning to inning, until the game is irretrievably lost. A catcher with a lame arm soon betrays his inability to throw to the bases; and the opponents steal second and then third, until his own nine feel that if a runner reaches first he has merely to trot around to third. Demoralization always follows, and the nine "goes to pieces."

The first problem to be studied, then, is how to avoid a lame arm; and the second, how to cure it if the misfortune comes. A lame arm is usually acquired early in the season; for, when the muscles are thoroughly trained and kept in good condition, lameness seldom results from any cause except some foolish overwork (such, for instance, as pitching several hard games a week for two or three weeks). This overwork is not the temptation to an amateur player that it is to the professional; but occasionally a combination of circumstances makes an unusual demand upon an amateur, and he is then even more likely than the professional to forget that his arm is not a machine. On this account it is well to state that two games a week should be the limit for the amateur pitcher. In fact, even that allowance, continued steadily, is very likely to weaken his pitching.

The preparatory training for the pitcher should be even more gradual than that for the other players. He should begin in the winter to take up all the exercises suggested for increasing the suppleness and strength of the muscles of the arm and shoulder, particularly the latter. He should use the light dumb-bells, going through as great a variety of motions as the most thorough system provides. He should vary the bells by exercises with the Indian clubs. After a week of this, he ought to do some rope-climbing and swinging on the flying-rings, if he enjoys the advantages of a well-equipped gymnasium. Every day he should throw a little, both overhand and underhand, but without attempting anything like speed; and he should avoid curves until he has had two weeks or more of this general exercise.

He may then begin upon the curves with a degree of safety — taking preferably the in-curves first, for a day or two, and later the out-curves. If a comrade can go through the work with him, nothing could be better, for they may be mutually useful, not only in keeping up the interest, but also by acting as massage operators upon each other. The arm and shoulder should be thoroughly rubbed and kneaded every day, and if there be any suspicion of lameness a little alcohol or cider-brandy may be rubbed in. The pitcher should not be called upon to pitch for any cage-batting except at his own desire, and even then he should not be allowed to do very much of it.

Having made a good beginning, and having with no apparent difficulty reached a point where he can get his curves and speed without any feeling of exhaustion or heaviness in the arm or shoulder, the next point of danger comes with the first outdoor practice. For this reason, it is an excellent plan for the pitcher to go into the open air for a little preliminary work some days before the rest of the nine are put into the field. In doing this he must remember that he should be almost as careful again as he was while getting broken in for the winter work. He should do no hard pitching for several days, and should have his arm and shoulder well rubbed with alcohol after his exercise. He should always wear a flannel sleeve covering the arm and shoulder. Until the weather is warm and settled, the pitcher should avoid hard pitching, or he will bitterly repent it. To cure a lame arm is a difficult task, but of course the treatment will vary with the nature and extent of the injury. Recovery is a question of rest and the encouragement of union by means of electricity, friction, or other gentle stimulus to the circulation through the part. As a rule, it is wise to seek at once a physician or surgeon.

Before entering upon a description of the work of the experienced pitcher after he is once started for the season, it is only fair to tell some of the younger aspirants for pitcher's honors something of the methods of acquiring the various curves and "shoots." There have been almost numberless articles written describing the theory of curving a ball. These are more interesting to theorists than to ball-players. The fact itself remains that a base-ball may be made to describe more or less of a curve while traversing the distance between the pitcher and the batsman; and that curve is accomplished by imparting a certain twist to the ball as it leaves the pitcher's hand. No matter how thoroughly one might explain to a man of no experience the way to balance upon a bicycle, the first attempt would result invariably in the machine and rider losing that balance. So the would-be pitcher must remember that no description will enable him to curve the ball at his first attempts. In fact, it is more discouraging than learning bicycle-riding, because there one feels at the very first trial the near possibility of success; whereas it is many a day before the novice can impart even a very slight curve to the base-ball. Perseverance will surely be rewarded eventually, however, in this as in any other practice.

The easiest curve, and the one to be acquired first, is the out-curve. The simplest method is to take the ball in the hand between the extended thumb and the first and second fingers, the third and little finger being closed. The ball rests against the middle joint of the third finger, but is firmly clasped by the first two and the thumb. If the arm be then extended horizontally from the shoulder, with the palm of the hand up, it will be seen that if the ball were spun like a top by the two fingers and thumb it would turn in the way indicated by the arrow in the diagram. This is the way it must twist to accomplish the out-curve. If this idea be borne in mind, and the ball be thus thrown, the thrower will immediately discover that the simpler way to impart this twist is not the spinning motion, but rather a snap as the ball is leaving the fingers, performed almost entirely without the aid of the thumb. The sensation is that of throwing the ball hard, but dragging it back with the ends and sides of the fingers just as it leaves the hand. In practising to acquire this curve, it is best to swing the arm not straight out, but bent at the elbow, with the ball just a little higher than the shoulder. When the curve is once acquired,

BASE-BALL — FOR THE PLAYER

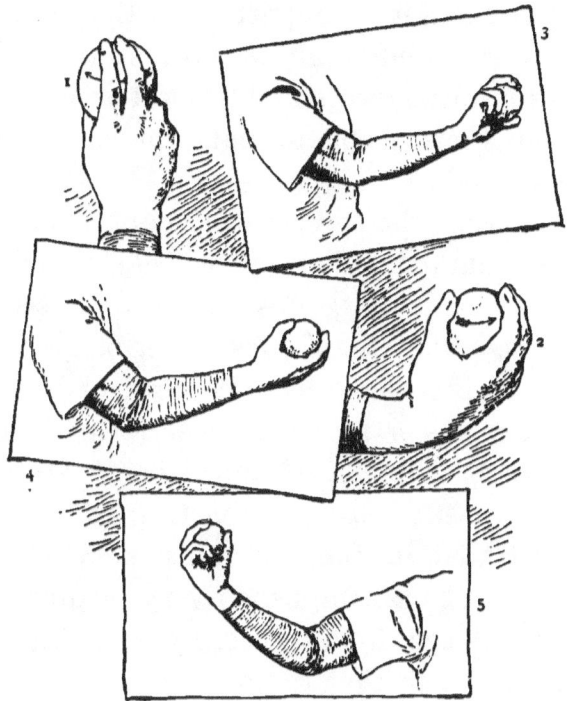

DIAGRAM OF PITCHER'S CURVES.

Fig. 1 shows the position of the ball and pitcher's fingers as seen when looking directly at the back of the hand, whether the pitcher is to deliver an out- or in-curve. For an in-curve, the pitcher lets the ball go from his hand so that it last touches the inside of the second finger, causing the ball to rotate in the direction indicated by the arrow; and Fig. 3 shows the position of the arm as it turns just previous to letting the ball go for this curve.

Fig. 2 shows the position of the ball and fingers as seen by one looking at the side of the hand, instead of at the back; and is the same, when the first motion of the arm begins, whether the pitcher is to deliver an "out" or an "in." If an out-curve be delivered, the pitcher will allow the ball to pass out of his hand so that it last touches that side of the forefinger nearest the thumb; thus causing the ball to rotate in the direction indicated by the arrow in Fig. 2.

Fig. 4 shows the position of the arm just previous to letting the ball go when an out-curve is delivered.

Fig. 5 shows the beginning of the motion; and as the arm comes forward, if an out-curve be delivered the hand turns with the motion of turning a screw; while if an in-curve is delivered the motion is reversed, or is as the hand would turn in extracting a screw.

it is simple enough to impart it to the ball, whether the arm is swinging high or low, straight or bent. None but the out-curve should be attempted until the pitcher finds himself able to make the ball take a quite perceptible bend.

The in-curve is the reverse of the out, and never can be made so marked. The ball is held as for the out-curve, but is made to go out between the second and third fingers. Both these curves can be accomplished by the use of the whole hand instead of the two fingers, but it is easier to learn to perform them in the way described. The "rise" and "drop" are also possible, and are effected by imparting to the ball the twists illustrated in the diagrams, page 241. These two curves can be accomplished very readily, after the out and in are acquired, by simply changing the position of the hand, so that the same twist as that which makes the ball curve out will make it curve up; while the twist which makes it curve in will make it drop. For instance, the hand held as in Fig. 4 will effect an out-curve, and when turned a little with the same twist will effect an up-curve or rise. The drop is sometimes also accomplished by allowing the ball to roll over the end of the fingers, this giving it the tendency to shoot down. The arm should be drawn up rather sharply as the ball goes over the tips of the fingers.

All these curves are susceptible of various combinations one with another, so that pitchers make use of the out-drop and the in-rise, the in-drop and the out-rise. Any combination to pitch what many writers have called a "snake ball" — that is, one which will have a change of curve, in effect, opposite to that with which it started — exists in the imagination only, unless the ball be blown out of its course by the wind. The effect of a strong wind upon the ball is very marked, and when it is toward the pitcher and against the ball, it aids materially in increasing the tendency to curve. When with the ball, it renders the curve less easy to produce and less marked. A left-handed pitcher is able to make much more of what to a right-handed batsman is an in-curve, for to such a pitcher it is the easiest one to produce; while its opposite, or the out-curve to a right-handed batsman, is correspondingly weak.

The training of the catcher has in it less variety, and is in consequence far more tedious than that of the pitcher. The work of strengthening the muscles of the shoulder and arm is the same as that described for the pitcher; but in the throwing practice the catcher should devote his attention to the short-arm throw. He should begin at the short distance of perhaps fifty feet, and increase that distance very gradually. In fact, he ought, even when he can readily throw the full distance from home to second with comparative ease, to do most of his throwing at two thirds that distance. After the nine have begun to work in the field, it is not advisable for the catcher to throw to second anything like the number of times the majority of amateurs attempt daily. Only after the nine have been out of doors for two or three weeks is so much of the full-distance throwing safe for any catcher who wishes to have his arm in good condition.

The position of the feet in throwing is all-important. If he be a strong man of moderate weight, he can, and should, throw without changing the position of his feet. To this object his gymnasium practice should be devoted. Standing steadily upon his feet in the exact position assumed at the moment of catching the ball, he should with a slight swing at the hips be able to send the ball down. Throwing in a cage with a low ceiling is the best thing possible for him, as it forces him to throw hard and on a line. A point of catcher's practice which does not enter into the work of the pitcher is that of toughening the hands. Rowing on the machines, climbing the rope, swinging on the flying-rings, and hand-ball, if there be any court for that excellent game, will all tend toward this end. He should consider, however, that it is not merely toughening the *skin* of the hands that is desirable, but also hardening the flesh so that it is not easily bruised. For this reason he should "pass ball" without gloves regularly every day. At the outset he should receive no swift balls, and should stop at the first feeling of anything beyond a moderate tingling of the palms. His hands should receive their full preparatory hardening before he goes out into the field, for ordinary carefulness demands that he should do no catching behind the bat after the season commences except with hands thoroughly protected by well-padded gloves. What is commonly called a "stone bruise" is one of the tenderest and most lasting mementos of carelessness in this respect. In his gymnasium practice he should wear the mask. This seems to most catchers a useless bore; but the captain or coach should insist upon it, and the mask should become almost a part of the catcher himself. All his throwing and passing should be performed with his eyes behind its wires, in order that, from becoming thoroughly accustomed to it, it may add no inconvenience to his work. The breastplate need not be so rigorously insisted upon, but even this should be worn frequently. The right-hand glove must always be worn when practising throwing, in order that this also shall offer no unusual difficulty in the later work. Many a catcher may think that it looks silly to stand up with a mask and glove on to throw at a mark; but he will appreciate the value of such practice when he stands accoutred on the field behind the batsman and with a runner on first.

As often as it is convenient, the catcher, particularly if a novice, should have some one swing the bat before him while he is "passing ball" in the gymnasium. By the time he gets out of doors, he should be thoroughly accustomed to the close proximity of the batsman and the swing of the bat, so that it does not disconcert him in the least or affect his holding the ball. It is no very difficult achievement for a novice to prepare for this part of the catcher's duties. He should begin by having a comrade swing the bat quite far from the actual course of the ball, say a foot above or below it, while the pitcher tosses the ball at slow speed. After several days more, the pitcher should slightly accelerate his delivery, and the batsman swing the bat within four or five inches of the ball. After a few days of this latter practice, the novice will find that he does not flinch at all, and from that time on all that he needs is daily practice behind the bat to become perfectly at home so far as catching the ball is concerned.

When the battery have left the gymnasium and are fairly settled down to regular field practice, they require the strictest supervision to prevent them from doing foolish things. For instance, all the nine have the strongest fancy for batting the delivery of the regular pitcher. They like the practice, and know that it is good for their batting. The pitcher, likewise, is prone to a vanity that urges him on to extreme effort when pitching to members of his own nine; and while such effort to a moderate degree is an excellent thing for him, it will be found that, left to himself, he will very likely enter into a duel with the batsman and pitch himself into exhaustion or a lame arm before the batsman will tire of the sport. He therefore should be permitted to pitch to one or, perhaps, two batsmen daily, just enough to give him a little interest; while the rest of his pitching practice should be very limited, and should have no element in it that would tempt him to pitch a single ball after his arm is tired. When the season is at its height, the games themselves will give him enough to do without any pitching to his own men — unless he may occasionally desire to try the effect of some new delivery upon the batsman. In that case he should be free to select his own victims as he may require them. The pitcher should also practice throwing to bases, paying particular attention to holding a runner close upon first base. He should aim to acquire such precision in this as habitually to throw four out of five balls successively in practically the same spot — namely, at about the height of the baseman's knee and just a little toward second. The same relative place is a good one for throwing to the other bases, for the purpose to be borne in mind is not to throw *at* the base, but to cut off the runner.

The catcher needs little watching, but the captain or coach must never allow him to stand before any swift pitching if his hands are sore. Sometimes a plucky fellow will not care to tell everybody that his hands are sore, and it therefore must be the captain's business to know all about this. The pitcher should tell the captain; for it is the pitcher who will notice the unavoidable wince that is the proof of a catcher's sore hand. The catcher should do a moderate amount of throwing to all the bases every day, and he ought also to practise receiving the ball from both in-fielders and out-fielders at the home plate, in order that he may be able to put the ball on a runner coming in from third. For general work, it is not a bad plan to have both catcher and pitcher bat to the in-fielders, as it gives them relaxation as well as exercise good for all-around development.

Their work with one another is of the most vital interest to the success of the nine, for in it lies the best part of the strength of the battery. If two men do not get on well together, it is an almost hopeless task to make of them a successful battery. In the matter of signals, as almost every one nowadays understands, they must be thoroughly accustomed to each other. These signals indicate what kind of ball is to be pitched, and sometimes the catcher gives them, sometimes the pitcher. If the catcher be a good judge of batsmen, and the pitcher be of a disposition inclining him to depend upon some one else, it is best that the catcher give the signals. It is also less likely to attract the attention of the coaches or batsmen, as the catcher can better conceal a gesture. The pitcher may, however, give them if it seems necessary. Signal systems of great ingenuity may be concocted, but as a rule the simpler they are, without too great risk of discovery, the better, as neither player should have his mind distracted from his work any more than is necessary by being obliged to think twice about a signal. A movement of the thumb or a finger, as the catcher stands with his hands on his knees preparatory to receiving the ball, is the most common; and if the catcher keep his hands on the inner sides of the legs in giving this signal, it is difficult for the coach to catch it. The height at which he holds his hands may indicate the kind of delivery he wants; a movement of the head, the position of the feet — all may be made useful in this way.

I remember one college catcher who gave the signals for an out-curve or an in-curve in a peculiar manner, and one which was never suspected by any one not in the secret. The signal consisted in the relative position to his eyes of a certain wire in the mask. If he looked over this wire, he wanted an in-curve; if under it, an out-curve. The change in the position of his head was almost imperceptible, but it was unmistakable to the pitcher who understood its significance. Ward once told a very good story apropos of signaling. A certain pitcher was giving the signals, and the man who was catching was comparatively a stranger to his delivery. It appears that the signals which the pitcher was giving were a smile and a frown; and after a time the first baseman, who had been in the habit of catching for the same pitcher, began to expostulate with the new catcher for his wretched work.

"Why," replied the poor fellow, "the sun is in that

CATCHER SIGNALING TO PITCHER BY RELATIVE POSITION OF THE MASK AND HIS EYES.

pitcher's eyes, and he squints his face up so that I can't tell, for the life of me, whether he's grinning or scowling!"

It is customary for the one of the pair who is not giving the signals to be perfectly free to shake his head if he does not approve of any particular delivery which has been signaled, and his comrade then gives the sign for a different curve. In a strong battery the man who is a good judge can in this way often be of great assistance to the other.

In his pitching to batsmen, the pitcher should bear in mind that it is by no means possible to strike out all, or even a moderate proportion, of the men who face him; whereas it *is* possible to prevent the majority from hitting the ball just where they wish. The first principle to keep before him, then, is to make the batsmen hit the ball either close up on the handle or out at the end of the bat. In either case the hit will probably be one which may be easily fielded so as to result in putting out the batsman. By the judicious use of the rise or drop, also, the pitcher may cause the batsman to hit flies or grounders, according to the delivery. If his out-field be exceptionally good, it is often good policy to make the batsman knock a fly. Again, a weakness in the out-field accompanied by unusual strength in the in-field may indicate that he should endeavor to make the batsman keep the ball on the ground. There are, correspondingly, occasions when, with men on the bases and less than two out, a pitcher can greatly relieve the feelings of his nine by striking out one or two men; and it is upon such an occasion that he should make an especial effort to accomplish this. All these things he should consider in practice as well as in games, and train himself accordingly. He should also think of his catcher; and, in a game, remember that he is giving the man behind the bat a deal more work to do if he continually labors to strike out the men than if he judiciously controls their hitting so that the rest of the nine share in the labor. When there is a man on first who is known to be a

A PITCHER'S VICTIM. OUT ON STRIKES.

good and daring base-stealer, it is also good policy to refrain from pitching the ball in such a manner as to give the catcher a poor opportunity for his throw, as, for instance, sending an in-shoot very close to the batsman, or a slow out-curve, which will give the runner a long lead on the ball. It is the pitcher's business to keep the base-runner as close to the base as possible, and to have his delivery of the ball to the batsman accompanied by as little preliminary step and swing as is consistent with good work, because in that way the runner cannot get very far toward second before the catcher receives the ball. The best of catchers cannot throw out even a moderately fast runner unless the pitcher assists in this way.

The catcher, on his part, must return the kindnesses of the pitcher by like consideration. He must begin by a resolution to try for everything, and to consider no ball beyond his reach, no matter how wild. If he cannot catch it, he may by an effort at least stop it; and nothing is so encouraging to the pitcher as to see that his catcher will try for even the wildest pitch. It is the fashion of some amateur catchers, if there has been a mistake in the signal, or a wild pitch, to stand a moment to cast a reproachful look at the pitcher before starting after the ball. This is, of course, absurd. It never does any good; it usually disgusts the pitcher and the rest of the nine, and allows the runner to take two bases instead of one. No matter what has happened, it is the catcher's business to *get the ball* as quickly as possible, and make any necessary explanation later. The catcher should also be very willing in the matter of trying for foul flies. It makes glad the heart of the pitcher to see a batsman go out on a foul fly, and the catcher should be mindful of this.

One very difficult ball for most catchers to handle is a high, swift rise which passes the batsman's face; and as it is, in the hands of a pitcher who uses it well, a

CATCHER RUNNING FOR A "FOUL FLY."

very effective ball, the catcher should devote plenty of practice to it, until he is absolutely sure of holding it. It will sometimes go a little higher than the pitcher intends, and, unless the catcher gives him good support, the pitcher becomes afraid to use it, and thus loses a strong feature of his delivery.

The catcher, even though he be an excellent thrower, should not fall into the error of throwing too frequently to first and third. An occasional throw, when there is a chance of catching a too venturesome runner, is good policy; but simply to return the ball to the pitcher by way of first or third is inviting the accident of a misplay which will give a runner a base and perhaps a run. Throwing to second has been dwelt upon already at considerable length; but one thing may be added, and that is, that a catcher will find it productive of the greatest improvement to his work in this respect if he will make a point of catching every ball, no matter whether there be a runner on first or not, exactly as if he must throw it to second. He will be astonished at the marked increase in quickness that comes from making this a habit. One word more for the catcher, and that in regard to returning the ball to the pitcher. Bearing in mind that the pitcher has a long task before him, the catcher should return the ball to him as accurately as possible; never falling into the slipshod habit of sending it back carelessly, so that the poor pitcher is kept dancing hither and yon to catch these returns. The ball should be so returned by the catcher as to go on a clean first bound almost into his very hands.

OUT-FIELDERS

THE importance of a strong out-field can hardly be overestimated. Nine out of every ten close games are won by the ability of the out-fielders to cover ground. When a grounder is batted to an in-fielder and he makes an error, it usually results that all runners who are on the bases advance each one base. But when there are men on first, second, and third, and a batsman drives a hard-line hit which the right-fielder misjudges and allows to go over his head, it results in three runs, and is likely to decide the game. No amount of time and labor should be grudged, therefore, in making these men strong and capable, for the outlay will be returned with interest in every close game the nine may play.

The out-fielders can be instructed generally as to the principles of their positions, but individual coaching is the only thing that will make them keep up to the mark. In the first place, all fielders are likely to fall into the habit of starting slowly, not moving until they see where the ball is coming, or they may become careless in their way of handling the ball. For this reason each man should receive some systematic coaching every day.

The left-fielder should work in harmony with the short-stop in the matter of taking the short flies. These two players should arrange beforehand which shall take the ball, although the fielder should take it if possible. There are two reasons for this: First, because the fielder is sure to be facing the diamond, while the short-stop may be running with the ball, and hence turned away from the in-field. Second, because the fielder should, from continual practice, be better able to handle quickly and return speedily ordinary flies.

The throwing of a left-fielder, beyond the ordinary return of the ball to the pitcher by way of short-stop or second base, is usually to third or home. He is seldom required to throw to first; as, in case of a fly to left when a runner is on first, there is usually ample time for this runner to return to his base, after the fly is caught, before the ball could reach that base. His throwing practice should therefore be directed toward third and home—principally to the latter. He should keep the ball down, sending it in as nearly as possible on a line and just a little to the third-base side of home. This last requirement, while it may seem to be asking too much of the fielder, is a vital one. If the ball come at all on the other side of the plate, there is little chance of its catching the runner, and for this reason the fielder should be persistently trained to. throw a trifle to the catcher's left. He must be continually cautioned not to make a high throw; but if he cannot put the ball directly into the catcher's hands on the fly, he must at least send it so that it reaches the catcher on the *first* bound. It is remarkable how little the progress of a low-thrown ball is delayed by its once touching the ground; and it is also noticeable how convenient it is for a catcher to handle a ball taken on the bound in putting it on a runner. When a left-handed man is at the bat, unless he have some well-known peculiarity of batting into left field, the left-fielder will do well to come in a little nearer.

The center-fielder occasionally has to be on the same terms with the second baseman, in regard to taking a fly, as those existing between the short-stop and the left-fielder; and about the same rules should govern the two players as those laid down for the short-stop and the left-fielder. His throwing, also, should be directed to third and home, but he will have an occasional opportunity of fielding to first after a fly catch. In case he has to throw to first, the pitcher should

CATCHER THROWING DOWN TO SECOND.

back up the first baseman, remembering that there is no short-stop on that side of the field to perform this duty. The center-fielder should always back up second quite closely, when the catcher throws down to that base, in order to prevent the runner from going on to third. All the fielders, after catching a fly, should exercise judgment about throwing home in order to cut off a runner, whenever there are other runners on the bases.

An excellent illustration of this feature of out-field play occurred during a match between the Yale nine and the Brooklyns, in a game played in the city of Brooklyn. It was the ninth inning, and the Yale nine were one run ahead. The Brooklyns were at the bat, with one man out, a man on second, and a man on third. The batsman knocked a fly to left. The ball was falling near the left-fielder. The man on third, knowing that if he made his run it would tie the score, stood on third ready to try for the plate whether the ball was dropped or caught. The man on second, feeling that his run would be needed to win, was naturally anxious to lead well off toward short, so that if the ball were dropped he could surely get in. He counted, of course, upon the fielder's attempting, if he caught the ball, to intercept the man who was running from third. The play happened exactly as this latter runner expected. The Yale left-fielder caught the ball and drove it home; but the runner beat it in, and the man on second had time to touch his base after the catch and still reach third. This tied the score, and Brooklyn eventually won. Had the left-fielder recognized his opportunity, he might easily have saved the game by fielding to second instead of home. The man starting from second would then have been the third man out; and he would have been put out while the runner from third was still several feet from the home-plate, so that no run would have been scored.

The right-fielder has, in addition to his throw to the plate, a throw to first. This latter is worth practising faithfully, as, if successful, it cuts off what would otherwise be a safe hit. The selection, however, of a man for this position on the strength of his throwing alone, and his ability to execute that one play, cannot be too strongly condemned. A man, to perform it successfully, should run up to meet the ball, and, after catching it, should throw it without appreciably slackening speed.

I have seen the professional player Kelly make this play as it should be made. It was in a game between the New Yorks and Chicagos, when he was a member of the latter nine. He had been catching, but having hurt a finger was replaced by Flint, and went out into right field. There were two men out and a man on third when one of the New Yorks sent a sharp hit past Anson on first base. The ball was whizzing along at a sharp pace; and Kelly, with his hair flying, came running in on it as if he were running for the plate. A scoop of his hands and a sharp drive of his arm, and the ball shot into Anson's hands a fraction of a second ahead of the runner, and the side was out.

BATTING AND BASE-RUNNING

In turning to the other, the aggressive side of the game, the batting, one finds even a greater necessity for education and experience than in the fielding. The majority of boys and men become fairly proficient in fielding long before they have acquired the ability to judge and to bat hard pitching. Occasionally a man will be found who, having a naturally good eye, will manage to use the bat fairly well as soon as he takes it up; but usually even such a man is entirely at the mercy of a skilled pitcher, and it is quite unusual to find among boys who have played for years more than a few good hitters. If, then, a boy will pay attention to the principles and try his best, he will, with practice, make himself more valuable to a nine than any of his comrades; for batting is more than half the game, although many amateur captains are led by the remarkably clever fielding of some players to forget this fact when making up their nines. A true eye, ability to concentrate the muscular force instantly, and plenty of courage, are the requisites for a good hitter. The batsman must endeavor to swing the bat as nearly on a line as possible, and must not "chop" at the ball. This proper swing he can readily acquire in his indoor practice. He should assume an easy position, slightly facing the pitcher, most of his weight resting upon the foot nearest the catcher. Just as the ball is delivered he should advance the foot nearest the pitcher, and, if the ball prove a good one, swing the weight of his body into the stroke as he meets the ball with his bat. He should not strike with all his might and main, as if he were intending to make nothing except a home-run, for these violent batsmen are not usually successful hitters. It does not require the greatest expenditure of muscular force to make a long hit, but the proper meeting of the ball and the putting the weight of the shoulders into the stroke. The bat should be firmly grasped and the arms well straightened and free from

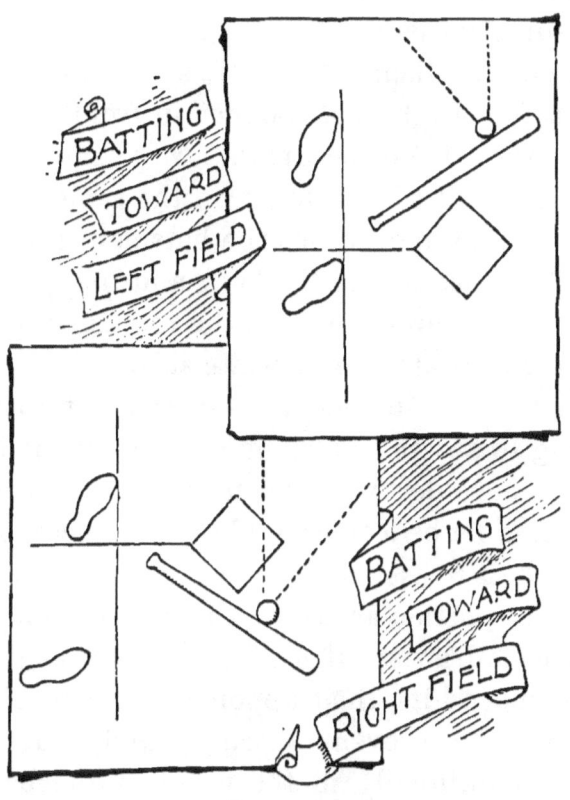

the sides when the ball is hit. The weight of the body should be coming forward, and the trunk should be slightly turning upon the hips. Early in the season it is best to strive to meet the ball squarely, rather than to hit out hard, for this method improves the eye and judgment far more rapidly than indiscriminate hard hitting. After a good eye has been acquired, the batsman may throw more force into his batting with a certainty of meeting the ball fairly. "Sacrifice" hitting and "placing" the ball are usually mere matters of luck to the average amateur; but a little attention to the principles of batting will enable any batsman to acquire some measure of control over the direction of his hitting. A diagram will illustrate the principles quite clearly. If the ball be met in front of the base, and the forward foot be drawn away slightly, the tendency of the ball will be to go on the same side of the diamond as that upon which the batsman stands; while if the ball be met behind the base, and the forward foot placed a little nearer the base, the tendency of the ball will be to go toward the opposite side.

The ordinary batsman will do well not to sacrifice his hitting to any false idea of placing *all* his hits; for he should consider that when there are no men on bases, unless he be a thoroughly experienced batsman, he will do best to assume his most natural position, and not be over-particular as to the exact point toward which the ball goes. If a nine will but keep the ball going by sharp hits, their opponents will be obliged to "play ball" to prevent scoring; and that thought should be continually in the mind of the batsman.

Base-running is hardly less important than batting; for by it the batting is made to yield what really count —namely, runs. Any one who follows the scores closely sees many cases where a nine make fewer base hits and more errors than their opponents, and yet win the game. This may be due to "bunching the hits," or to a lucky combination of hits and errors, but it is usually accompanied by good base-running. Whenever a close game is played, superiority in base-running is usually enough to determine the winner. The necessity of quick starting has already been dwelt upon, and is the underlying principle of success. Good judgment comes next; for when a man is on a base and

BASE-RUNNER KEEPING ON TO THIRD.

the ball is batted, he may take chances up to what appears to be the very limit of recklessness, and yet seldom make the mistake of being put out. He does this through reliance upon his knowledge of what his opponents can and will do at each moment.

A few instances will illustrate this. A runner is on first base, and the batsman drives a grounder between first and second. The average amateur will run to second, and turn to see whether the right-fielder has the ball; and if the fielder has stopped the ball the runner will not go further. If, however, the runner has thoroughly thought out this particular combination, he will be ready to take a more daring view of the play, and, instead of stopping at second, he will go straight on for third. This is not nearly so reckless as it appears, provided the runner be fast, and also provided that he has made up his mind at the start exactly what he will do. It is not an easy throw from right field to third, and the right-fielder, if he be playing at all close in, is very likely to be thinking of throwing the runner out at first; and he will therefore lose track entirely of the other runner. Another excellent feature of the attempt is that if the right-fielder make a wild throw, as he often does in his surprise, there is a strong probability of the runner's going on to the home-plate. Thus, what was only an opportunity to take second may be quite easily turned into a run. The majority of amateurs are thoroughly familiar with the advisability of coming home from second on a base-hit, but when the hit is made very few of them are really in the best position to take advantage of it. The runner should not try to take too great a lead before the pitcher lets the ball go, but should move well up as the ball is delivered, so that if the hit be made he may have a flying start. He should not be just in the base-line, but slightly back of it, so that he may not have quite so sharp a turn to make in going by third. There are, of course, innumerable combinations that may arise, any one of which lends some new element for the consideration of the base-runner, but there are a few facts which are worth remembering. One of these is, that a fielder who has made an error by dropping or fumbling a ball is very prone to make another error in his throw if the base-runner take a daring chance. Yet another point is, never to assist a fielder by letting him touch the runner with the ball when the fielder is seeking to make a double play. This is most likely to happen when a man is on first and another on second, and the ball is batted between third and short, but so that either of those fielders stops it. A third point for the consideration of the runner is, always to force the fielders to throw the ball when it can be done without sacrifice on his part. This can be accomplished frequently, and it always affords an opportunity for an error. The same rule applies to tempting a pitcher to throw to bases. To lead him to throw frequently will probably make his pitching irregular, and this favors the batsman and troubles the catcher.

One of the most delicate points of base-running is taking advantage of fly catches. Naturally, every one is thoroughly familiar with the act of running home from third on a long fly caught by an out-fielder, for this is the simplest case; but the taking a base on a fly catch when the apparent odds are not so strongly on the side of the runner requires good judgment and a cool head. For instance, there is a runner on second and a high foul fly is batted over first base almost into the crowd of spectators. The first baseman is running for the ball and away from the plate, so that his back is turned toward third. The clever runner on second stands with his toe just touching the bag, and the instant the first baseman catches the ball he is away like a shot for third. The first baseman, whose mind has been thoroughly occupied in catching the ball and not falling in the crowd, is startled by the cry, "Look out for third!" and he turns hastily and throws; but the

SHUTTING OFF A RUNNER AT THE HOME-PLATE.

distance is a long one, his position poor for throwing, and the runner's lead enables him to make the base before the ball reaches the third baseman.

There are many emergencies in base-running which call for attempts when desperate chances must be taken. But every runner should always have the possibilities of the situation in his mind at all times; then, if it seem wise at the critical moment to take the chance, he will be prepared to make the most of it.

To sum up, the duty of the player, as soon as he becomes a base-runner, is to be one bundle of activity, actuated by the keenest desire to take advantage of any misjudgment or weakness of his adversaries.

REMINISCENCES

When old college ball-players get together, they are always glad to recall the exciting game or games of their college course; and I have noticed that as a rule the players of the present day are by no means disinclined to listen to the tales. Sometimes, I confess, the younger players seem rather skeptical of certain incidents narrated by the veterans; and I must admit that the magnifying mist of a few years' distance may perhaps lead the older players into exaggeration. However, I shall conclude this series with a few of these stories. I wish to play over again, "for fun," a few incidents from games upon which once seemed to hang my stake of happiness for the time. If I exaggerate, I hope the boys will forgive me and remember that they, too, may some time need a little leeway in telling how they won or lost.

Of all games in which I have played, the most remarkable for a sudden revulsion of feeling was one between Harvard and Yale, played upon Jarvis Field, in June of 1882. It was in the days of the Intercollegiate Association, and Yale had already lost a game to Brown and one to Harvard, so that it was the general impression that Yale would lose this game and be practically out of the race for the championship.

About seven thousand people were gathered about the field, and they seemed an unbroken mass of crimson. Just a few stray bits of blue showed where an occasional Yale sympathizer sat. Yale went first to the bat, but failed to score. Harvard followed suit. In the second inning, a muff by the Harvard first baseman, followed by the Yale catcher's making a "two-bagger," gave Yale a run. Our happiness was short-lived, however, for in the third inning Harvard made two runs, followed by another in the fifth. Yale scored one in the seventh, but Harvard matched it with one in the eighth, so that we began the ninth with Harvard four to Yale's two. I think we had not the least hope of winning.

I remember feeling, as we came in for the ninth inning, that this defeat would settle our chances of the championship, and thinking how the crowd of boys who, as I knew, were sitting on the Yale fence awaiting the news, would hear it and dwindle away in silence to their rooms. Our first man at the bat in the ninth inning went out quickly, and our catcher followed with the same result. Wilcox, the last man on our batting list, came to the bat. Two men out, two runs to reach even a tie, and three to win! I noticed that the crowd was leaving the field, and that the young rascal who had charge of our bats was putting them into the bag.

"Here, you! stop that!" cried I, for we all were superstitious about packing up the bats before the last man was out. Besides, I was the next batter, if Wilcox should by any chance reach his base, and I wanted my bat. "Two strikes," I heard the umpire call, and

"WE CROSSED THE HOME-PLATE WITHIN THREE FEET OF EACH OTHER."

TYING THE SCORE YALE vs HARVARD -1881-

then at the next ball, to my great joy, "Take your base," and Wilcox trotted away to first. I remember thinking how much I would give for a home-run, and then there came a good ball just off my shoulder, and I hit it with all my power. It went between third and short-stop on a swift drive, but bounded high, as I afterward learned, for I was meanwhile running at my best speed toward first. When I was fifteen feet from that base, I saw the baseman give a tremendous jump up into the air, and I knew somebody had made an overthrow. How I ran then!—for every base I passed I knew was one nearer to tying the score. As I came dashing past third base, I saw Wilcox just ahead of me, and we crossed the home-plate within three feet of each other. Our next batter took his base on poor pitching, and stole second; the next followed with a base-hit past second, which brought the first runner home with the winning run. We then went into the field, put three Harvard men out, and won the game: when probably half the seven thousand spectators were already on their way home with a victory for Harvard in their minds.

I remember a singular case of an undecided match which was played at New Haven in 1881, between the New Yorks and the Yale nine. Brouthers, who has since become so remarkable a batsman, was on the New Yorks at that time. The case in dispute occurred in the sixth inning, but owing to the indecision of the umpire no settlement was reached, although the nine innings were played, leaving the score a tie, according to Yale's claim, or a victory by one run for the professionals, if their claim was allowed. Yale was at the

"THE UMPIRE DID NOT SEE GARDNER AT ALL, AND WAS THEREFORE WHOLLY UNABLE TO SAY WHETHER THE RUN COUNTED OR NOT."

bat with two men out, and Gardner—a Yale man—was running to second when the ball was pitched. Walden, our striker, sent a base-hit, upon which he tried to take second. The fielder, instead of throwing home, as he had at first intended, seeing Gardner well along between third and home, fielded the ball to second. The umpire, as soon as he saw the fielder change the direction of his throw, forgetting the necessity of noting the time when Gardner crossed the plate, ran down into the diamond to obtain a nearer view of the play at second. Walden was put out, but so far as human eye could judge exactly at the moment when Gardner crossed the plate. The umpire did not see Gardner at all, and was therefore wholly unable to say whether the run counted or not. At the end of the ninth inning the New Yorks refused to play further, claiming the game. It was some slight satisfaction to the college nine that just a week later they met the New Yorks again and defeated them by a score of ten to four.

One of the most exciting contests in which I ever took part was a game with the Providence League nine in 1881. Yale had had a remarkably strong nine the previous year, and many of the players had remained in college, so that our nine was really a veteran organization. We, as well as the college in general, had been looking forward to this game with more than usual interest, as the Providence nine had some old scores to settle with us. Yale lost the toss and we went to the bat. The first two men were put out easily, but Walden came to the rescue with a three-base hit. Allen, our next batsman, drove a swift ball to short-stop, which gave him a base-hit, and Walden scored. Allen started for second on the first ball pitched, which the batsman hit safely, and Allen scored. Our next man went out at first, leaving Gardner on second, but Yale with two runs for a beginning. We took the field, and easily retired the first two men on the Providence list. Then Farrell came to the bat and knocked a two-base hit. Ward stepped up to the plate and broke our hearts by sending the ball out into the track for a clean home-run, Farrell of course scoring. The next man went out to first, and we came in to the bat with the score tied. Our first batter sent a high fly into the field, but luckily it was not caught. The batter then attempted to steal second, but was put out. The next striker reached first base safely, but was forced out at second by his successor's ground hit. With a man on first and two out, we had but little hope of scoring; but Hutchison, our batsman, made a safe hit, upon which the runner managed to take third. Hutchison went to second on the first ball pitched, and Lamb brought them both home by a double. The third man went out on a fly, but Yale was jubilant with the score four to two.

Providence failed to score in her half. The third inning went by without a run; but in the fourth each side scored one, thus keeping Yale still in the lead, five to three. In the fifth inning neither side crossed the plate, although Providence had two men on the bases who were retired by a double play. The sixth inning went by, the excitement growing more and more intense, and both sides playing a perfect game. In the seventh Providence again had men on bases, but another double play swept them off. The eighth inning was another blank, and Yale came to the bat in the first half of the ninth, with the score five to three in her favor. Two runs seemed like a safe lead, but we were anxious to increase it. One man out, two men out, and Badger came to the plate. Two balls were pitched, and then he hit a beauty into left center for a home-run! How the crowd cheered! The next man went out easily, but six to three was surely safe.

Providence came in, and I well remember that Joe Start and Johnny Ward looked anything but pleased at the prospect. After one man went out they seemed to find the ball, and Gross, Matthews, and Denny each made a hit which, with clever base-running, brought in two runs. Denny stole third by a desperate slide, having gone to second on a throw home which failed to catch Matthews. One man out, a man on third, one run to tie the score! — the Yale audience hardly dared breathe as McClellan came to the bat. He hit a sharp grounder to Hopkins, who was playing first base for Yale, and Denny came down the line for home as if his life depended upon that run. Hopkins took the ball cleanly, and drove it into the plate just as Denny, in a cloud of dust, threw himself across it! "Safe!" said the umpire, and the score was tied. McClellan had gone straight on to second, and, as old Joe Start took his place at the plate, I know more than one of us felt that the victory we had counted on was gone. McClellan took all the lead he dared, on every ball, for he meant to come home on a hit. The third ball pitched suited Start, and he hit it squarely along the ground, but straight at Hutchison, who was our short-stop. McClellan was within three feet of third when Hutchison got the ball and sent it over to Hopkins, putting out Start. Meanwhile McClellan was taking his run home just as fast as he knew how. But Hopkins was too swift for McClellan: the catcher put him out, and six to six was the score!

I don't know how it was with the spectators, but I know that the nine Yale men in uniform were glad the inning was over.

The tenth inning had no long-drawn-out suspense about it. Lamb, who was first at the bat for Yale, made a single. Walden, the next batsman, immediately followed with a three-base hit; Gardner took first on wild pitching; and the writer had the pleasure of sending them both home by batting a single — being, later, the third man out on a double play. Then the Providence players went out one, two, three, and we rode home with our heads in the air.

Perhaps you think that all the games I remember are those in which Yale won. Naturally those are the ones I like best to recall, but in the same year that we had rejoiced over such a game won from Providence, we visited Princeton and learned that some other boys could play ball too. The game was not of particular interest until the fourth inning, when Yale by a home-run of Hutchison's had just left the score six to one in her favor. Princeton came in to the bat and set about overcoming this long lead. Their first man took first base on balls, stole second on a passed ball, third on a fielder's error, and came home as Schenck, a Princeton batsman, drove the ball past short-stop. Then Harlan, their next batsman, went out, short to first, and his successor, Winton, struck out. Archer, who came next, brought Schenck home with a hit, but the following batter ended the inning by a fly. Score, six to three in Yale's favor. There was no scoring in the fifth and sixth innings, although Yale succeeded each time in getting men on bases. In the seventh Yale again began with a single, but failed to do anything more, and Princeton came to the bat. Winton struck three times, but the Yale catcher dropped the third ball and then threw wild to first. Archer struck out. Winton then came home on a wild pitch and a passed ball, the Yale battery evidently going to pieces. The next Princeton batter went to first on balls. Then another was put out, and a Princeton player named Wadleigh came to the bat. He was quite equal to the occasion, and sent a fine three-base hit into left field, bringing a run home. But the succeeding batsman went out, and the eighth inning opened with the score six to five in Yale's favor. The game was becoming decidedly interesting. One, two, three, Princeton put us out as we came to the plate. We returned the compliment when they came to the bat, so far as two men were concerned, but under these circumstances Princeton proceeded to brace again. Harlan hit for three bases, Winton followed with a single, on which Harlan came in and tied the score. Archer followed with another single, on which Winton took third and scored what proved to be the winning run, while the next batter was striking out. We came to the bat for the ninth, and after two men were out Platt made a two-base hit for Yale, and I succeeded him, with a chance to tie the score by batting him in. I hit the ball hard, driving it, as we all thought, over the head of a Princeton fielder named Loney; but by a magnificent jump he reached and held it, and the game was over. Then a sad and quiet little band of men stole away to the train and left New Jersey.

When asked what play I recall as most singular in my remembrance of college games, I tell the tale of a game Yale once played with Brown University at Providence. The field there was backed by a stone church behind center, and an occasional very long hit would strike it. In an open field such a hit would have resulted in a home-run. Yale had, I believe, made some objection to the ground on that account; but on this particular occasion, as it proved, the church assisted Yale very materially. The game was a commonplace one up to the ninth inning, Yale having scored six runs and Brown none. When Brown came in to complete the game, in the ninth, the crowd had already become considerably diminished, and the few remaining were standing about the edge of the field making ready to go home. The first man at the bat made a hit, the second followed with another. The third man went out on a fly to the Yale pitcher. The next batsman made a base-hit, which was so slowly handled in the field that the first two men scored, the batter going on to second on the throw home. The next man at the plate hit a grounder to second, who attempted to throw the runner out at third, but threw wild, and both men scored, thus making the score: Yale, six; Brown, four. The next batter took first base on balls. The Yale pitcher struck out the following batter. The runner who had taken his base had meantime stolen second.

A home-run now would tie the score, and the Brown man at the bat evidently realized this, for he made a long drive into center field. The Brown crowd yelled madly with delight; but the ball struck the church and bounded back to the fielder, who turned instantly and fielded it home, putting out the man who was running in from second by the veriest scratch I ever saw on the ball-field.

I don't know that any man on the Yale nine ever earned the heartfelt gratitude of its every member to such an extent as did George Clark, our right-fielder in a game at Cambridge in 1880. We had scored two runs in the first inning, and Harvard had scored one. From the end of that first inning both sides had been struggling desperately to score, but without success. Repeatedly men had been on the bases, and some one or two had been thrown out at the home plate. Harvard came to the bat for the ninth inning, and their first batter went out by a throw from short-stop to first base; a second batsman followed with a base-hit; a third went to first base on an error, which gave the runner second. The next man batted to third, thus forcing out the runner at that base. The next batsman, whose name was Fessenden, came to the bat and hit what certainly appeared to all of us and to the spectators to be a home-run over the low rail fence on the right-field side. Clark had started on the instant the ball was batted, and, coming to the rail just as the ball was passing over, he reached far out, and to our supreme delight caught and held it, leaving us winners.

APPENDIX

FOR REFERENCE IN CASES WHERE FORMS OF AGREEMENT ARE REQUIRED, THE FOLLOWING SETS OF RULES, CONSTITUTIONS, AND AGREEMENTS ARE APPENDED:

Foot-ball.— Intercollegiate Foot-ball Rules.
Base-ball.— Base-ball Rules governing principal College Games of 1893.
Rowing.— Original Harvard-Yale Boating Agreement.
Track Athletics.— Deed of Gift and Rules governing Harvard-Yale Track Athletic Contests.
Constitution.— Constitution of last Base-ball League of Harvard, Princeton, and Yale.
Contract.— Contract for Grounds, as used by Princeton and Yale when hiring Manhattan Field.

	In Goal.	
Touch-in-goal.		Touch-in-goal.
	Goal-line. Goal-line.	
	(18½ feet.)	
	(Goal.)	
	160 feet.	

Touch or Bounds.   25-yard-line Limit of Kick-out.   Touch or Bounds.

In Touch.   330 feet.   330 feet.   In Touch.

Touch or Bounds.   25-yard-line Limit of Kick-out.   Touch or Bounds.

	160 feet.	
	(Goal.)	
	(18½ feet.)	
	Goal-line. Goal-line.	
Touch-in-goal.		Touch-in-goal.
	In Goal.	

FOOT-BALL RULES OF THE AMERICAN INTER-COLLEGIATE ASSOCIATION

RULE 1. (*a*) A drop-kick is made by letting the ball fall from the hands and kicking it at the very instant it rises.

(*b*) A place-kick is made by kicking the ball after it has been placed on the ground.

(*c*) A punt is made by letting the ball fall from the hands and kicking it before it touches the ground.

(*d*) Kick-off is a place-kick from the center of the field of play, and cannot score a goal.

(*e*) Kick-out is a drop-kick, or place-kick, by a player of the side which has touched the ball down in their own goal, or into whose touch-in-goal the ball has gone, and cannot score a goal. (See Rules 32 and 34.)

(*f*) A free-kick is one where the opponents are restrained by rule.

RULE 2. (*a*) In touch means out of bounds.

(*b*) A fair is putting the ball in play from touch.

RULE 3. A foul is any violation of a rule.

RULE 4. (*a*) A touch-down is made when the ball is carried, kicked, or passed across the goal-line and there held, either in goal or touch-in-goal. The point where the touch-down scores, however, is not necessarily where the ball is carried across the line, but where the ball is fairly held or called " down."

(*b*) A safety is made when a player guarding his goal receives the ball from a player of his own side, either by a pass, kick, or a snap-back, and then touches it down behind his goal-line; or when he himself carries the ball across his own goal-line and touches it down; or when he puts the ball into his own touch-in-goal; or when the ball, being kicked by one of his own side, bounds back from an opponent across the goal-line and he then touches it down.

(*c*) A touch-back is made when a player touches the ball to the ground behind his own goal, the impetus which sent the ball across the line having been received from an opponent.

RULE 5. A punt-out is a punt make by a player of the side which has made a touch-down in their opponents' goal to another of his own side for a fair catch.

RULE 6. A goal may be obtained by kicking the ball in any way except a punt from the field of play (without touching the ground, or dress, or person of any player after the kick) over the cross-bar or post of opponents' goal.

RULE 7. A scrimmage takes place when the holder of the ball puts it down on the ground, and puts it in play by kicking it or snapping it back.

RULE 8. A fair catch is a catch made direct from a kick by one of the opponents, or from a punt-out by one of the same side, provided the catcher made a mark with his heel at the spot where he has made the catch, and no other of his side touches the ball. If the catcher, after making his mark, be deliberately thrown to the ground by an opponent, he shall be given five yards, unless this carries the ball across the goal-line.

RULE 9. Charging is rushing forward to seize the ball or tackle a player.

RULE 10. Interference is using the hands or arms in any way to obstruct or hold a player who has not the ball. This does not apply to the man running with the ball.

RULE 11. The ball is dead:

I. When the holder has cried down, or when the referee has cried down, or when the umpire has called foul.

II. When a goal has been obtained.

III. When it has gone into touch, or touch-in-goal, except for punt-out.

IV. When a touch-down or safety has been made.

V. When a fair catch has been heeled. No play can be made while the ball is dead, except to put in play by rule.

RULE 12. The grounds must be 330 feet in length and 160 feet in width, with a goal placed in the middle of each goal-line, composed of two upright posts, exceeding 20 feet in height, and placed 18 feet 6 inches apart, with cross-bar 10 feet from the ground.

RULE 13. The game shall be played by teams of eleven men each; and in case of a disqualified or injured player a substitute shall take his place. Nor shall the disqualified or injured player return to further participation in the game.

RULE 14. There shall be an umpire and a referee. No man shall act as an umpire who is an alumnus of either of the competing colleges. The umpire shall be nominated and elected by the Advisory Committee. The referee shall be chosen by the two captains of the opposing teams in each game, except in case of disagreement, when the choice shall be referred to the Advisory Committee, whose decision shall be final. All the referees and umpires shall be permanently elected and assigned on or before the third Saturday in October in each year.

RULE 15. (*a*) The umpire is the judge for the players, and his decision is final regarding fouls and unfair tactics.

(*b*) The referee is judge for the ball, and his decision is final on all points not covered by the umpire.

(*c*) Both umpire and referee shall use whistles to indicate cessation of play on fouls and downs. The referee shall use a stop-watch in timing the game.

(*d*) The umpire shall permit no coaching, either by substitutes, coaches, or any one inside the ropes. If such coaching occur he shall warn the offender, and upon the second offense must have him sent behind the ropes for the remainder of the game.

RULE 16. (*a*) The time of a game is an hour and a half, each side playing forty-five minutes from each goal. There shall be ten minutes intermission between the two halves. The game shall be decided by the score of even halves. Either side refusing to play after ordered to by the referee shall forfeit the game. This shall also apply to refusing to commence the game when ordered to by the referee. The referee shall notify the captains of the time remaining not more than ten nor less than five minutes from the end of each half.

(*b*) Time shall not be called for the end of a three-quarter until the ball is dead; and in the case of a try-at-goal from a touch-down the try shall be allowed. Time shall be taken out while the ball is being brought out either for a try, kick-out, or kick-off.

RULE 17. No one wearing projecting nails or iron plates on his shoes, or any metal substance upon his person, shall be allowed to play in such a match. No sticky or greasy substance shall be used on the person of players.

RULE 18. The ball goes into touch when it crosses the side-line, or when the holder puts part of either foot across or on that line. The touch-line is in touch and the goal-line in goal.

RULE 19. The captains shall toss up before the commencement of the match, and the winner of the toss shall have his choice of goal or of kick-off. The same side shall not kick-off in two successive halves.

RULE 20. The ball shall be kicked off at the beginning of each half; and whenever a goal has been obtained, the side which has lost it shall kick-off.

RULE 21. A player who has made and claimed a fair catch shall take a drop-kick, or a punt, or place the ball for a place-kick. The opponents may come up to the catcher's mark, and the ball must be kicked from some spot behind that mark on a parallel to touch-line.

RULE 22. The side which has a free-kick must be behind the ball when it is kicked. At kick-off the opposite side must stand at least ten yards in front of the ball until it is kicked.

RULE 23. Charging is lawful for opponents if a punter advances beyond his line, or in case of a place-kick, immediately the ball is put in play by touching the ground. In case of a punt-out, not till ball is kicked.

RULE 24. (*a*) A player is put off-side if, during a scrimmage, he gets in front of the ball, or if the ball has been last touched by his own side behind him. It is impossible for a player to be off-side in his own goal. No player when off-side shall touch the ball, or interrupt or obstruct opponent with his hands or arms until again on side.

(*b*) A player being off-side is put on-side when the ball has touched an opponent, or when one of his own side has run in front of him, either with the ball, or having touched it when behind him.

(*c*) If a player when off-side touches the ball inside the opponents' five-yard line, the ball shall go as a touch-back to the opponents.

RULE 25. No player shall lay his hands upon, or interfere by use of hands or arms with, an opponent, unless he has the ball. The side which has the ball can only interfere with the body. The side which has not the ball can use the hands and arms as heretofore.

RULE 26. (*a*) A foul shall be granted for intentional delay of game, off-side play, or holding an opponent unless he has the ball. No delay arising from any cause whatsoever shall continue more than five minutes.

(*b*) The penalty for fouls and violation of rules, except otherwise provided, shall be a down for the other side; or, if the side making the foul has not the ball, five yards to the opponents.

RULE 27. (*a*) A player shall be disqualified for unnecessary roughness, hacking or striking with closed fist.

(*b*) For the offenses of throttling, tripping up, or intentional tackling below the knees, the opponents shall receive twenty-five yards, or a free-kick, at their option. In case, however, the twenty-five yards would carry the ball across the goal-line, they can have half the distance from the spot of the offense to the goal-line, and shall not be allowed a free-kick.

RULE 28. A player may throw or pass the ball in any direction except toward the opponents' goal. If the ball be batted in any direction, or thrown forward, it shall go down on the spot to opponents.

RULE 29. If a player when off-side interferes with an opponent trying for a fair catch, by touching him or the ball, or waving his hat or hands, the opponent may have a free-kick, or down, where the interference occurred.

RULE 30. (*a*) If a player having the ball be tackled and the ball fairly held, the man so tackling shall cry "Held," the one so tackled must cry "Down," and some player of his side put it down for a scrimmage. The snapper-back and the man opposite him cannot pick out the ball with the hand until it touches a third man; nor can the opponents interfere with the snapper-back by touching the ball until it is actually in play. Infringement of this nature shall give the holders of the ball five yards for every such offense. The snapper-back is entitled to full and undisturbed possession of the ball. If the snapper-back be off-side in the act of snapping back, the ball must be snapped again, and if this occurs three times on same down the ball goes to opponents. The man who first receives the ball when snapped back from a down, or thrown back from a fair, shall not carry the ball forward under any circumstances whatever. If, in three consecutive fairs and downs, unless the ball crosses the goal-line, a team shall not have advanced the ball five or taken it back twenty yards, it shall go to the opponents on spot of fourth. "Consecutive" means without leaving the hands of the side holding it, and by a kick giving opponents fair and equal chance of gaining possession of it. When the referee, or umpire, has given a side five yards, the following down shall be counted the first down.

(*b*) The man who puts the ball in play in a scrimmage cannot pick it up until it has touched some third man. "Third man" means any other player than the one putting the ball in play and the man opposite him.

RULE 31. If the ball goes into touch, whether it bounds back or not, a player on the side which touches it down must bring it to the spot where the line was crossed, and there either —

I. Bound the ball in the field of play, or touch it in with both hands, at right angles to the touch-line, and then run with it, kick it, or throw it back; or,

II. Throw it out at right angles to the touch-line; or,

III. Walk out with it at right angles to touch-line any distance not less than five nor more than fifteen yards, and there put it down, first declaring how far he intends walking. The man who puts the ball in must face field or opponents' goal, and he alone can have his foot outside touch-line. Anyone, except him, who puts his hands or feet between the ball and his opponents' goal is off-side. If it be not thrown out at right angles, either side may claim it thrown over again, and if it fail to be put in play fairly in three trials it shall go to the opponents.

RULE 32. A side which has made a touch-down in their opponents' goal *must* try at goal, either by a place-kick or a punt-out. If the goal be missed, the ball shall go as a kick-off at the center of the field to the defenders of the goal.

RULE 33. (*a*) If the try be by a place-kick, a player of the side which has touched the ball down shall bring it up to the goal-line, and, making a mark opposite the spot where it was touched down, bring it out at right angles to the goal-line such distance as he thinks proper, and there place it for another of his side to kick. The opponents must remain behind their goal-line until the ball has been placed on the ground.

(*b*) The placer in a try-at-goal may be off-side or in-touch without vitiating the kick.

RULE 34. If the try be by a punt-out, the punter shall bring the ball up to the goal-line, and, making a mark opposite the spot where it was touched down, punt-out from any spot behind line of goal, and not nearer the goal-post than such mark, to another of his side, who must all stand outside of goal-line not less than fifteen feet. If the touch-down was made in touch-in-goal, the punt-out shall be made from the intersection of the goal- and touch-lines. The opponents may line up anywhere on the goal-line except space of five feet on each side of punter's mark, but cannot interfere with punter, nor can he touch the ball after kicking it until it touch some other player. If a fair catch be made from a punt-out, the mark shall serve to determine positions as the mark of any fair catch. If a fair catch be not made on the first attempt, the ball shall be punted over again; and if a fair catch be not made on the second attempt, the ball shall go as a kick-off at the center of the field to the defenders of the goal.

RULE 35. A side which has made a touch-back or a safety must kick out, except as otherwise provided (see Rule 32), from not more than twenty-five yards outside the kicker's goal. If the ball go into touch before striking a player, it must be kicked out again; and if this occurs three times in succession, it shall be given to opponents as in touch on twenty-five-yard line on side where it went out. At kick-out opponents must be on twenty-five-yard line, or nearer their own goal.

RULE 36. The following shall be the value of each point in the scoring:

Goal obtained by touch-down	6
Goal from field-kick	5
Touch-down failing goal	4
Safety by opponents	2

PLAYING-RULES OF BASE-BALL FOR PRINCIPAL COLLEGE MATCHES OF 1893

THE BALL GROUND

The ground must be an inclosed field, sufficient in size to enable each player to play in his position as required by these rules.

The in-field must be a space of ground thirty yards square.

THE BASES

The bases must be four in number, and designated as first base, second base, third base, and home base.

The home base must be of whitened rubber twelve inches square, so fixed in the ground as to be even with the surface, and so placed in the corner of the in-field that two of its sides will form part of the boundaries of said in-field.

The first, second, and third bases must be canvas bags, fifteen inches square, painted white, and filled with some soft material, and so placed that the center of the second base shall be upon its corner of the in-field, and the center of the first and third bases shall be on the lines running to and from second base and seven and one half inches from the foul lines, providing that each base shall be entirely within the foul lines.

All the bases must be securely fastened in their positions, and so placed as to be distinctly seen by the umpire.

THE FOUL LINES

The foul lines must be drawn in straight lines from the outer corner of the home base, along the outer edge of the first and third bases, to the boundaries of the ground.

THE POSITION LINES

The pitcher's lines must be straight lines forming the boundaries of a space of ground, in the in-field, five and one half feet long by four feet wide, distant fifty feet from the center of the home base, and so placed that the five and one half feet lines would each be two feet distant from and parallel with a straight line passing through the center of the home and second bases. Each corner of this space must be marked by a flat round rubber plate six inches in diameter, fixed in the ground even with the surface.

The catcher's lines must be drawn from the outer corner of the home base, in continuation of the foul lines, straight to the limits of the ground back of home base.

The captain's or coacher's line must be a line fifteen feet from and parallel with the foul lines, said lines commencing at a line parallel with and seventy-five feet distant from the catcher's lines, and running thence to the limits of the grounds.

The player's lines must be drawn from the catcher's lines to the limits of the ground, fifty feet distant from and parallel with the foul lines.

The batsman's lines must be straight lines forming the boundaries of a space on the right, and of a similar space on the left of the home base, six feet long by four feet wide, extending three feet in front of and three feet behind the center of the home base, and with its nearest line distant six inches from the home base.

The three-foot lines must be drawn as follows: from a point on the foul line from home base to first base, and equally distant from such bases, shall be drawn a line on foul ground, at a right angle to said foul line, and to a point three feet distant from it; thence running parallel with said foul line, to a point three feet distant from the first base, thence in a straight line to the foul line, and thence upon the foul line to point of beginning.

The lines designated in the above Rules must be marked with chalk or other suitable material, so as to be distinctly seen by the umpire. They must all be so marked their entire length, except the captain's and player's lines, which must be so marked for a distance of at least thirty-five yards from the catcher's lines.

THE BALL

The ball must not weigh less than five or more than five and one quarter ounces avoirdupois, and measure not less than nine nor more than nine and one quarter inches in circumference. The Spaulding League Ball must be used in all games played under these rules.

For each championship game two balls shall be furnished by the home club to the umpire for use. When the ball in play is batted over the fence or stands, on to foul ground out of sight of the players, the other ball shall be immediately put into play by the umpire. As often as one of the two in use shall be lost a new one must be substituted, so that the umpire shall at all times after the game begins have two for use. The moment the umpire delivers a new or alternate ball to the pitcher it comes into play, and shall not be exchanged until it, in turn, passes out of sight on to foul ground. At no time shall the ball be intentionally discolored by rubbing it with the soil or otherwise.

In all games the ball or balls played with shall be furnished by the home club, and the last ball in play becomes the property of the winning club. Each ball to be used in championship games shall be examined, measured, and weighed by the secretary of the association, inclosed in a paper box and sealed with the seal of the secretary, which seal shall not be broken except by the umpire in the presence of the captains of the two contesting nines after play has been called.

Should the ball become out of shape, or cut or ripped so as to expose the yarn, or in any way so injured as to be — in the opinion of the umpire — unfit for fair use, the umpire, on being appealed to by either captain, shall at once put the alternate ball into play and call for a new one.

THE BAT

The bat must be made wholly of wood, except that the handle may be wound with twine, or a granulated substance applied, not to exceed eighteen inches from the end.

It must be round, except that a portion of the surface may be flat on one side; but it must not exceed two and one half inches in diameter in the thickest part, and must not exceed forty-two inches in length.

THE PLAYERS AND THEIR POSITIONS

The players of each club in a game shall be nine in number, one of whom shall act as captain, and in no case shall less than nine men be allowed to play on each side.

The players' positions shall be such as may be assigned them by their captain, except that the pitcher must take his position within the pitcher's lines, as defined in the rule. When in position on the field, all players will be designated "fielders" in these rules.

Players in uniform shall not be permitted to seat themselves among the spectators.

Every club shall be required to adopt uniforms for its

players, and each player shall be required to present himself upon the field during said game in a neat and cleanly condition; but no player shall attach anything to the sole or heel of his shoes other than the ordinary base-ball shoe plate.

THE PITCHER'S POSITION

The pitcher shall take his position facing the batsman with both feet square on the ground, one foot on the rear line of the "box." He shall not raise either foot unless in the act of delivering the ball, nor make more than one step in such delivery. He shall hold the ball, before the delivery, fairly in front of his body, and in sight of the umpire. When the pitcher feigns to throw the ball to a base he must resume the above position and pause momentarily before delivering the ball to the bat.

THE BATSMEN'S POSITION — ORDER OF BATTING

The batsmen must take their positions within the batsmen's lines, as defined in the rule, in the order in which they are named on *the score,* which must contain the batting order of both nines, and be submitted by the captains of the opposing teams to the umpire before the game, and when approved by him THIS SCORE must be followed except in the case of a substitute player, in which case the substitute must take the place of the original player in the batting order. After the first inning the first striker in each inning shall be the batsman whose name follows that of the last man who has completed his turn — time at bat — in the preceding inning.

When a side goes to the bat, the players of that side must immediately return to and seat themselves upon the players' bench and remain there until the side is put out, except when they are batsmen or base-runners. All bats not in use must be kept in the bat racks, and the two players next succeeding the batsman, in the order in which they are named on the score, must be ready with bat in hand to promptly take position as batsmen; provided, that the captain and one assistant only may occupy the space between the players' lines and the captain's lines to coach base-runners.

No player of the side at bat, except when batsman, shall occupy any portion of the space within the catcher's lines, as defined in Rule 6. The triangular space behind the home base is reserved for the exclusive use of the umpire, catcher, and batsman, and the umpire must prohibit any player of the side "at bat" from crossing the same at any time while the ball is in the hands of or passing between the pitcher and catcher while standing in their positions.

The players of the side "at bat" must occupy the portion of the field allotted them, but must speedily vacate any portion thereof that may be in the way of the ball, or of any fielder attempting to catch or field it.

PLAYERS' BENCHES

The players' benches must be furnished by the home club, and placed upon a portion of the ground outside of and not nearer than twenty-five feet to the players' lines. They must be twelve feet in length, and must be immovably fastened to the ground. At the end of each bench must be immovably fixed a bat rack, with fixtures for holding twenty bats; one such rack must be designated for the exclusive use of the visiting club, and the other for the exclusive use of the home club.

THE GAME

Every championship game must be commenced not later than two hours before sunset.

A game shall consist of nine innings to each contesting nine, except that—

(*a*) If the side first at bat scores less runs in nine innings than the other side has scored in eight innings, the game shall then terminate.

(*b*) If the side last at bat in the ninth inning scores the winning run before the third man is out, the game shall terminate.

A TIE GAME

If the score be a tie at the end of nine innings to each side, play shall only be continued until the side first at bat shall have scored one or more runs than the other side, in an equal number of innings, or until the other side shall score one or more runs than the side first at bat.

A DRAWN GAME

A drawn game shall be declared by the umpire when he terminates a game on account of darkness or rain, after five equal innings have been played, if the score at the time is equal on the last even innings played; but if the side that went second to bat is then at the bat, and has scored the same number of runs as the other side, the umpire shall declare the game drawn without regard to the score of the last equal innings.

A CALLED GAME

If the umpire calls "Game" on account of darkness or rain at any time after five innings have been completed, the score shall be that of the last equal innings played, unless the side second at bat shall have scored one or more runs than the side first at bat, in which case the score of the game shall be the total number of runs made.

A FORFEITED GAME

A forfeited game shall be declared by the umpire in favor of the club not in fault, at the request of such club, in the following cases:

If the nine of a club fail to appear upon the field, or being upon the field fail to begin the game within five minutes after the umpire has called "Play," at the hour appointed for the beginning of the game, unless such delay in appearing or in commencing the game be unavoidable.

If, after the game has begun, one side refuses or fails to continue playing, unless such game has been suspended or terminated by the umpire.

If, after play has been suspended by the umpire, one side fails to resume playing within *one minute* after the umpire has called "Play."

If a team resorts to dilatory practices in order to gain time for the purpose of having the game called on account of darkness or rain, or for any other reason whatsoever.

If, in the opinion of the umpire, any one of these rules is wilfully violated.

If, after ordering the removal of a player, as authorized by rule, said order is not obeyed within five minutes.

In case the umpire declares a game forfeited, he shall transmit a written notice thereof to the president of the association within twenty-four hours thereafter.

NO GAME

"No Game" shall be declared by the umpire if he shall terminate play on account of rain or darkness before five innings on each side are completed; except in a case when the game is called the club second at bat shall have more runs at the end of its fourth inning than the club first at bat has made in its five innings, then the umpire shall award the game to the club having made the greatest number of runs, and it shall be a game and be so counted in the championship record.

SUBSTITUTES

In every championship game each team shall be required to have present on the field, in uniform, one or more substitute players.

Any such player may be substituted at any time by either club, but no player thereby retired shall thereafter participate in the game.

The base-runner shall not have a substitute run for him, except by consent of the captains of the contesting teams.

CHOICE OF INNINGS — CONDITION OF GROUND

The choice of innings shall be given to the captain of the home club, who shall also be the sole judge of the fitness of the ground for beginning a game after rain.

THE DELIVERY OF THE BALL — FAIR AND UNFAIR BALLS

A fair ball is a ball delivered by the pitcher while standing wholly within the lines of his position and facing the batsman, the ball so delivered to pass over the home base, not lower than the batsman's knee, nor higher than his shoulder, provided a ball so delivered that touches the bat of the batsman in his position shall be considered a batted ball, and in play.

An unfair ball is a ball delivered by the pitcher, as in above rule, except that the ball does not pass over the home base, or does pass over the home base, above the batsman's shoulder, or below the knee.

BALKING

A balk is —

Any motion made by the pitcher to deliver the ball to the bat without delivering it, and shall be held to include any and every accustomed motion with the hands, arms, or feet, or position of the body assumed by the pitcher in his delivery of the ball, and any motion calculated to deceive a base-runner, except the ball be accidentally dropped.

The holding of the ball by the pitcher so long as to delay the game unnecessarily; or,

Any motion to deliver the ball, or the delivering the ball to the bat by the pitcher when any part of his person is upon ground outside of the lines of his position, including all preliminary motions with the hands, arms, and feet.

DEAD BALLS

A dead ball is a ball delivered to the bat by the pitcher, that touches the batsman's bat without being struck at, or any part of the batsman's person or clothing while standing in his position without being struck at, or any part of the umpire's person or clothing while on foul ground, without first passing the catcher.

In case of a foul strike, foul-hit ball not legally caught out, dead ball, or base-runner put out for being struck by a fair-hit ball, the ball shall not be considered in play until it is held by the pitcher standing in his position.

BLOCK BALLS

A block is a batted or thrown ball that is stopped or handled by any person not engaged in the game.

Whenever a block occurs the umpire shall declare it, and base-runners may run the bases, without being put out, until the ball has been returned to and held by the pitcher standing in his position.

In the case of a block, if the person not engaged in the game should retain possession of the ball, or throw or kick it beyond the reach of the fielders, the umpire should call "Time," and require each base-runner to stop at the last base touched by him until the ball be returned to the pitcher standing in his position.

THE SCORING OF RUNS

One run shall be scored every time a base-runner, after having legally touched the first three bases, shall touch the home base before three men are put out. Exception: if the third man is forced out, or is put out before reaching first base, a run shall not be scored.

THE BATTING RULES

A fair hit is a ball batted by the batsman, standing in his position, that first touches the ground, the first base, the third base, any part of the person of a player, umpire, or any object in front of or on the foul lines, or batted directly to the ground by the batsman, standing in his position, that (whether it first touches foul or fair ground) bounds or rolls within the foul lines, between home and first or home and third bases, without interference by a player.

A foul hit is a ball batted by the batsman, standing in his

position, that first touches the ground, any part of the person of a player, or any object behind either of the foul lines, or that strikes the person of such batsman, while standing in his position, or batted directly to the ground by the batsman, standing in his position, that (whether it first touches foul or fair ground) bounds or rolls outside the foul lines, between home and first or home and third bases without interference by a player. Provided, that a foul hit not rising above the batsman's head and caught by the catcher playing within ten feet of the home base, shall be termed a foul tip.

BALLS BATTED OUTSIDE THE GROUNDS

When a batted ball passes outside the grounds, the umpire shall decide it fair should it disappear within, or foul should it disappear outside, of the range of the foul lines, and rules are to be construed accordingly.

A fair-batted ball that goes over the fence shall entitle the batsman to a home run, except that should it go over the fence at a less distance than two hundred and thirty-five feet from the home base, when he shall be entitled to two bases, and a distinctive line shall be marked on the fence at this point.

STRIKES

A strike is —

A ball struck at by the batsman without its touching his bat; or,

A fair ball legally delivered by the pitcher, but not struck at by the batsman.

Any obvious attempt to make a foul hit.

A foul strike is a ball batted by the batsman when any part of his person is upon ground outside the lines of the batsman's position.

THE BATSMAN IS OUT—

If he fails to take his position at the bat in his order of batting, unless the error be discovered and the proper batsman takes his position before a fair hit has been made; and in such case the balls and strikes called must be counted in the time at bat of the proper batsman. Provided, this rule shall not take effect unless *the out* is declared before the ball is delivered to the succeeding batsman.

If he fails to take his position within one minute after the umpire has called for the batsman.

If he makes a foul hit, other than a foul tip, as defined in previous rule, and the ball be momentarily held by a fielder before touching the ground. Provided, it be not caught in a fielder's hat or cap, or touch some object other than a fielder, before being caught.

If he makes a foul strike.

If he attempts to hinder the catcher from fielding or throwing the ball, by stepping outside the lines of his position, or otherwise obstructing or interfering with that player.

If, while the first base be occupied by a base-runner, three strikes be called on him by the umpire, except when two men are already out.

If, while making the third strike, the ball hits his person or clothing.

If, after two strikes have been called, the batsman obviously attempts to make a foul hit, as mentioned in previous rule.

Base-running Rules

WHEN THE BATSMAN BECOMES A BASE-RUNNER

The batsman becomes a base-runner—

Instantly after he makes a fair hit.

Instantly after four balls have been called by the umpire.

Instantly after three strikes have been declared by the umpire.

If, while he be a batsman, his person—excepting hands or forearm, which makes it a dead ball—or clothing be hit by a ball from the pitcher, unless—in the opinion of the umpire—he intentionally permits himself to be so hit.

Instantly after an illegal delivery of a ball by the pitcher.

BASES TO BE TOUCHED

The base-runner must touch each base in regular order—viz., first, second, third, and home bases; and when obliged to return (except on a foul hit) must retouch the base or bases in reverse order. He shall only be considered as holding a base after touching it, and shall then be entitled to hold such base until he has legally touched the next base in order, or has been legally forced to vacate it for a succeeding base-runner.

ENTITLED TO BASES

The base-runner shall be entitled, without being put out, to take the base in the following cases:

If, while he was batsman, the umpire called four balls.

If the umpire awards a succeeding batsman a base on four

balls, or for being hit with a pitched ball, or in case of an illegal delivery, and the base-runner is thereby forced to vacate the base held by him.

If the umpire calls a "balk."

If a ball delivered by the pitcher passes the catcher and touches the umpire, or any fence or building within ninety feet of the home base.

If upon a fair hit the ball strikes the person or clothing of the umpire on fair ground.

If he be prevented from making a base by the obstruction of an adversary.

If the fielder stops or catches a batted ball with his hat, or any part of his dress.

RETURNING TO BASES

The base-runner shall return to his base, and shall be entitled to so return without being put out.

If the umpire declares a foul tip (as defined in previous rule) or any other foul hit not legally caught by a fielder.

If the umpire declares a foul strike.

If the umpire declares a dead ball, unless it be also the fourth unfair ball, and he be thereby forced to take the next base, as provided in previous rule.

If the person or clothing of the umpire interferes with the catcher, or he is struck by a ball thrown by the catcher to intercept a base-runner.

WHEN BASE-RUNNERS ARE OUT

The base-runner is out, if, after three strikes have been declared against him while batsman, and the catcher fails to catch the third-strike ball, he plainly attempts to hinder the catcher from fielding the ball.

If, having made a fair hit while batsman, such fair-hit ball be momentarily held by a fielder before touching the ground or any object other than a fielder. Provided, it be not caught in a fielder's hat or cap.

If, when the umpire has declared three strikes on him while batsman, the third-strike ball be momentarily held by a fielder before touching the ground. Provided, it be not caught in a fielder's hat or cap, or touch some object other than a fielder, before being caught.

If, after three strikes or a fair hit, he be touched with the ball in the hand of a fielder *before* he shall have touched first base.

If, after three strikes or a fair hit, the ball be securely held by a fielder, while touching first base with any part of his person, *before* such base-runner touches first base.

If, in running the last half of the distance from home base to first base, while the ball is being fielded to first base, he runs outside the three-foot lines, as defined in previous rule, unless to avoid a fielder attempting to field a batted ball.

If, in running from first to second base, from second to third base, or from third to home base he runs more than three feet from a direct line between such bases to avoid being touched by the ball in the hands of a fielder; but in case a fielder be occupying the base-runner's proper path, attempting to field a batted ball, then the base-runner shall run out of the path and behind said fielder, and shall not be declared out for so doing.

If he fails to avoid a fielder attempting to field a batted ball, in the manner described in sections of this rule; or if he in any way obstructs a fielder attempting to field a batted ball, or intentionally interferes with a thrown ball. Provided, that if two or more fielders attempt to field a batted ball, and the base-runner comes in contact with one or more of them, the umpire shall determine which fielder is entitled to the benefit of this rule, and shall not decide the base-runner out for coming in contact with any other fielder.

If, at any time while the ball is in play, he be touched by the ball in the hands of a fielder, unless some part of his person is touching a base he is entitled to occupy. Provided, the ball be held by the fielder after touching him; but (exception as to first base), in running to first base, he may overrun said base without being put out for being off said base, after first touching it, provided he returns at once and retouches the base, after which he may be put out as at any other base. If, in overrunning first base, he also attempts to run to second base, or, after passing the base, he turns to his left from the foul line, he shall forfeit such exemption from being put out.

If, when a fair or foul hit ball (other than a foul tip, as referred to in previous rule) is legally caught by a fielder, such ball is legally held by a fielder on the base occupied by the base-runner when such ball was struck (or the base-runner be touched with the ball in the hands of a fielder), before he retouches said base after such fair or foul hit ball was so caught. Provided, that the base-runner shall not be out in such case, if, after the ball was legally caught as above, it be delivered to the bat by the pitcher before the fielder holds it on said base, or touches the base-runner with it; but if the base-runner, in attempting to reach a base, detaches it before being touched or forced out, he shall be declared safe.

If, when a batsman becomes a base-runner, the first base, or the first and second bases, or the first, second, and third bases, be occupied, any base-runner so occupying a base shall cease to be entitled to hold it, until any following base-runner is put out, and may be put out at the next base or by being touched by the ball in the hands of a fielder in the same manner as in running to first base, at any time before any following base-runner is put out.

If a fair-hit ball strikes him *before touching the fielder*, and in such case no base shall be run unless forced by the batsman becoming a base-runner, and no run shall be scored, or any other base-runner put out.

If, when running to a base or forced to return to a base, he fails to touch the intervening base or bases (if any) in the order prescribed in previous rule, he may be put out at the base he fails to touch, or by being touched by the ball in the hands of a fielder, in the same manner as in running to first base.

If, when the umpire calls "Play," after any suspension of a game, he fails to return to and touch the base he occupied when "Time" was called before touching the next base.

WHEN BATSMAN OR BASE-RUNNER IS OUT

The umpire shall declare the batsman or base-runner out, without waiting for an appeal for such decision, in all cases except those otherwise provided for, where such player is put out in accordance with these rules.

Coaching Rules

The coachers are restricted to coaching the base-runner only, and are not allowed to address any remarks except to the base-runner, and then only in words of necessary direction; and shall not use language which will in any manner refer to or reflect upon a player of the opposing club, or the spectators; and not more than two coachers, who may be one player participating in the game and any other player under contract to it, in the uniform of either club, shall be allowed at any one time. To enforce the above, the captain of the opposite side may call the attention of the umpire to the offense, and upon a repetition of the same the club shall be debarred from further coaching during the game.

The Umpire

The umpire shall not be changed during the progress of a game, except for reason of illness or injury.

HIS POWERS AND JURISDICTION

The umpire is master of the field from the commencement to the termination of the game, and is entitled to the respect of the spectators, and any person offering any insult or indignity to him must be promptly ejected from the grounds.

He must be invariably addressed by the players as Mr. Umpire; and he must compel the players to observe the provisions of all the playing rules, and he is hereby invested with authority to order any player to do or omit to do any act as he may deem necessary, to give force and effect to any and all of such provisions.

SPECIAL DUTIES

The umpire's duties shall be as follows:

The umpire is the sole and absolute judge of play. In no instance shall any person be allowed to question the correctness of any decision made by him on a play, and no player shall leave his position in the field, his place at the bat, on the bases or players' bench, to approach or address the umpire, except on an interpretation of the playing rules, and only that shall be done by the captains of the contending nines. No manager or any other officer of either club shall be permitted to go on the field or address the umpire, under a penalty of a forfeiture of a game.

Before the commencement of a game, the umpire shall see that the rules governing all the materials of the game are strictly observed. He shall ask the captain of the home club whether there are any special ground rules to be enforced, and if there are, he shall see that they are duly enforced, provided they do not conflict with any of these rules. He shall also secure from the captains of the contesting teams their respective batting orders, which, upon approval, shall be followed as provided in the rule.

The umpire must keep the contesting nines playing constantly from the commencement of the game to its termination, allowing such delays only as are rendered unavoidable by accident, injury, or rain. He must, until the completion of the game, require the players of each side to promptly take their positions in the field as soon as the third man is put out, and must require the first striker of the opposite side to be in his position at the bat as soon as the fielders are in their places.

The umpire shall count and call every "unfair ball" delivered by the pitcher, and every "dead ball," if also an unfair ball, as a "ball," and he shall also count and call every "strike." Neither a "ball" nor a "strike" shall be counted or called until the ball has passed the home base. He shall also declare every "dead ball," "block," "foul hit," "foul strike," and "balk."

For the special benefit of the patrons of the game, and because the offenses specified are under his immediate jurisdiction, and not subject to appeal by players, the attention of the umpire is particularly directed to possible violations of the purpose and spirit of the rules, of the following character:

Laziness or loafing of players in taking their places in the field, or those allotted them by the rules when their side is at the bat, and especially any failure to keep the bats in the racks provided for them; to be ready to take position as batsmen, and to remain upon the players' bench, except when otherwise required by the rules.

Any attempt by players of the side at bat, by calling to a fielder, other than the one designated by his captain, to field a ball, or by any other equally disreputable means seeking to disconcert a fielder.

The rules make a marked distinction between hindrance of an adversary in fielding a batted or thrown ball. This has been done to rid the game of the childish excuses and claims formerly made by a fielder failing to hold a ball to put out a base-runner. But there may be cases of the base-runner so flagrantly violating the spirit of the rules and of the game in obstructing a fielder from fielding a thrown ball, that it would become the duty of the umpire to declare the base-runner "out" (and to compel base-runners to return to the bases last held by them). For example: If the base-runner plainly strikes at the ball while passing him, to prevent its being caught by a fielder; if he holds a fielder's arms so as to disable him from catching the ball; or if he runs against or knocks down the fielder for the same purpose.

CALLING "PLAY" AND "TIME"

The umpire must call "Play" promptly at the hour designated by the home club, and on the call of "Play" the game must immediately begin. When he calls "Time," play shall be suspended until he calls "Play" again, and during the interim no player shall be put out, base be run, or run be scored. The umpire shall suspend play only for an accident to himself or a player (but in case of accident to a fielder, "Time" shall not be called until the ball be returned to and held by the pitcher, standing in his position), or in case rain falls so heavily that the spectators are compelled, by the severity of the storm, to seek shelter, in which case he shall note the time of suspension, and should such rain continue to fall thirty minutes thereafter, he shall terminate the game; or to enforce order in case of annoyance from spectators.

The umpire is only allowed, by the rules, to call "Time" in case of an accident to himself or a player, a "block," as referred to in the rules, or in case of rain, as defined by the rules. The practice of players suspending the game to discuss or contest a decision with the umpire is a gross violation of the rules.

Field Rules

No club shall allow open betting or pool-selling upon its grounds, nor in any building owned or occupied by it.

No person shall be allowed upon any part of the field during the progress of the game, in addition to the players in uniform, the manager on each side, and the umpire, except such officers of the law as may be present in uniform, and such officials of the home club as may be necessary to preserve the peace.

No umpire, manager, captain, or player shall address the spectators during the progress of a game, except in case of necessary explanation.

Every club shall furnish sufficient police force upon its own grounds to preserve order, and in the event of a crowd entering the field during the progress of a game, and interfering with the play in any manner, the visiting club may refuse to play further until the field be cleared. If the ground be not cleared within fifteen minutes thereafter, the visiting club may claim, and shall be entitled to, the game by a score of nine runs to none (no matter what number of innings have been played).

General Definitions

"Play" is the order of the umpire to begin the game, or to resume play after its suspension.

"Time" is the order of the umpire to suspend play. Such suspension must not extend beyond the day of the game.

"Game" is the announcement by the umpire that the game is terminated.

"An inning" is the term at bat of the nine players representing a club in a game, and is completed when three of such players have been put out as provided in these rules.

"A time at bat" is the term at bat of a batsman. It begins when he takes his position, and continues until he is put out or becomes a base-runner; except when, because of being hit by a pitched ball, or in case of an illegal delivery by the pitcher, as in previous rule.

"Legal" or "legally" signifies as required by these rules.

FORM OF BOATING AGREEMENT

(YALE-HARVARD EIGHT-OARED RACES)

I

ALL previous agreements entered into between the Harvard and Yale Boat Clubs are hereby abrogated and annulled.

II

These rules shall stand until repealed by the consent of both boat-clubs. By mutual agreement in writing, duly signed by the respective captains of the two university crews, however, any one or more of Rules VI, VII, XII, XIV, XIX, XXIV may be temporarily suspended or waived by and with the written consent and approval of the referee.

III

Additional agreements concerning things for which provision has not been made in these rules may be entered into in the same way as under Rule II. Such additional agreements, however, shall be temporary in their nature, and shall not last longer than is necessary to fulfil the purpose or purposes which gave rise to them.

IV

The race between Harvard and Yale shall be deemed an annual event; but in case of the inability of either party to send a crew to participate in such annual race, notice of such inability shall be sent to the other party prior to the first day of December of that college year; and if such notice shall be sent, no race will occur in that college year.

V

The referee shall be a graduate of some neutral college; and each boat-club shall name the referee on alternate years—Yale naming him in 1886. The name of the person proposed as referee shall be submitted by the proposing club to the other club at least one month before the day set for the race, and such nomination shall be acted upon within one week after its receipt.

In case of objection to the person proposed, written notice of such objection must be sent to the proposing club within one week from time the nomination is received. Within one week after the receipt of such notice, the proposing club must submit another name (or names) to the other club, which must be acted upon in the same manner as before. In case no objection be sent within the time specified above, the person whose name has been thus submitted shall be deemed the choice of both clubs for referee.

VI

In 1886 Yale shall have choice between the first Thursday and Friday after the last Wednesday in June as the day set for the annual race, after which the choice between the aforesaid days shall rest alternately with Harvard and Yale.

VII

The race in the years 1886–90 shall take place at New London, Conn.

VIII

The race shall be rowed on ebb tide, and shall be started within two hours of high water at the starting-line.

IX

There shall be a central line of buoys which shall be situated at each half-mile point, and either boat may be disqualified if at any point during the race it shall be nearer than ten feet to, or more than one hundred feet from, the central line of buoys.

X

The referee shall have absolute power in the interpretation of these rules, and his decision shall be final in all cases. Should any unforeseen difference of opinion arise, it shall be referred to the referee for decision.

XI

Both boats shall be at the starting-point at the time agreed upon. If either boat can not appear, the captain of such boat shall, before said time, personally report to the referee, who shall at once proceed to start the other boat, unless the delay has been caused by a *bona fide* accident.

XII

All races shall be started in the following manner: The referee shall ask the question, "Are you ready?" and receiving no reply after waiting not more than five nor less than three seconds, shall give the word "Go"; and if either boat starts before the word is given by the referee, it shall be recalled and a new start made as soon as possible. A start shall be unfair if during the first ten strokes either of the competing boats shall be disabled by a *bona fide* accident.

XIII

In any case an appeal must be made to the referee by the competitors themselves, or by the judge, before the crew leaves its boat.

XIV

In case of a dead heat the race shall be declared a tie for that year; no flags shall be awarded, and neither college shall claim the championship for that year on any pretext whatever.

XV

No boat shall be allowed to accompany a competing boat for the purpose of directing its course, or affording any other assistance.

XVI

The championship flags shall be placed in the referee's hands before the race, and shall be by him presented to the captain of the winning crew as soon as the race shall have been decided. These flags shall be provided by each college in turn — Yale to provide them in 1886. Each college shall contribute one half their cost.

XVII

If he thinks proper, the referee may reserve his decision, provided that in every case such decision be given on the day of the race. Pending his decision, no one shall be admitted to the presence of the referee except the judges and such witnesses as they and the referee may summon.

XVIII

The crews shall row in each successive year on alternate courses. In 1886 Yale shall have the east course and Harvard the west course, provided the race be rowed at New London. If rowed elsewhere, Yale is to have the choice of courses in 1886, after which the choice shall alternate between the two colleges.

XIX

The starting line shall be moved down from the present starting line the distance of sixty feet toward the finish line, and shall be at right angles to the central line of buoys. Each boat shall be provided with a metal staff, or rod, eighteen inches high, carrying a flag, 9×5 inches, of the color of its university, such rod to be fixed perpendicularly at the stern of shorter boat, and on longer boat at a distance forward from center of said boat equal to one half the length of the shorter boat. Each boat shall be started even by these flags so fixed on the starting line, and shall be adjudged to have completed the course when said flags shall have crossed the finish line.

XX

Five days before the race a suitable referee's boat shall be provided—such boat to be provided in 1886 by Yale, and alternately thereafter by Harvard and Yale.

XXI

Each university shall name two judges and one timekeeper—one of these judges to be located at the finish; the other, with the timekeeper, to accompany the referee. The appointment of the judges and timekeepers shall be reported to the referee when made.

XXII

The referee shall appoint as a third judge at the finish, a graduate of some neutral college, whose duty it shall be to decide, in case of disagreement between the other judges, which boat, if either, first crossed the line at the finish; such decision to be final.

XXIII

Each of the two judges at the finish shall be provided with a flag of his college color, which he shall drop as a signal to the timekeepers when the boat of his college crosses the finish line.

XXIV

A boat shall be provided for the judges at the finish by the club which does not provide the referee's boat. The boat shall be so placed that the referee and timekeepers may easily see the flags when they fall.

XXV

On the day of the race, the referee, accompanied by the judges, shall go over the course and personally satisfy himself that everything is in proper position.

XXVI

Any man shall be eligible to row in the university race who is duly entered as a student in one of the recognized departments of the university. The appearance of his name in the annual catalogue, or a certificate of membership signed by the dean or other acting head of the department in which he is a student, stating that he entered such department prior to December 1st of the same college year, shall be deemed conclusive evidence in favor of the eligibility of any candidate or member of the crew. Either boat-club, by giving at least one week's notice before the day set for the race, may require such evidence to be submitted to the referee on or before the day set for the race. Failure to comply with these requirements will authorize the referee to deprive the person objected to of a seat in the boat on the day of the race, if he shall deem such action advisable after a full consideration of all the circumstances of the case.

ALFRED COWLES, JR.,
PAUL K. AMES,
GEORGE A. ADEE,
G. S. MUMFORD,
LAWRENCE E. SEXTON.

CONDITIONS

GOVERNING THE HARVARD-YALE CONTESTS FOR THE UNIVERSITY TRACK ATHLETIC CUP

Deed of Gift

THE undersigned hereby offer to the students of Harvard University and Yale University a cup, to be known as the University Track Athletic Cup, for the encouragement of track athletics, and to foster a friendly rivalry between the students of the two universities in track and field athletics.

A track athletic contest between the students of the two universities is to be held annually between May 1st and July 1st of each year from 1891 to 1899 inclusive, provided this contract be renewed annually to the entire and mutual satisfaction of the universities. The cup shall become the property of the university whose students shall win the majority of the nine contests herein provided for, to be held as a trophy. If either or both universities shall withdraw before the completion of the nine-years' term, the cup shall be disposed of in such manner as may be agreed upon by a majority of the trustees appointed by the donors. Said trustees shall have the power by unanimous vote to amend this deed of gift.

The time and place for holding each contest, the number and nature of the events, the points that are to count, the rules regulating each contest and each event, the method of counting, the rules regulating the eligibility of contestants, and all incidental matters, including the construction of all rules, shall be determined, and may from time to time be changed and amended, by the representatives of the two universities herein named, and their successors as herein provided, except as otherwise herein stated. Voting by proxy shall be permitted. To make any change or amendment, an affirmative vote of at least five shall be necessary. As representing Harvard University, the following persons are appointed —

namely, Wendell Baker, of New York; George B. Morison, of Boston, Massachusetts; the captain, from time to time, of the Harvard Track Athletic Team; and one undergraduate, to be selected by the Executive Committee of the Harvard Athletic Association prior to January 1st of each year. An additional undergraduate, not a senior, to be selected by the Executive Committee of the Harvard Athletic Association, shall be allowed to attend the meetings of this committee and join in debate, without power to vote. Vacancies shall be filled by the other representatives of Harvard University. As representing Yale, the following persons are appointed — namely, Walter Camp; Henry Stanford Brooks; the captain, from time to time, of the Yale Track Athletic Team; and one undergraduate, to be selected by the Executive Committee of the Yale Athletic Association prior to January 1st of each year. An additional undergraduate, not a senior, to be selected by the Executive Committee of the Yale Athletic Association, shall be allowed to attend the meetings of this committee and join in debate, without power to vote. Vacancies shall be filled by the other representatives of Yale University.

Dated March 16, 1891.

(Here follow signatures of Harvard and Yale graduate subscribers.)

CONSTITUTION AND RULES

As authorized by the foregoing deed of gift, the University Track Athletic Cup Committee, having met on April 4, 1891, adopted the following constitution and rules:

Constitution

I

1. The annual contest shall be held on the afternoon two weeks before the last Saturday in May.
2. Each university shall have the privilege of naming the place of contest in alternate years; the privilege of naming the place in 1891 to be with Harvard.

II

1. DEFINITION.—An amateur is a person who has never competed in an open competition, either for money or under a

false name, or with a professional for a prize, or with a professional where gate-money is charged; nor has ever at any time taught, pursued, or assisted at athletic exercises for money, or for any valuable consideration; or whose association with the university was not brought about or does not continue because of any mutual understanding, expressed or implied, whereby his association would be of any pecuniary value to him whatever, direct or indirect. But nothing in this definition shall be construed to prohibit the competition between amateurs for medals, cups, or prizes other than money. And it is hereby expressly declared that this definition is not retroactive, and that all past acts of amateurs shall be judged in accordance with the provisions of the constitution of the I. C. A. A. A. adopted on the 25th day of February, 1888. The above definition shall take effect on and after April 4, 1891.

To prevent any misunderstanding in reading the above, attention is drawn to the following explanations:

An athlete has forfeited his right to compete as an amateur, and has thereby become a professional, by—

(*a*) Ever having competed in an open competition,—that is, a competition the entries to which are open to all, irrespective as to whether the competitors are amateurs or professionals, and, whether such competition be for a prize or not, in any athletic exercises—namely, base-ball, rowing, cricket, etc.

(*b*) Ever having competed for money in any athletic exercise.

(*c*) Ever having competed under a false name in any athletic exercise.

(*d*) Ever having knowingly competed with a professional for a prize, or where gate-money is charged, in any athletic exercise.

(*e*) Ever having taught or pursued as a means of livelihood any athletic exercise.

(*f*) Ever having directly or indirectly accepted or received remuneration for engaging in any athletic exercise.

An athlete shall hereafter forfeit his right to compete as an amateur, and shall thereby become a professional, if, at any time after the foregoing definition shall take effect, he shall—

(1) Directly or indirectly receive payment for training or coaching any other person in any athletic exercise.

(2) Directly or indirectly receive payment for services personally rendered in teaching any athletic exercise.

(3) Directly or indirectly receive payment for services rendered as referee, judge, umpire, scorer, manager, director, or in any other capacity at any professional exhibition or contest of any athletic exercise whatsoever.

NOTE.—Nothing herein shall be construed to prohibit the acceptance by any amateur of his necessary traveling expenses incurred as referee, judge, umpire, scorer, or starter in going to and from the place of any amateur contest.

(4) Directly or indirectly run, manage, or direct, for prospective profit, any professional exhibition or contest.

An amateur shall not forfeit his right to compete as an amateur and shall not become a professional by —

(*a*) Receiving compensation for services rendered as ticket-taker or ticket-seller at any contest or exhibition of amateur athletics.

(*b*) Receiving compensation for services personally rendered as secretary, treasurer, manager, or superintendent of any amateur athletic club.

(*c*) Receiving compensation as editor, correspondent, or reporter of, or contributor to, any sporting, athletic, or other paper or periodical.

(*d*) Running, managing, or directing, for prospective benefit, any sporting, athletic, or other paper or periodical.

(*e*) Receiving compensation for services personally rendered as official handicapper under the direction and authority of any amateur athletic association.

(*f*) Receiving from a club of which he shall be a member the amount of his expenses necessarily incurred in traveling to and from the place of any amateur contest.

(*g*) Nothing in this rule shall be construed so as to consider a man a professional for playing on a college team against a professional team.

2. No one shall represent either university who is not an amateur under the above definition, and who has not been a member of that university, in good and regular standing, for at least one college year prior to said meeting. In case a competitor's qualifications are questioned, he shall furnish to the U. T. A. C. Committee a certificate, signed by three members of the faculty of said university, stating that he regularly attends lectures and recitings amounting to at least five hours a week at such university, and has done so since the beginning of the college year prior to said meeting.

III

A student shall be allowed to compete at four meetings and no more.

IV

The starter of the games shall be a professional of known integrity and ability.

V

The officials who control the games shall be composed entirely of non-college men. The clerk of the course and the scorers, with their assistants, shall be deemed exempt from this rule.

VI

The U. T. A. C. Committee shall decide all protests on the eligibility of competitors.

VII

1. Entries to the games shall close at least two weeks before the day assigned for the games.
2. At least twelve days before the annual games a list of all the entries shall be sent by the secretary of each college association to the secretary of the other association and to the chairman of the U. T. A. C. Committee. Protests must be sent to the chairman of the U. T. A. C. Committee as soon as this list is received. The latter shall at once notify the members protested and all members of the U. T. A. C. Committee.
3. He shall also send to the members protested a printed certificate of qualification, to be signed according to Article II, Section 2. This certificate must have said section printed plainly upon its face, with a space below for signature.
4. These certificates, signed, must be sent by protested contestants to the chairman of the U. T. A. C. Committee at least three days before the game.

VIII

The events shall include —
Running 100 yards; running 220 yards; running one quarter mile; running one half mile; running one mile; hurdle-racing, 120 yards, 10 hurdles, 3 feet 6 inches; hurdle-racing, 220 yards, 10 hurdles, 2 feet 6 inches; walking one mile; running high jump; running broad jump; pole-leaping; putting the shot, 16 pounds; throwing the hammer, 16 pounds; bicycle-racing, 2 miles.

IX

Each university shall be limited in number of contestants in each event as follows:
Running 100 yards, six; running 220 yards, six; running one quarter mile, three; running one half mile, four; running

one mile, six; hurdle-racing, 120 yards, four; hurdle-racing, 220 yards, four; walking one mile, six; bicycle-racing, four; field events, no limit.

X

The order of events shall be as follows:

TRACK EVENTS

(1) 100-yard dash, trial heats; (2) 120-yard hurdle, trial heats; (3) two-mile bicycle, trial heats; (4) 440-yard run; (5) 120-yard hurdle, final heat; (6) 100-yard dash, final heat; (7) one-mile run; (8) one-mile walk; (9) 220-yard hurdle, trial heats; (10) two-mile bicycle, final heat; (11) half-mile run; (12) 220-yard dash, trial heats; (13) 220-yard hurdle, final heat; (14) 220-yard dash, final heat.

FIELD EVENTS

(1) Throwing the hammer; (2) pole vault; (3) running high jump; (4) running broad jump; (5) putting the shot.

XI

1. The expenses of the annual games, including prizes of a standard and number to be fixed by the Committee on Prizes, subject to the approval of the Games Committee, shall be paid from the gate receipts. Any surplus receipts shall be divided between the two universities equally. In case there is a deficit, the same shall be borne equally by each university.

2. Training expenses and cost of transportation are not to be included in the expenses as considered above.

XII

The cup referred to in the deed of gift shall be awarded each year to the team scoring the greater number of points. The points are to be counted as follows: first place, five; second place, two; third place, one. In case of a tie, the cup shall be awarded to the team winning the greater number of first prizes. If the tie still exists, the team winning the greater number of second prizes shall be awarded the cup. If necessary, third prizes shall decide in the same way.

XIII

Each contestant shall be allowed the exclusive use of his own shot, pole, and hammer.

XIV

The arrangements for the games shall be under the control of a Games Committee, consisting of the four active undergraduate members of the U. T. A. C. Committee. The chairman of the committee shall be chosen from the university having the choice of grounds.

XV

A special meeting of the U. T. A. C. Committee shall be called by the chairman at the request of any member of that committee.

Athletic Rules

I

The officials of the games shall be appointed by the U. T. A. C. Committee, and shall be as follows:

One referee; three judges at the finish; three timekeepers; one judge of walking, with assistants, if necessary; one starter; one clerk of the course, with assistants, if necessary; three or more field judges; two or more inspectors; two scorers.

II. CLERK OF THE COURSE

He shall record the name of each competitor who shall report to him; shall give him his number for each game in which he is entered, and notify him before the start of every event in which he is engaged. He shall, so far as possible, arrange to have a Yale and a Harvard contestant in each heat. The assistants shall do such portion of his work as he may assign them.

III. STARTER

He shall have entire control of competitors at their marks, and shall be the sole judge of fact as to whether or not any man has gone over his mark.

IV. JUDGE OF WALKING

He shall have entire control of competitors during the race, and his decision as to unfair walking shall be final and without appeal. The assistants shall do such portions of his work as he may assign to them.

V. SCORER

He shall record the laps made by each competitor, and call them aloud, when tallied, for the information of the contestants. He shall record the order of finishing and the times of the competitors as given him by the timekeepers in walking and running races. The assistants shall do such portions of his work as he may assign to them.

VI. TIMEKEEPERS

Each of the three timekeepers shall time every event; and in case two watches agree and the third disagrees, the time marked by the two shall be official time; if all three watches disagree, the time marked by the watch giving the middle time shall be the official time. If there be but two timekeepers, and their watches do not agree, the time marked by the slower watch shall be the official time. Time shall be taken from the flash of the pistol.

VII. JUDGES AT THE FINISH

Two shall stand at one end of the tape, and the third at the other. One shall take the winner, another the second man, and the other the third man; they shall also note the distances between the first three as they finish. In case of disagreement, the majority shall decide. Their decision as to the order in which the men finish shall be final and without appeal.

VIII. FIELD JUDGES

They shall make an accurate measurement and keep a tally of all trials of competitors in the high and broad jumps, the pole vault, and the weight competitions. They shall act as judges of these events, and their decisions shall likewise be without appeal. In case of disagreement a majority shall govern.

IX. REFEREE

He shall, when appealed to, decide all questions whose settlement is not otherwise provided for in these rules. His decision shall be final and without appeal. In case a race has been drawn in heats, and no more contestants appear than enough to make one heat, the referee shall be empowered to see that the race is run in one heat.

X. INSPECTORS

It shall be the duty of an inspector to stand at such a point as the referee may designate; to watch the competition closely, and in case of a claim of foul to report to the referee what he saw of the incident.

XI. PROTESTS

Verbal protests may be made at or before any athletic meeting, against a competitor, by any member of either university; but such protest must subsequently, and before action be taken thereon, be made in writing and duly presented to the U. T. A. C. Committee.

XII. INNER GROUNDS

No person whatever shall be allowed inside the track except the officials and properly accredited representatives of the press. Competitors not engaged in the game actually taking place shall not be allowed inside or upon the track.

XIII. TRACK

The measurements of tracks shall be eighteen inches from the inner edge, which edge shall be a solid curb raised above the level of the track.

XIV. ATTENDANTS

No attendants shall accompany a competitor on the scratch or in the race.

XV. STARTING SIGNALS

All races (except time handicaps) shall be started by report of pistol; the pistol shall be fired so that its flash may be visible to the timekeepers. A snap cap shall be no start. There shall be no recall after the pistol is fired except as especially provided for in the bicycle race. Time handicap shall be started by the word "Go."

XVI. STARTING

When the starter receives a signal from the judge at the finish, that everything is in readiness, he shall direct the competitors to get on their marks. Any competitor starting before the signal shall be put back one yard; for the second offense, another yard; and for the third, shall be disqualified. He shall be held to have started when any portion of his body touches the ground in front of his mark. Stations count from the inside.

XVII. KEEPING PROPER COURSE

In all races on a straight track each competitor shall keep his own position on the course from start to finish. In the 100- and 220-yard dash, courses for contestants shall be marked out by stakes protruding three feet from the ground, and connected at the top by a cord or wire plainly marked.

XVIII. CHANGE OF COURSE

In all races other than on a straight track a competitor may change toward the inside whenever he is two strides ahead of the man whose path he crosses.

XIX. FOULING

Any competitor may be disqualified by the referee for jostling, running across, or in any way impeding others.

XX. THE FINISH

The finish shall be represented by a line between two finishing posts, drawn across and at right angles to the sides of the track. Three feet above this line shall be placed a tape drawn tightly from post to post. A finish shall be counted when any part of the winner's body, except his hands or arms, shall touch this tape. The tape is to be considered the finishing line for the winner, and the order of finishing across the track-line shall determine the positions of the other competitors.

XXI. WALKING

The judge shall caution for any unfair walking, and the third caution shall disqualify the offender. On the last one eighth (220 yards) of a mile, an unfair walker shall be disqualified without previous caution.

XXII. HURDLES

120-yard hurdle races shall be over ten hurdles, each 3 feet 6 inches high. The first hurdle shall be placed 15 yards from the scratch, and there shall be 10 yards between each hurdle. 220-yard hurdle races shall be over ten hurdles, each 2 feet 6 inches high. The first hurdle shall be placed 20 yards from the scratch, and there shall be 20 yards between each hurdle.

Hurdle races of different distances, and with different numbers and heights of hurdles, may be given. No record shall be made in a hurdle race unless each of the hurdles, at the time the competitor jumps the same, is standing.

XXIII. JUMPING

No weights or artificial aid shall be allowed in any jumping contest except by special agreement or announcement. When weights are allowed, there shall be no restrictions as to size, shape, or material.

XXIV. RUNNING HIGH JUMP AND POLE-LEAPING

The jump or leap shall be made over a bar resting on pins projecting not more than three inches from the uprights. The height of the bar at starting and at each successive elevation shall be determined by the measurers. Three tries allowed at each height. Each competitor shall make one attempt in the order of his name on the program; then those who have failed (if any) shall have a second trial in regular order, and those failing on this trial shall take their final trial. Displacing the bar counts as a "try." A line shall be drawn six feet in front of the pole and parallel therewith in pole-leaping, and three feet in front of the bar and parallel therewith in high jumping; and stepping over such line, to be known as the balk-line, in an attempt, shall count as a balk. Three balks count as a "try." A competitor may omit his trials at any height; but if he fails at the next height, he shall not be allowed to go back and try the height he omitted. Each competitor shall be credited with the best of all his jumps or leaps.

XXV. RUNNING BROAD JUMP

The competitors shall have an unlimited run, but must take-off from or behind the scratch. The scratch-line shall be a joist five inches wide, the ground in front of which shall be removed to the depth of three and the width of six inches. Stepping over the scratch in an attempt shall be no jump, but shall count as a "try." Each competitor shall be allowed three "trials," and the best three men shall have three more trials each. Each competitor shall be credited with the best of all his jumps. The measurement shall be from the outer edge of the joist to the nearest break of the ground made by any part of his person. A line shall be drawn six feet in front of the scratch-line, and stepping over such line in an attempt shall count as a balk; three balks count as a "try."

XXVI. PUTTING THE SHOT

The shot shall be a metal sphere weighing sixteen pounds. It shall be put from the shoulder with one hand, and during the attempt it shall not pass behind nor below the shoulder. It shall be put from a circle seven feet in diameter, two feet of whose circumference shall be a toe board four inches in height. Foul puts, which shall not be measured, but which shall count as puts, are as follows:

1. Letting go of the shot in an attempt.
2. Touching the ground outside of the circle with any portion of the body while the shot is in hand.
3. Touching the ground forward of the front half of the circle with any portion of the body before the put is measured. Each competitor shall be allowed three puts, and the best three men in the first trial shall be allowed three more puts. Each competitor shall be credited with the best of all his puts. The measurement of the puts shall be from the nearest edge of the first mark made by the shot to the point of the circumference of the circle nearest such mark.

XXVII. THROWING THE HAMMER

The hammer-head shall be a metal sphere weighing sixteen pounds; the handle shall be of wood, and the combined length of the head and handle shall be four feet. The hammer shall be thrown from a circle seven feet in diameter. Foul throws, which shall not be measured, but shall count as throws, are as follows:

1. Letting go of the hammer in an attempt.
2. Lifting from the ground the foot nearest the circumference of the circle while the hammer is in hand.
3. Touching the ground outside the circle with any portion of the body while the hammer is in hand.
4. Touching the ground forward of the front half of the circle with any portion of the body before the throw is measured. Each competitor will be allowed three throws, and the best three men in the first trial shall be allowed three more throws. Each competitor shall be credited with the best of all his throws. The measurement of the throw shall be from the nearest edge of the first mark made by the head of the hammer to the point of the circumference of the circle nearest such mark.

XXVIII. BICYCLING

1. The referee shall have general supervision of the race-meeting. He shall give judgment on protests received by him;

shall decide all questions or objections respecting foul riding, or offenses which he may be personally cognizant of, or which may be brought to his notice by an umpire or other officer. He shall act as he may think for the best in cases of misconduct by attendants, and shall disqualify any competitor who may become liable to disqualification. He shall decide all questions whose settlement is not otherwise provided for in these rules. His decision shall be final.

2. It shall be the duty of the starter, when it has been reported to him by a clerk of the course that all the competitors are ready, to see that the timekeeper is warned, and before starting the men to say, "Mount"; in a few seconds after to say, "Are you ready?" and if no answer to the contrary be given, to effect the start by report of pistol. The starter may at his discretion put back for a distance not exceeding ten yards any competitor starting before the signal is given. In case of a false start the competitors shall be called back by the starter and re-started. Any competitor refusing to obey shall at once be disqualified. In case of a fall within ten feet of the scratch-line, the contestants shall be recalled and the race started over again. Time handicaps shall be started by the word "Go."

3. Choice or change of machine and choice of costume are not limited. In races distinctly stated on the program of events to be for a peculiar class of machine, this rule shall not apply so far as choice or change of machine is concerned. Safety-bicycle races shall be limited to machines whose driving-wheel does not exceed 32 inches in diameter. Safety bicycles shall not be ridden in "ordinary" bicycle races.

4. When races are run in heats and a final, the winner of the fastest heat shall take the pole in the final.

5. All starts, bicycle or tricycle, shall be from a standstill, with the left hand toward the curb; and the machines are to be held in position by an attendant (the front wheel touching the starting-line) until the signal is given by the starter. Attendants, when pushing off competitors, must have and keep both feet on the ground behind the mark from which the competitor actually starts. Should the attendant overstep that mark with either foot while touching the 'cycle, the competitor shall be disqualified. Any competitor shall be at liberty, with the consent of the referee, to start from a mark behind the one allotted him in the race; but in such case, as in all others, the point of contact of the front wheel of the machine with the ground shall be considered the starting-mark as regards the attendant.

6. The finish of all races shall be judged by the first part of the front wheel which touches a tape fastened flat on the ground at the winning-post.

7. Riders must pass on the outside (unless the man passed be dismounted), and must be at least a clear length of the 'cycle in front before taking the inside. The inside man must allow room for his competitor to pass him on the outside. A competitor overtaking another may pass between him and the pole if there be ample room, but he does so at his risk; and should a foul be claimed, the referee must decide if the rider was justified in his course. Riders are cautioned that they must not pass inside, except as a last resort.

8. Any competitor guilty of foul riding will be disqualified and debarred from any place or prize.

9. Any protest against a competitor, respecting foul riding or breach of rules, must be made to the referee immediately after the heat is finished. A competitor, upon being disqualified, shall forfeit any entry fee he may have paid.

10. Competitors may dismount during a race at their pleasure, and may run with their 'cycles if they wish to, but they must keep to the extreme outside of the path whenever dismounted. If a rider be dismounted by accident or to change his machine, he shall not be allowed a push-off in starting again, but an attendant may hold his machine while he mounts it, and he must so mount at the extreme outside of the path.

11. Competitors will not be permitted to fall behind one lap, or more, and continue on the track with the other competitors, for the purpose of pacing. Pacing, if so attempted, shall disqualify both the competitor and the pace-maker.

WENDELL BAKER,
GEO. B. MORISON,
E. C. MOËN,
J. P. LEE,
JOSEPH HOWLAND HUNT,

HENRY STANFORD BROOKS,
WALTER CAMP,
HOWELL CHENEY,
 for H. W. WOLCOTT,
HENRY L. WILLIAMS.

FORM OF CONSTITUTION AS ADOPTED IN OLD LEAGUE OF HARVARD, PRINCETON, AND YALE

ARTICLE I

The name of this association shall be the College Base-ball League.

ARTICLE II

SECTION 1. The following colleges shall constitute the League: Harvard, Princeton, and Yale.

SEC. 2. An annual tax of $33⅓ shall be levied on each club of the League, payable on or before the first day of May. Said tax to be expended for the purchase of a pennant for the champion nine. A tax shall also be levied to provide suitable salaries for the umpires. [See Article 8.]

SEC. 3. No college other than those named shall be admitted to membership except by two thirds vote of the League.

ARTICLE III

SECTION 1. The officers shall consist of a president, to be elected from the college holding the championship; a vice-president, a secretary and treasurer, and a Judiciary Committee. All officers shall be elected by ballot except the Judiciary Committee.

SEC. 2. The Judiciary Committee shall consist of the captains of the clubs in the League. Each college shall have one vote. In case of disagreement the matter shall be referred to the Advisory Committee hereafter provided for.

ARTICLE IV

The series of games shall consist of four of each college, two to be played on the home ground of each. Games commonly agreed upon and published as such in the official schedule shall be the championship games. The championship shall be awarded to the club having won the greatest number of games. In case of a tie for championship or second place, one game shall be played by each club thus tying with each of the other tying clubs; said games to be played on neutral grounds within ten days after the last scheduled championship game; said neutral grounds to be decided by mutual agreement or by lot.

ARTICLE V

Each club shall be entitled to its own gate receipts, and pay its own expenses, unless mutually agreed otherwise.

ARTICLE VI

SECTION 1. Any club having agreed to play a championship game with another club on a certain day, and refusing or failing to meet its engagement, shall, unless the failure be caused by an unavoidable accident in traveling, or the game be prevented by rain, or postponed with the consent in writing of the other club, forfeit its membership in the League. A certificate, signed by at least three members of the faculty, shall be also considered a sufficient excuse for failure to play a schedule game. Said certificate must be forwarded to the other nine within one week after the failure to play.

SEC. 2. Tie games shall be considered the same as postponed games.

SEC. 3. In case of a postponed or tie game the visiting club shall, within three days after said postponed or tie game, furnish to the home nine three dates, one of which shall be a Saturday; said dates to fall before the commencement day of the home nine, if possible; but if not, then on the Saturday next succeeding said commencement day. No one of these dates shall fall within three days of the scheduled championship game of the home nine except by mutual consent.

SEC. 4. A postponed game may be forfeited to the home club only when such forfeiture cannot affect the decision of the championship, and provided forfeiture is made by the agreement of the two clubs.

ARTICLE VII

Any student who has been pursuing a course of study through the entire collegiate year, and whose college expenses are in no way borne by men connected with base-ball interests, shall be eligible for college nine. Any student who shall play on a professional base-ball nine as a member thereof, or receive pay therefor, shall not be eligible. Questions of eligibility to be investigated and decided by the Advisory Committee on the application of any college.

ARTICLE VIII

Umpires shall be appointed by a unanimous vote of the Judiciary Committee. The umpires shall be two in number. Their duties shall be assigned and salary fixed by unanimous vote of the Judiciary Committee. In case of a tie game for championship, the umpire shall be decided by lot.

ARTICLE IX

The annual meeting of the League shall be held on the third Saturday of January, in New York and Boston, in alternate years. The meeting in 1888 to be held in New York. Each college shall be represented by not more than three delegates.

ARTICLE X

SECTION 1. There shall be an Advisory Committee, to consist of three graduates, one to be appointed by the base-ball association of each college. It shall be the duty of this committee to decide all questions referred to it by the League in cases in which no decision can be reached by the League or the Judiciary Committee.

SEC. 2. All questions that cannot be decided according to the provisions of this constitution must be referred to the Judiciary Committee.

ARTICLE XI

A unanimous vote of the League shall be required to amend this constitution. All votes shall be taken by colleges.

BY-LAWS

It shall be the duty of the president to preside at the meetings of the League, and to call a special meeting whenever one college shall so request. It shall be the duty of the vice-president to assume the duties of the president in the absence of the latter. It shall be the duty of the secretary and treasurer to keep a record of all the meetings of the League; to serve notices; to collect and disburse all moneys of the League; and to keep a record of official averages of players. He shall make a complete report at the annual meeting of the League.

The vote of the colleges for the disposition of the pennant shall be taken at the regular convention immediately after the election of officers. The money for said pennant shall thereupon be given to the manager of the winning club.

FORM OF CONTRACT BETWEEN CLUBS AND GROUND OWNERS

USED BY YALE AND PRINCETON WITH MANHATTAN FIELD OWNERS

This agreement, made this..........................day of....................eighteen hundred and ninety-..........

Between..
and..
of the first part, and ....
of........................city, of the second part,

Witnesseth, that the said party of the second part, in consideration of the sum of money hereinafter agreed to be paid to them by the party of the first part, hereby covenants and agrees to lease unto the parties of the first part, their athletic grounds, grand stands, seats, and accommodations, situated at the corner of One Hundred and Fifty-seventh Street and Sixth Avenue, in the city of New York, to be used on the eighteenth day of June next, between the hours of 10 A. M. and 6 P. M., by the parties of the first part, for the playing of a game of base-ball, to which the public shall be admitted upon paying such an admission-fee as shall be determined upon by the parties of the first part.

The party of the second part hereby further covenants and agrees, that on said eighteenth day of June the base-ball diamond and field shall be in perfect order, the ground thoroughly rolled, the diamond marked and lined with lime, the base and base-bags properly staked and secured, and the grounds conformed in all respects to the rules of the National League and American Association.

The party of the second part hereby further agrees to furnish comfortable seats for ten thousand persons, six thousand of which seats, at least, shall be in the grand stand, and shall be reserved for the persons purchasing the same.

They hereby further agree to furnish at their own cost, and without charge to the parties of the first part, a proper police force to maintain order, both within and about said grounds, and the entrance and exits thereto and therefrom.

They hereby further agree to furnish at their own cost ticket-sellers and ticket-takers at the entrance to said grounds, if required so to do by the parties of the first part.

They hereby further agree to furnish at their own cost all tickets of admission and for reserved seats, and to have the six thousand, more or less, tickets for reserved seats in the grand stand printed by The American Bank Note Company.

They hereby further agree that they will deliver to the parties of the first part the said six thousand reserved-seat tickets at least by June first next ensuing; and that all sales of tickets shall be made by the parties of the first part, if they, the parties of the first part, shall so desire.

They hereby further agree to furnish to the parties of the first part three blue prints of the stand diagram for use in the sale of tickets.

The said party of the second part hereby further assumes all liability for any damage that may occur to any person or persons on said grounds, or in said grand stand, or upon any part of said grounds and the seats thereon, so far as said damage is charged to negligence in the construction or management of the seats, grounds, or buildings.

In consideration whereof, and the faithful performance of all and singular the covenants and agreements hereinbefore made by the party of the second part, we, the parties of the first part, hereby covenant and agree to pay to the party of the second part twenty-two and one half percentum of all the gross receipts of the sales of tickets of admission and for reserved seats for the said game of June eighteenth aforesaid.

In witness whereof, the parties to these presents have hereunto set their hands and seals the day and year first above written.

Signed, sealed, and delivered }
in the presence of }

www.ingramcontent.com/pod-product-compliance
Lightning Source LLC
Chambersburg PA
CBHW031854220426
43663CB00006B/620